THE WAY OF THE
SPIRITUAL WARRIOR

THE TIMELESS PATH TO ENLIGHTENMENT

IMRE VALLYON

Sounding-Light

The Way of the Spiritual Warrior: The Timeless Path to Enlightenment
by Imre Vallyon

ISBN 978-0-909038-49-6
First Edition: January 2016

Sounding-Light Publishing Ltd
PO Box 771, Hamilton 3240, New Zealand
www.soundinglight.com

A NOTE ON SANSKRIT USAGE
~

The Sanskrit language is SAṄSKṚTA, meaning "well-made, perfectly polished". It is also called DEVANĀGARĪ, "God's writing". It is the most ancient sacerdotal (priestly) language of India, used for writing the scriptures, mythologies and sciences of the ancient Indian Subcontinent.

Sanskrit is a multi-layered language. It is a language which has the highest number of esoteric, spiritual and religious words, terms and expressions. There is no other language like it on Earth. The spiritual and esoteric terms run into thousands and thousands.

This work describes the pronunciation of the Sanskrit words by way of transliterated spellings, along with esoteric and spiritual meanings, as perceived in Higher Consciousness. Note that usage will in general vary from popular adaptations. The Sanskrit word KARMA, for instance, translates literally as "action" and may refer either to a cosmic principle (action and reaction, cause and effect) or to one's accumulated *karmas* or "actions".

To help preserve their original sound-structures, Sanskrit words are pluralized using a small 's' (Nirmānakāyas), except for those commonly used in English (mantras, gurus). A pronunciation guide can be found at the back of the book.

CONTENTS
~

PART I

The Spiritual Warrior School: The Practical Teaching

PART II

The Spiritual Warrior School: The Universal Teaching

CONTENTS

~

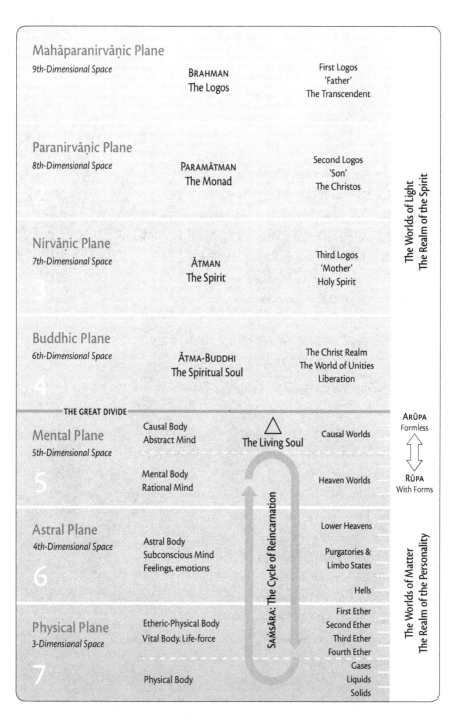

The Seven Great Planes of Being

PART ONE

~

THE SPIRITUAL WARRIOR SCHOOL

THE PRACTICAL TEACHING

THE WARRIOR JOURNEY
BEGINS WITH SELF-ASSESSMENT

The Way of the Spiritual Warrior is so profound that very few people in the world today understand it. Even in the olden days, when there were great spiritual civilizations, the Way of the Warrior was an extremely subtle path, an exclusive path. We hope to unveil the magnificence of this path, which is infinitely more than even those who are well versed in the martial arts know.

The Spiritual Warrior Path used to be *the* path for Humanity, but it was forgotten when the way of the monks, nuns and renunciates came into being. That was about four thousand years ago, when people decided to renounce the world and suppress the mind, the emotions and all activities of life and disconnect from life itself. Ever since then people have thought that the spiritual way of life has to do with suppressing normal human activities and living without a family, job and material possessions and not dealing with anything in the world. This Piscean Age view is still strong in the world, but it is the wrong view and it will be displaced as the ancient Way of the Spiritual Warrior becomes the new way again in the New Age.

The Spiritual Warrior Path begins with your self—self-assessment and assessment of your situation in life, your vision and goal, where you are going. (By *Spiritual Warrior Path* we mean a path to Enlightenment and a way of living life.) Unless you start with assessing yourself, where you are at and what your goal in life is, you will never get there. It can't be hit and miss, an accident or an attitude that maybe you will get there. It does not work that way. It has to be precise; it has to be with complete knowledge and understanding of how you are developing yourself. This is so even if you want to become a doctor, a lawyer or anything in life: you have to assess your abilities and whether you are suited for what you want to be.

When you begin any journey you first have to make preparations and plan out your journey. This is true in physical life and in spiritual life too, and for the Way of the Warrior it is essential. The reason why so many people fail in the spiritual quest is simply because they have no clue what they are doing, why they are doing it and where they are heading. If you are aspiring to be a Spiritual Warrior, therefore, you have to have a plan: you have to ask yourself, what talents do you have, what are your strengths and weaknesses; what do you have to do on this journey and what will you need in order to do them; and what is the final goal. Unless you do this you will not be successful.

You start off with who you are and the world reality you are in. Six to eight thousand years ago people's lives were oriented towards spirituality. People thought about spiritual things and tried to live a spiritual life. At present we are living in a materialistic age, where the emphasis of life is in gathering material things. As part of your self-assessment, therefore, you have to accept that this is a materialistic society and you are not going to get much help on your spiritual journey; on the contrary, you are going to have immense opposition from this materialistic society.

So you have to work out whether you are able to sacrifice and work hard for the vision of what you want to achieve. Are you here to gather more money and more goodies and maybe in your spare time do a bit of spiritual meditation? Or are you really desperate for Enlightenment in this lifetime? Is that really what drives you in life? These are important questions.

Many people are not clear about their goal in spite of being on the Path for a long time, mainly because they were brought up with the Piscean Age thinking of suppressing the personality and renouncing the world. If you still think this way you will never succeed on this particular path, because on the Path of the Warrior you do not suppress your mind, emotions or physical body. On the contrary, you cultivate and expand them. The Warrior trains the body, trains the mind, trains the emotions so that the personality becomes larger, more comprehensive, more powerful and more *useful*—unlike monks and nuns and the sādhus of India, who are of no use to themselves or to society.

The whole idea of the Warrior training is to improve on what you already have, not what you don't have. This is why you start off with yourself and pay no attention to what somebody else has. On the level of Divine Consciousness you are neither better nor worse than anybody else. The pervasive competition in politics, education, science, art—in all facets of human life—is evil. It presumes that somebody is better than you. But nobody can be better than you. You have your talents, others have their talents, and everybody is part of the same Universal Reality. There is no need for competition and there is no need to try to be like somebody else. What is needed is to become more and more oneself, because within us is the infinite horizon of Goodness and Wisdom.

The Way of the Spiritual Warrior is to be in the world. The Spiritual Warrior realizes that this world is real, whereas the Piscean-type religions think it is an illusion, or they say that it is not the creation of God, that it is "of the devil". Millions of people still believe that this world is evil. For the Spiritual Warrior, however, *this* world is part of God, part of the Divine Reality, an aspect of the Divine Consciousness that manifests in this (the physical) realm of Creation. As a Spiritual Warrior you do not fight this Creation; you understand it and, having understood it, work with it in order to liberate yourself to greater awareness, greater union with the total Reality.

So the real competition is within you and has to do with your own growth and development, with unveiling or uncovering the spiritual regions within you; that is where the effort should be, not in competing with somebody else.

In reality, spiritual development is multidimensional—it embraces your personality, your Soul and the Spirit or Divinity within you—and you cannot measure your own status. Only people with spiritual vision can see your true status in life. The Way of the Spiritual Warrior is an individual development within the whole. Each tree in the forest grows by itself and each tree is part of the forest. As you are, you are a tree, responsible for your own growth in the forest, and you are part of the forest of trees, neither better nor worse than any other tree. And remember that even the littlest tree is beautiful in the Kingdom of God; even the least of the least is perfect in the Kingdom of God.

In the real Way of the Warrior, therefore, there are no comparisons. The Way is within you and you awaken the Divine Warrior within you as part of your own unfoldment, without comparing yourself to anybody else. There will always be people who are better than you at something or another, but that is their path, not yours. If you want to be better, you have to better yourself through the power inherent within you, the Divine as it expresses itself through you and in you.

If you can be yourself, the power comes to you more and more, but if you try to be somebody else, the effort of trying to be that other person takes away your power. By focusing your energy inside and developing yourself to be more powerful day by day, the current of energy inside you grows and unveils more and more of Reality from within. You become a Spiritual Warrior in your own Light, according to your own develop-ment—your own dharma, or destiny.

The Way of the Spiritual Warrior is an individual attainment but not because you are selfish, not because you want to be isolated or separated from society; on the contrary, it is simply because you are attaining your own spiritual horizons. At the same time, however, you know that others in the Spiritual School are doing the same thing for themselves, and together you form one hierarchy of evolving sentient beings—one hierarchy, one school, one reality. In the Inner Worlds there is only one Spiritual School, and only one Spiritual Hierarchy of enlightened Adepts or, if you like, Spiritual Warriors.

This School that I'm talking about has nothing to do with a particular religion, nothing to do with a particular culture, nothing to do with a particular *way*. It is the unveiling of the Divinity within each single person who enters the School, unveiling the Light within that person, because the Light shines uniquely within each person.

That is what we are trying to do, and it does not involve escaping the world. In the time of the Buddha that idea was already well established, and the Buddha also taught that you are supposed to escape from this dimension and absorb yourself into Nirvāṇa. But we do not say that you have to escape this world and enter Nirvāṇa. We say that you enter Nirvāṇa and enter this world; you enter the total Reality, because Nirvāṇa is just another part of the Inner Worlds in the Mind of God.[1]

In the process of attaining Nirvāṇa, moreover, two things happen: first, to get there, all that matters to you is your own Liberation, so you are useless to the world; and second, when you get there you are absorbed in a tremendous Bliss Consciousness, so again you are no help to the world and its evolution. People who are already in Nirvāṇa cannot liberate this world or help planetary evolution because they are tuned up and have no tuning-down devices. They are in a state of consciousness where they cannot even perceive the world condition; to them it does not exist anymore.

The Spiritual Warrior, however, perceives the world condition and is able to put the Light of Nirvāṇa, the Divine Consciousness, into the world, to change the planetary structure, the very atomic vibration of the

---

1. See the diagram *The Seven Great Planes of Being* at the front of this book.

planet. As a Spiritual Warrior you start off *here*, using your physical body and the physical world as a base, and then slowly expand outwardly and inwardly, extending your circle of awareness towards the inner dimensions and absorbing ever-larger realities. And when you enter Nirvāṇa as a Spiritual Warrior, Nirvāṇa becomes part of that all-inclusiveness, part of the vast embrace of the Warrior, the outer region of that embrace. But all the while you are still centred in the world, still actively working to liberate Humanity from its worldly condition.

Remember that this is a non-selfish path. You attain Enlightenment so that you can help the world and help the evolution of human consciousness.

The reason this particular age is an extremely materialistic age has to do with the current astrological setup. As the planet moves through the zodiac it comes under different influences that condition planetary life. We are now in the Aquarian Age and therefore the vibration from that group of stars is influencing our planet. Unfortunately the Aquarian vibration is materialistic and mental, which means that it is geared towards Physical Plane expression and Mental Plane expression. That is why scientific development has shot up in a steep curve since the Aquarian Age started in 1875.

This is what most people do not understand: The Buddha was a Spiritual Warrior; the Christ was a Spiritual Warrior; Moses was a Spiritual Warrior; Muhammad was a Spiritual Warrior; Kṛṣṇa was a Spiritual Warrior; Arjuna was a Spiritual Warrior, Lao Tzu was a Spiritual Warrior. All the great spiritual reformers of the past belonged to the Spiritual Warrior School—*without exception*. Which means they followed the Path of the Warrior that we are describing, not symbolically but in the literal sense of the word. They put the energy of Enlightenment into the world to transform the world with the Understanding and Inner Wisdom they had gained. They did it because they were Warriors—true Warriors following the true Spiritual Warrior Path.

Under the influence of Aquarius, therefore, science will continue to evolve and material goods will increase, and so will the ability of the mind to understand, to reason and to do research and other scientific work. But notice that the Aquarian energy has these two vibrations, the vibration of matter and the vibration of mind, but it has no vibration of the Soul or the Spirit.

So this age will be the age of gadgets and it will satisfy everyone's immediate mental and physical needs, but it will not provide a spiritual understanding of life—the sense of devotion to the Divine, the sense that there is another invisible reality, the sense that there is a larger destiny for Mankind. This is why it is important that the Spiritual Way is taught to people because it will be increasingly forgotten. If materialism wins, in a hundred years' time spirituality will just become a mythology, and the only reality will be science and the accumulation of wealth.

So it is important to understand that the Spiritual Warrior Path is a real path and it begins and ends with you, but in combination with the others travelling with you. And this is the beauty of this Path: You walk the path within you but you are walking together with others, and every discovery you make within you helps the others and, believe it or not, it helps Humanity. This is why the Buddha said, "Be a light unto yourself" and the Christ said, "I am the light of the world" (John.8: 12).

Once the Light shines within you it shines out towards the whole world—not symbolically but actually. An invisible Light shines out of you that stimulates other people's minds and understanding, improving their consciousness, their knowledge, their way of living. This Light shatters the materialistic illusion of people, because materialism is a grand illusion. It says you are separated from everybody else as a unique little island and you have to fight for your own rights. When the Light shines within you, you know that you are one with everybody and everybody is equal. So you do not have to struggle to conquer somebody else because they are part of you.

The ancient Way of the Warrior is the Noble Path because it asks you to live your normal life, whatever is normal for you. It is a Western way for Westerners. By this I mean it takes care of your materialistic consciousness, your materialistic environment, your materialistic background and education—the way you have been brought up—and within *that* context you walk the Path. You start off exactly where you are. You base your spirituality on yourself, the Westerner you are, with the understanding that the Way is within you and that it evolves out of your Soul. On this Path, it is being what you are that gives you the success to become more and more. ⚔

THE WARRIOR AND HEALTH

The problem with this materialistic age is its one-percent vision of life—the physical world is all there is. That is only one percent of Reality. So the whole medical system relies on what can be objectively seen and touched and heard in the objective physical world. I know there are some doctors or counsellors who are different, who may be spiritual, but I am talking about the vast majority who are materialistic. It is the mass that counts, not the few individuals who are different.

So in the materialistic view, the only thing that is real is the solid physical body, the solid physical world and whatever you can produce from the solid physical world—which is why the medical profession relies so much on drugs. If it were true that the physical world is all there is, then naturally what they are doing would be absolutely correct. I mean you would have to rely on the physical world system and everything you can get from it. But the problem is, the materialistic view of life is completely wrong; that is *not* how reality is.

Therefore, to the ancient Warriors and all the great enlightened Sages, healing and health had very much to do with the Invisible Worlds, the other ninety-nine percent of the Cosmos, and the invisible you, the other ninety-nine percent of *You*. In other words, the question of healing and the question of health are more complicated than what they appear to be.

Now, materialists do not even believe in the mind. They think the mind is the brain and the nervous system. They do not know that the mind is a separate living reality from the physical body and the physical brain. So all the healing methods, techniques and knowledge based solely on the physical are bound to be insufficient, for the simple reason that a human being is not just a physical body and the mind is not the brain or the nervous system.

The Four "Wheels" of the Personality

When the medical profession (or any profession) says that the physical is the only thing and tries to base all solutions on that, it's like trying to run a car on one wheel. Have you ever tried to run a car on one wheel? It can be done but it is rather difficult.

The personality runs on four wheels: you have a physical body; an etheric-physical body, which is your vital body; an astral body, your feeling nature; and a mental body, or your mind. You are a car running on four wheels. So if you want to keep your car running you have to maintain the health of your physical body, your etheric body, your astral body and your mental body.

Remember, this is not You; it is your personality, the car you are driving around in this world. The health systems in every country do not acknowledge the other three wheels of the car, let alone the Soul within, the spiritual entity you are, and let alone the Divine Spark, your Spiritual Source. They are not even dreamed about!

So the human personality is composed of the physical body and its vibrations and qualities, the so-called genes, cells, and so on. You also have an invisible etheric body, which is technically what we call the *vital force*. This is not a myth; it is as real as electricity or any other physical force. The ancient Greeks called it PNEUMA and the ancient Romans, SPIRITUS. Spiritual Warriors use it, drawing the etheric vital force out of the environment, and so do some healers. So-called *prana-healers* and people who lay hands on the sick use the etheric force from the environment or from a plant or from within themselves. Nowadays, of course, we don't believe in such "nonsense" as a vital force; that idea was chucked out in the nineteenth century.

You also have an astral body, which is your emotional body. Again, materialists think that emotions are simply changes in your brain cells or your nervous system. Yes, the brain reacts to everything you do, but the brain is not the *cause*. Materialists think that the brain is the cause of everything. (There's no use talking to them because they will not admit any possibility beyond their one-percent view of life. They will force every explanation into that view and refuse to acknowledge that there can be a larger view.)

Healing has to do with harmonizing the four wheels of your car, because they are all continually interacting with each other. For instance, you may be lucky to be born with a healthy physical body because your mom and dad had good genes. But if you have negative emotions all the time, if you get angry or depressed or feel sorry for yourself, you will still get sick, no matter how good your genes are. Similarly, if you overwork your mind it will affect your emotions and your physical body and your vitality. And if you are one of those superactive people who do extreme sports, you overuse your etheric vital body. If you exhaust your vital body you will exhaust your physical body.

This is because your mental body, astral body, vital body and physical body are structures and therefore have limitations. So if you abuse any one of them it affects the others. All four wheels of your car work together, influencing one another all the time: the wrong kinds of emotions will affect your mind, your vital body and your physical body; the wrong kinds of thoughts will affect your emotional body, physical body and vital body; and the wrong kinds of energies will impact on all your bodies, no matter where the abuse is or where you are overusing or wrongly using the energy. The wrong use of any body will affect the others because the car is driven on four wheels, *simultaneously*; a car has to have all four wheels turning at the same time.

There are many people in the health field, some working on the physical body level, some on the emotional level and some on the mind level, but it does not matter what healing profession you belong to, you must consider all four wheels of the person. Doctors nowadays specialize in parts of the body, which is rather unfortunate because they are even limiting their one-percent view of life, specializing in one percent of the one percent. They look at smaller and smaller parts of the picture, and within that narrow view they are all correct, but the problem is that they do not have the larger vision.

Health and the Law of Karma

It is only in the alternative medicine field that there are healers who believe that a human being is actually more than a physical body and they need to treat the whole person—the mental nature, the emotional nature, the vitality nature and of course the physical body. That is, they have the vision that they should treat people in a more holistic or comprehensive way to attain health. They try to heal people by telling them about breathing properly so their vital body will be healthy, about not having negative emotions and about right thinking and having the right understanding of life. But the healing field is not an easy field at all. Even if you understand that you need a more complex treatment that looks at the whole life, even if you get people to do everything correctly, it will still not be enough—because there are *causes* of illness that are beyond the personality level.

A human being is a Soul, a Reincarnating Ego, and has a causal body having all the past life impressions within it. And those impressions express themselves in the present incarnation according to the Law of Karma.

The factor of Karma is simple: in every lifetime you bring something to work out from past lifetimes. You are a Living Soul in your causal body, and before you incarnate you consider what you did in your past lives and the unbalance of forces you created (your so-called bad karma), and you decide that in this lifetime you are going to work out some of that unbalance. This is all crystal clear when you are in your causal body, in Soul-Consciousness, but when you are born, unfortunately, it is all forgotten.

So you are born in your personality and do all the right things according to the textbook of alternative health, but you still get sick or something bad happens to you. This means that your Soul decided that you should not cruise along all your life in perfect health, with everything going your way and not the slightest problem. No, your Soul decided to pay off a certain amount of bad karma and rebalance your karmic record, so you, the present personality, are going to cop it. Of course, you do not know that; you just get all kinds of suffering. This is what many people do not understand; even if you do everything right, you may have to go through a lot of suffering—physical, emotional and mental.

Krishnamurti, for example, was a holy man and he suffered from a steady migraine from about the age of twenty-nine until he died. He did not have the kind of stress in his life that would normally cause severe migraines, but he suffered because he was working out past karma. His Soul knew that he had to work out a certain amount of karma to keep his level of Liberation or lift him up so that he could reach a higher level and be freer in the Inner Worlds.

Karma is much like borrowing money from a bank and then setting up a repayment system. You try to pay back as little each month as possible, of course, but bankers are smart enough to know that you won't pay your debt by the time you are dead and will expect you to pay enough each month. That is how it is with Karma.

You borrowed the money, which is to say, you borrowed certain consequences of actions that are multidimensional—physical, emotional, mental—and involve the whole personality, so you stored up debt in your causal body that your Soul feels needs to be paid back. The Soul says, "If I suffer from cancer or have a car accident, I can balance up this part of the account." The Soul does not think of this as a problem but a way of adjusting the karmic balance sheet. It becomes a problem for the personality, who does not understand what is actually going on.

To put it another way, if the causes of ill health are in the present circumstances or situation on any personality level (physical, etheric, emotional or mental), then the problem can be remedied. But if they are karmic, that is to say, the Soul is working out karma through that illness, then it is more difficult to remedy. It is not impossible, but you have to get the approval of the Soul.

Health and Culture

You may think this is the whole story, but there is more to it still. Believe it or not, your health is also influenced by your environment—the country you live in, the people you associate with, your culture, religion, society; they all help or hinder your health expression.

If your family has problems and is fighting all the time, you are naturally going to be influenced by that. If you live in a society that is

---

Suppose you are living a normal, ordinary life and your country goes to war with another country, and you get wounded and suffer for the rest of your life. You could say that you did not deserve to suffer, that you were living a good life and did not hate anybody. But you are simply part of the karma of your nation, or national karma, the karma being worked out between nations, between races, between religions. You are caught up in mass karma that has absolutely nothing to do with you.

In New Zealand, for example, there was warfare between the British and the Māori in the nineteenth century and the karmic consequences are still being felt today. Of course, the present generation does not understand why things are happening to them that they have not created, but events in the Cosmos flow in sequence like waves upon waves upon waves, and a wave started in the past will affect the present generation even though it had nothing to do with producing it.

prone to violence, where there is wrong thinking, wrong feeling, wrong action, you will take that karma on as well. You may be raised in a reasonably healthy family environment and with reasonably normal mental, physical, emotional and vital functions, but if you happen to go to a rough school, you will pick up the wrong energy of the rough kids.

In other words, health also depends on external factors. This is another thing that modern health professionals do not understand: the people who come to see them bring their family, culture, religion and country with them, because they bring their environment with them. It is like the fish in the sea: they breathe in the sea and breathe out the sea, and if the sea is poisoned, the fish are poisoned. The human being is like that, too. If you personally do the right thing and live a reasonably balanced life but are living in a chaotic, unbalanced environment, you pick up that environment and it affects your health, because you are like the fish in the sea: you are part of your environment.

So it is important for health professionals to consider that a person is not an isolated unit, that apart from a person's health problems they should also consider the person's environment. This was partially understood by doctors of the seventeenth, eighteenth and nineteenth centuries. In those days, if you lived in a big city like London and were suffering from a disease, doctors had a simple solution: they recommended that you go out into the countryside and spend a few months there. Did they understand the occult reason for that? No. But they knew that if you went out into the countryside and were in a natural, healthy environment for a few months, it would be better for you than being in the city.

People living in big cities often lack energy simply because they do not get enough sunshine or fresh air. They go to work, they go home; they are never in Nature, just concrete, brick and stone. So they lack vitality because their etheric body does not commune with Nature. We get energy from the Sun; the etheric vibration of the Sun gives energy to our etheric vital body. So if a person is cooped up indoors all the time, they have increasingly less and less energy and get more and more tired. But basically this is a health problem that can be easily remedied: they should go to a beach or walk in a forest, just be in Nature and allow the energies of Nature to re-energize their etheric vital body.

The point is that an individual's health depends on their school environment, work environment, home environment and the environment of the country. If the country is always at war, like certain countries where wars between rebels and government forces go on for decades, or if the country has a corrupt government and there is no social order, individuals will naturally suffer health problems because of the massive negative characteristics and tendencies of society itself, which reflect back on the individual. If hate and violence permeate the atmosphere that you live in and breathe in, you become hateful and violent.

Health professionals therefore have to think on a large scale: community-wide, nationwide and even worldwide. They have to consider that this planet is sick because of the mass effect of wrong vibrations—the wrong thinking, wrong feelings and wrong actions cast off by the seven billion human beings in incarnation. These impact the planetary structure and atmosphere and produce floods, earthquakes, tidal waves, fires and other disasters, because Nature has to react to work out karma and recover from all that negativity, which impacts Humanity on a large scale. The materialistic consciousness says, "This is unfair. Why does God allow these disasters to happen?" God does not have anything to do with it; much of it is a human creation.

To heal the planet we need to have enlightened beings who understand the big picture, where the real causes are and how they are working themselves out in the present, and what this generation can do so that the next generation will not have the same problems. But this does not seem to be happening on the planet at the moment because there are not enough people with enough intelligence to understand what is going on.

Spiritual Healing

Healing, from the ancient Warrior point of view, has to do with the condition of the four bodies of the personality and how the bodies relate to the Soul (because the Soul determines the personality's karma) and then how the Soul relates to the Spirit within. This is an even deeper layer of understanding because in the ancient system of healing the Warriors had to understand the relationship between "Heaven and Earth", which means the relationship between the outer world and the Inner Worlds. They also had to understand how the Inner Worlds relate to the unknowable Absolute, the final point of reference of Reality.

So they had to understand not only what karma the Soul was working out but also how the Soul related to the Spirit within and how to improve that relationship. That is to say, there is another, even deeper side to healing which is about how the Soul relates to the Divinity within, because that relationship is changing all the time as you evolve and get closer to Reality, as your Soul Nature contains more Light, more Purity, more Harmony, more Grace, and becomes more in tune with the Infinite.

For the Ancients, the final solution, the final healing knowledge was the Enlightenment process—to meditate and go into higher states of consciousness and have superior experiences—because it is through meditation that the Soul and Spirit connection is made and the whole equation of personal existence is radically changed as the person goes onto a completely different, higher evolutionary level. In the future, when healing is a spiritual art, people will be taught how to meditate and the steps to attaining inner levels of consciousness, to getting in touch with their higher Self, because that will be part of the understanding of how to be healthy.

All the great Warrior Schools had all kinds of herbal medicines and healing techniques—Sound healing, Colour healing, meditation—all kinds of remedies based on the ancient knowledge that a human being is a multidimensional entity and the Cosmos is a multidimensional cosmos, and that they are continually interacting. And this is precisely what is missing in the modern world—consideration of the visible and invisible worlds and of the invisible nature of human beings. ✗

~ 3 ~

THE CAUSES OF DISEASE

Physical Energy

The Spiritual Warrior's understanding of health is radically different from the modern view of health. Nowadays, there are all kinds of healers offering all kinds of remedies, but few explain the causes of disease and how to prevent disease. The Way of the Spiritual Warrior is about prevention of disease, about being in perfect health and vitality. So we will deal with what causes problems in the first place, so that you won't have to give heaps of money to the drug companies; I'm going to teach you how to reduce their level of income.

There is a tendency in modern society to concentrate on food. Health fanatics think that by eating this or not eating that they will attain health, which might be true if there were nothing to the human being except the physical body. But the problem is that the food we eat is only a fragment of the absolute Reality; it does not give all the answers to anything and everything.

So we will go step by step from the most obvious causes of health to the subtlest and slowly build up the concept of what a Spiritual Warrior understands by health and how the great ancient Warriors maintained themselves in perfect condition year in and year out. You will understand that it involves a bit more than the food you eat.

I will start with the most obvious: the physical world, the one percent of Reality that is visible, what everybody is most aware of. Your physical body has a biorhythm, which is how your physical body normally functions when you allow it to, and planet Earth has a biorhythm, which we call the seasons or the weather, and the two are inseparable and work together.

Biorhythm refers to the rhythm of life within the body, whether it's a human, animal or plant body. Everything that lives, everything that has a physical body, has a biorhythm. In an ideal condition the Earth would be functioning normally and the energies of Nature would flow naturally through each part of the Earth, with the four seasons flowing into each other and with the biorhythms of all the human beings following the biorhythms of Nature, with no physical diseases and everything in harmony.

That is an ideal picture, of course, which does not exist these days, for many reasons. First of all, there is pressure from the Cosmos because the Sun is undergoing a major revolution of a higher frequency; therefore, it is putting pressure on planet Earth.[2] This means that the normal biorhythms, the normal weather patterns that have been observed for centuries in each part of the globe, have been broken. Snow falls in places where it has never snowed before, while the polar ice is melting. This impacts the human beings living on the planet because our physical bodies cannot readjust suddenly to a different biorhythm, so we are susceptible to bugs and viruses.

So, one part of the problem is that Nature is not functioning smoothly anymore for cosmic reasons. Another part of the problem of why people fall ill is their wrong lifestyle, or wrong behaviour patterns that are not in tune with Nature. In the early days we were in tune with Nature: when the Sun came up we got up and started our activities; when the Sun

2. This is described in more detail in: Imre Vallyon, *Planetary Transformation: A Personal Guide to Embracing Planetary Change* (Sounding-Light Publishing, 2010), 75–83.

went down we went to sleep. We followed the biorhythm of the planet in relationship to the Sun, and we were healthier and lived longer.

The rhythm of Nature is based on how things have been established in Creation, so when the Sun comes up you receive the Sun's rays, the physical vibration of the Sun, which stimulates your physical body into activity; therefore you can do things. And when the Sun goes down you have to produce the energy that is no longer there. The Moon's rays stimulate our astral consciousness, so we are supposed to be out of the body, sleeping, while we are active in the Astral World in our dreams.

But what do people do? They sleep during the day, under the rulership of the Sun, and mess up their whole biorhythm. This is partly because of the invention of electricity and artificial light, but there is more to it than that: much of the problem is partying or staying up all night because it's the cool thing to do. The early part of the morning is when the positive energy of the rising Sun is entering into your system. If you sleep then, your physical body gradually becomes weaker, more susceptible to physical diseases. You are out of tune with Nature, and I'm not even talking about the invisible side of Nature but the physical side. Your lifestyle is wrong, not what Nature originally intended.

Early to bed and early to rise makes a man healthy, wealthy and wise. Wealthy? Maybe. Wise? No. For that you have to do other things. But it certainly makes you healthy.

In the early days people used to have a nap at midday because at that time the Sun is so powerful that it overcharges you. Have you ever been at a beach in the sun for three or four hours and found that you were totally exhausted? Well, if you are in the sun for half an hour it increases your energy and you feel vital and strong, but if you're in the sun for longer than what your physical body can absorb, you can lose consciousness as a self-defence mechanism. But in the shade you can stay outside longer and it will recharge your physical body because the shade does not prevent the energy of the Sun from penetrating into your body.

But the main lesson here is the irregular lifestyle, the sleeping and waking at the wrong times. I know you can become habituated to work at night and to sleep during the day, and after a while the body takes up that new rhythm, but the body will be fighting against the natural tendency, so it has to work twice as much. If you work at night using the Moon energy, therefore, your physical resources will be more easily depleted than if you were working during the daytime, because your body has to get energy from another source than what Nature intended.

Another physical cause of illness is what may be called chaotic living. Chaotic living—which is prevalent nowadays—is where you have absolutely no idea what you are going to do next and you just let things happen as they happen. Your daily activities are chaotic; you senselessly move from one thing to another without purpose. Millions of people live like that. They have no direction or rhythm in their physical bodily life. The body needs a rhythm. Without it, the body will be prone to physical illness. It is as simple as that. Eighty percent of colds and other illnesses could be vanquished if people just lived how Nature intended them to live.

Of course, Nature itself is being messed up nowadays, so you have to be even more cautious. For instance, suppose you are trying your best to go along with Nature, there is still the problem of a sudden seasonal change. The Sun has been shining for a week and then suddenly the weather is back in the middle of winter. Unfortunately, the physical body reacts because it has no defence mechanism against sudden changes of weather. This means that you have to be more aware of protecting yourself.

So far we have been dealing with the physical body; now we will consider the invisible side, the ninety-nine percent of Life.

Etheric Energy (Prāṇa)

The four etheric dimensions[3] are still physical—what we call the *subtle physical*—but they are invisible because they vibrate at a slightly higher pitch than the three regions of the dense physical (solids, liquids and gases). Now, as I mentioned previously, a human being is composed of more than just a physical body. The etheric body is within the physical body, the etheric world (the etheric body of the planet) is within the dense physical world and the etheric Sun is within the dense physical Sun—and they all extend beyond their physical counterparts. The etheric Sun, etheric world and etheric body interact with the dense physical Sun, physical world and physical body, and this is where the picture changes again.

Have you ever been walking in the mountains or in Nature or on a city street on a nice, crisp winter morning and suddenly felt really happy and full of life and vitality? Well, that was because your etheric body was in tune with the etheric world (the etheric part of your environment), which happened to be in tune with the vibration of the etheric Sun at that time, making you feel charged and buzzing with energy inside. In other words, the whole physical and etheric environment was full of energy—Prāṇa—and that got communicated to you through your etheric body. So there is a connection between your physical body, your etheric body, the etheric world and the etheric Sun and that is how you get your life-force, which is technically what life really is.

On the other hand, have you ever been walking in a smoggy city or on a dark winter night and felt heavy and depressed, like you could hardly lift one leg after the other? Again, your physical body was not receiving etheric energy from the etheric environment, which was not receiving etheric energy from the Sun, so you felt sluggish and heavy.

---

3. In spiritual language we use the word *dimensions* in terms of worlds or planes of being, not the mathematical or scientific definition of the word.

The vitality, or Prāṇa, in the environment can change from country to country or within a country or a region, so one area can have more vitality than another. It depends on how that part of the country relates to the etheric body of the planet and how that environment relates to the etheric body of the Sun.

You can actually see Prāṇa, by the way. I'll tell you an interesting experience I had when I was a small child. I was lying in bed and looking at the ceiling when I saw bluish white droplets or lines coming down like rain. I thought, "That's peculiar; I don't think it's raining." I kept watching and then got a sense that they were intelligent, so I started to play with them. I imagined them moving sideways and they started

---

Prāṇa and Breatharians

There have been many Saints in India who lived on air only, but this is where the new agers went wrong back in the sixties and seventies. We had a case in New Zealand where a woman, the head of a New Age community, decided to be a breatharian and live on air only. Of course she died soon thereafter. That's because the Yogīs and Saints who live on breath only are in a state of Higher Consciousness. They work with cosmic energies and can absorb the Prāṇic currents in the air—and they do nothing physically. They are not laying bricks or rushing off to the office or organizing a family. They just sit and meditate and breathe air.

There were also Christian Saints who lived on air. Saint Theresa, for instance, lived only on one communion wafer, given by the priest at Mass every day, and the breath of the Spirit. But she also did not *do* anything. If she had to do heavy physical work every day she would have needed to densify her body vibration and get more in touch with the earth.

This is where a little knowledge is a dangerous thing and many breatharians fade away and die or become anorexic because they don't understand that it is not the right thing for them to do, especially if they are active in the world. There are Himalayan Yogīs who spend all their lives in caves meditating and doing nothing else. Of course, they can live on fresh air. But for a westerner who is beginning to learn meditation to decide to become a breatharian and live on Prāṇa, well, the disaster is already in the making.

moving sideways; then I imagined them going up and they started moving up. Later on, I realized that it was Prāṇa, the life-force of the planet, and at other times I perceived it as little, pearl-shaped globules of light. Of course, it is all the same Prāṇa, the life-force that comes from the Sun and is absorbed by the planet through its etheric body (and by us through our etheric bodies).

So your etheric body and how it relates to the etheric body of the world and how that relates to the etheric body of the Sun all play a part in your health.

Causes of Diseases Originating in the Astral World

Now we come to a different level of Reality. As I said, your astral body interpenetrates your etheric body and your etheric body interpenetrates your physical body. So immediately this gives you a clue: your health is directly affected not only by what happens to you on the physical level, not only by what happens to you on the etheric level, but also by what happens to you on the astral level. This has to be understood, because you function as a unit. As I mentioned previously, you are a four-wheel drive car and all four wheels function together as a unit.

The astral body of the Sun extends throughout the Solar System and beyond it, and within that great astral field is the astral body of our planet Earth, the Astral World. The Astral World provides your vitality and energy and it provides vitality and energy for the astral bodies of the plants, animals, elemental beings and angelic hierarchies living in the physical and non-physical dimensions of the planet. That is to say, these myriads of astral bodies are fed by the Astral World, which is fed by the Astral Sun.

Diseases in the Astral World can be caused by cosmic factors, such as the astral body of the Earth not receiving the full astral force of the Sun, or by human factors, the astral energies being warped by human emotions. For us, therefore, the big problem is how the astral energies are shaped by human moods, desires and emotions, and in turn how the astral energies impact on the moods, desires and emotions of humans. This is the key to emotional or psychological ill health; all the so-called psychological diseases would disappear if humans could relate to the astral realm correctly.

So it is important to know how the human astral body and the Astral World relate to each other, which can be summarized as follows:

If your astral body vibrates with the right moods, desires, feelings and emotions, you produce the right kind of energy, which connects you to the right part of the Astral World, where the energies are in accordance with the positive nature of your emotions. If your emotions are wrong, that is to say, negative, they link you to astral energies that are negative and in turn impact on you with even more negativity.

This is not the teaching of the Pope, the Buddha or the Dalai Lama; it is a natural law, a cosmic law.

In the real world, therefore, your emotions impact on your astral body, then on the Astral World, and then back onto you again. Your astral body is like a large, egg-shaped oval around you, and when it's functioning correctly it is full of beautiful colours—red, orange, green, yellow, violet—all shining brightly. This means that you are a perfectly healthy person on the Astral World, that is, your emotional structure is in harmony with the Cosmic Law and you therefore attract only those kinds of energies in the Astral World that are in accordance with that law. So you get energies of joy, bliss, lightness, happiness, grace, and so on, because your positive emotions invoke positive astral energies.

Negative emotions like self-pity, jealousy, fear, anger, depression, worry and tension warp the energy of the astral body: with self-pity, your astral body energies become darker and curl in like big claws inside you; with jealousy, your aura (astral body) turns a murky green; with fear, anger and depression, it is murky brown, dark red or black; worry is dark grey in colour and tension appears like bright red jagged lines. Your whole vibrational nature (the colours in your astral body) changes according to the negative moods, desires and feelings you have, and these attract, from the astral currents, astral energies that are like in nature, because in the Inner Worlds, like attracts like. Then you will be swamped by your negative moods and feelings and be even more miserable than you were before. In the case of fear, for example, the warped energy of the Astral World that produces fear swamps your system, and you will be afraid to even get into an elevator. (Many phobias are due to the reinforcement of a negative emotional energy from the Astral World.)

I'm trying to say that a negative emotion has a certain frequency of vibration that warps your astral body, which attracts an energy with the same vibration from the Astral, which in turn increases the negative voltage of the astral body. Over time this affects the etheric body and destroys its vitality, that is, the capability of the etheric body to defend you. So this negativity impacts on the physical body, and lo and behold, you begin to have *physical symptoms*—a part of your physical body begins to react and produces the negative condition—and you have what is called a psychosomatic disease.

The Warrior Life: Preventative Medicine

Spiritual practices like meditation, breathing techniques, chanting and intonation prevent psychological illnesses, because they put you in the right emotional state, the right vibration. Look at the great Warriors of the past; they were shining, bright, positive and purposeful, not sickly and lying in a hospital bed all day taking pills. The whole Spiritual Path, the Way of the Warrior, is preventative medicine: how to *attain* harmony and how to *maintain* that harmony once you have attained it. It is a scientific system.

Part of the defence mechanism of the Spiritual Warrior is to be positive all the time, to always be radiating rays of positivity from your aura so that it is difficult for the normal negativity from others to enter your sphere. It is all part of the Art of the Spiritual Warrior, who is a Warrior on all levels, not only on the physical but also on the astral, mental and causal, all the way to the Heart of Divinity.

Causes of Diseases Originating in the Mental World

So far we have covered various causes of diseases up to the Astral World, and now we are going to consider the causes of diseases originating in the next dimension, the Mental World (the Mental Plane).

Your mental body is real: it is an ovoid-shaped body within your astral body and it extends beyond it (just as your astral body is within and extends beyond your etheric body, which is within and extends beyond your physical body). So your mental body is larger than your astral body and it is made of a finer substance or matter. The physical body is made of the densest matter, the etheric-physical body of lighter matter, the astral body of still lighter matter and the mental body is made of even lighter matter. But they are all made of *matter*, of visible substance. To clairvoyants, people's mental bodies and auras look just as real and solid as physical objects. On the Mental Plane, a mental "object" (a thought) is just as solid for your mental body as a physical object is solid for your physical body.

The relationship between your mental body and the Mental Plane has to be understood. There is always an interrelationship between you and the world around you—your physical environment, etheric-physical environment, astral environment and mental environment (which, of course, you are related to through your mental body, your mind). So the first thing to understand is that your mental state, your mental attitude, either enlivens your mental body or poisons it. By the Law of Reaction, therefore, whatever happens in your mental body will impact *you*—first your astral body and from there your etheric body and then your physical body, where it finally manifests as a physical, mental or psychological disease in your physical organs, brain, nervous system, and so on.

So it is important to understand the poisonous mental states that produce illness inside you, because they are so prevalent among Mankind, which is why there are always so many people who are sick.

We will start with *self-centredness*, which is a mental condition pervading the minds of hundreds of millions of people. If you are self-centred, whatever substance or life-force or energy you have in your mind, your mental body, is turned inward, toward yourself. Your mental body is surrounded by the Mental World like an ocean, so if you are habitually self-centred as a way of life, you cannot draw life-force or energy from the Mental Plane because your way of being is focused on yourself, your own little, narrow world. (This is why self-centred people are highly opinionated and narrow in their thinking.) Your mental structure becomes your whole universe and you have no way to sense the larger realities outside of you. What is more, if your mental body is contracted and not able to function normally, your astral body and your vital body will also be contracted, so you will not get energy from the *vital plane*, the etheric dimensions, and you will suffer from lack of lustre, lifelessness and debility.

Thought Pools

The opposite of self-centredness is openness. When your mental body is open, all the mental energies flow through you and you are able to receive inspiration, to tune into higher realities; you are able to receive *Thought Pools*.

The Astral World is like an ocean interpenetrating the Physical World, and the Mental World is also like an ocean interpenetrating the Astral and the Physical. And like a real ocean, the astral substance and the mental substance contain waves and whirlpools. The whirlpools in the Mental World are what we call *Thought Pools*—imprints of the greatest minds of the planet that stay on the Mental World in the form of pools of swirling energies.

If you are a person with an open mind, you will be able to tune into the Thought Pools of the minds of the Buddha, the Christ, Kṛṣṇa, Rāma, Lao Tzu, Moses, Mohammad; the minds of the greatest Mystics, Saints and Masters; the minds that were creative in any field, not just the spiritual field; the minds of the great musicians, scientists and philosophers who have gone before or are alive today. Through your mental body, you can tune into the mental structure created in the Mental World by the greatest minds because their Thought Pools are maintained in the mental dimensions for the benefit of Mankind, as positive forces in the evolution of our planet, the evolution of Humanity.

Another cause of disease that springs from the mind body is *malicious thinking*. This too is common; many people have what I call an evil mind. They always look for faults in people and, when they find them, happily talk about them to other people. They have an evil way of working the mind, tearing people down, either openly or subtly. If you could see the mental body of such a person, it would have large black and dark reddish swirls which act as destructive cells within the mental body, similar to cancer or other cells that destroy the physical body. So although malicious thinkers manage to damage other people, what they don't know is that in that process they also damage their own mental bodies, and that damage filters down into their physical body so that they will become sick as a result of their malicious thinking.

Another problem is *mental pride*. A mentally proud person is one who thinks he or she is above everybody else, a know-it-all who cannot be taught anything. They are proud of their attainments, knowledge, education, status in life, family history or whatever—people have mental pride for all kinds of different reasons. The mental aura of such a person contains big, murky, dark yellowish globules, and if there are many of these dark globules they block the free flow of energy in the mental body, which, again, filters down into the physical body and blocks out the life-force, weakening the person physically.

Another problem is *competitiveness*. Competitiveness—in sports, religion, business—permeates society because everybody thinks it's a good thing. Well, actually, it isn't. A little bit of competitiveness may be okay because it stimulates you into action—a *little bit*. But what if this is the way people live all the time, in every place and situation? At school you have to compete against everybody in your class and everybody in the other classes, and your school has to compete against all the other schools. This idea of competing against everybody all the time seems to be the salvation of Mankind, but all it does is create stress in the mind body. And if you compete a lot, you stress out your mental body, your astral body and your etheric body, and it comes out as severe headaches or a nervous breakdown. So competitiveness is another cause of ill health.

Another mental cause of disease that afflicts hundreds of millions people is *lack of direction*. The mind—the mental body—likes to work in a systematic, directed manner; otherwise, it goes into a self-destruct state. I'll give you an example. Suppose you are a creative artist and are writing a book, composing a piece of music, carving a sculpture, preparing a talk or acting in a movie. While you are doing that your mind is positively engaged. It has a sense of direction and purpose and is attracting a large amount of energy from the Mental Plane, which works down to the physical level, giving you extra energy and power. So you are happy.

But when that work comes to an end—you gave your talk, you finished your sculpture, you composed your music, you wrote your book, your movie is finished—then you fall into a slump. When this happens, people start drinking and popping pills and they often end up in the gutter and have to go into rehabilitation. This is the story of artists that is repeated over and over again, and the simple reason is that while their mind is engaged in a positive action, it is functioning correctly, in a holistic, coherent, purposeful, directed manner. But after the work of art is finished, the mind no longer has a direction and the downward spiral begins. It does not have to be like this, but most people do not know that. The solution is simple: they can redirect their mind into another field of action and set themselves another goal, and their mind will be positively engaged again.

Many people get into states of depression and other negative states and suffer from physical illnesses from lack of purpose and intelligent direction in their existence. They need to have a purpose in life. It can be an artistic, religious, political or academic purpose. What the purpose is doesn't matter; what matters is the coherent functioning of the mind, that the mind has a plan and works toward it systematically. That keeps the mental body together in a positive, healthy way, which works down to the other levels.

Related to this is the problem of doing too much. As I said, when you are doing something your mind is directed and functioning normally, it has a plan and purpose, and all the energies are working coherently towards that purpose. But what if you decide that you are going to become a taxi driver and at the same time study for a PhD in chemistry and become a ballerina? Then, one part of your mind is pushing energy this way, another part that way and another part in a third way. Of course, the cross currents in the mental dimensions get more and more entwined and entangled until you end up in the local mental hospital. So doing too much, having too many purposes at the same time, is another problem.

There is one more cause of disease that is more deadly than all the rest of the mental diseases: *materialistic thinking*. In fact, materialism produces more mental and physical illnesses than all the others combined. By *materialism* I mean the belief that your body is the real you and this physical world is the only reality and beyond it there is nothing. Millions of people believe that, which means that all their thoughts, all their internal energy and resources, their whole life current is restricted to *this* reality only, and they cannot breathe in or draw from the larger energies and realities of the spiritual dimensions inside themselves. They have a narrow view of life, and therefore the life-force inside them can only function at perhaps one percent of what it could be. So they are susceptible to be attacked by diseases from the outside.

The Ultimate Cause of All Diseases

Now we are going to go one level higher than the Mental World to the Causal World, which is the source of the cause of all diseases!

The biggest cause of disease—the cause of causes, the cause from which all diseases originate—is simply this: lack of Soul Awareness. You are a Soul in a causal body in the Causal World under the all-pervading Luminous Causal Sun. The fact that people live in the personality structure without Soul Awareness is the single cause of all diseases. They have no Soul direction in their lives, no Luminous Causal Sun to illumine their being, no consciousness of the tremendous beauty, grace, harmony and bliss of the Causal World.

This is why in every great spiritual tradition the first thing you are taught is to meditate, meditate, meditate, so that you will regain your Soul connection and know yourself as a Soul, the perfection of Beauty, Harmony, Joy and Love.

Your Soul, your causal body, is also where you store up karma. You have been born thousands of times and after each lifetime there was an assessment of the total meaning of your life. This assessment is not like an examination in which Saint Peter asks, "Well, my son, tell me what you did so I can send you either up or down." In this assessment, your whole life-wave (all your experiences from the time you were born until the time you died) is concentrated into a *knowledge-atom*, a causal atom of *Intelligence* that summarizes the meaning of that particular lifetime.

The Soul, the Self within you, is covered by four layers, or structures—the "four wheels of the personality"—the mental body, the emotional body, the vital body and the physical body. We have these bodies simply so that we can be in touch with their corresponding worlds. The physical body enables us to see things, hear things and register things in the physical dimension. The astral body enables us to see things, hear things and register things in the astral dimension after we die. And the mental body enables us to think and connect to thought processes in the mental dimension.

But in themselves these bodies are not geared to lead you to awareness of yourself as a Soul in the Causal World; they are simply geared for you to function in their corresponding realms, and that is all they do. You can be physically conscious for two million years and you will not experience yourself as a Soul through your physical consciousness.

To experience who you really are, that shining Self with all the miraculous possibilities of Higher Consciousness, you have to make a conscious effort to withdraw your attention from the outside and start to go within. That is why you have to meditate.

Since you have been born many times, your causal body is filled with these concentrated atoms, which are like sparks of Light of various sizes and frequencies, and you keep adding to them in each lifetime, that is, you keep accumulating karma.

Now, you as a Soul are more intelligent than you as a thinking personality—infinitely more intelligent. You as a Soul in the Causal World have the sensation of a continuum in your awareness of past and future possibilities, a feeling of how you relate to total existence, a sense that you should be going along in the great Stream of Life in a certain way, or along a certain path. In other words, you as a Soul are aware of what I call your *destiny line.*

So when you return to the Causal World and arise in Causal Consciousness and become the Living Soul, you (the Soul) make a decision. And you make that decision because you are in tune with all the knowledge-atoms of your past lives, which, as I said, sum up everything you ever did in each life—not as actions, but more as the stress resulting from your actions. Then you know that in your next lifetime you will have to release a certain amount of this stress (karma) so that you will be moving along your destiny line. All you have to do after that is just be born, which means that you have to build yourself a mental body, an astral body, and an etheric body, and then find some parents who hopefully are intelligent enough on the physical level to be able to help you. But you will have already set in motion your destiny.

With some people the destiny line is strong. Those are usually the more evolved Souls, what are called *Old Souls* or *Wise Souls.* They know before they are born what they are going to do in their new lifetime, and after they are born their internal energies are moving toward the goal of their destiny line. These are people who arrive in the world with a destiny, with a plan and purpose, which they start working on as soon as they can crawl. The average human being is not aware of their destiny but is swept along by it anyhow. This is because the Soul has to work out its karma, so on the physical level the personality is pushed along its destiny line by the interior Soul forces, whether the person is aware of it or not. But for an advanced Soul the personality consciously works at its destiny from an early age, working along the appointed line decided by the Soul.

With the even more advanced Souls, the *Spiritual Souls*, the personality works in conjunction with others, usually members of the Spiritual Hierarchy who arrange the birth of that particular person because he or she has a certain job to do in the world. These people are helped by the Spiritual Hierarchy throughout their life, right from the day they are conceived (and even before) to make sure that their destiny is fulfilled. These are the spiritually directed Souls, directed from the inner dimensions, and they have a tremendous impact on the world.

For the average person in the world, karma can produce havoc in one's life, physically, emotionally and mentally, as decided by the Soul. But for special people it is even more complicated, because when they are incarnating the Soul may decide to work out past karma at the same time as it goes along its destiny line. In that case, there is tremendous upheaval in that person's life because the karma and the destiny line merge, creating a situation in which the person is apparently doing a great good for Mankind and at the same time is suffering from a horrible illness or ends up being crucified or tortured. This explains why spiritual people have to go through suffering; they have chosen to do that in combination with their world service. ✸

The Spiritual Hierarchy

The Spiritual Hierarchy is known by many names: the Spiritual Kingdom, the Christ-Hierarchy, the Kingdom of Light, the Brotherhood of Light, and so on. It is the hierarchy of Saints, Masters, Yogīs and Teachers who have attained Enlightenment and are now evolving on the Causal, Buddhic and Nirvāṇic Planes. From there they send down Avatāras, Divine Incarnations or Divine Messengers, to remind human beings of who they really are, and to teach Humanity about the Kingdom of God.

THE HEALING POWER
OF RĀM

So far I have talked about where illnesses come from, on all the different dimensions, but I haven't suggested any remedies except that not doing all the wrong things will automatically be a preventative process. However, if you have already done those wrong things, you will need to have something to restore your health.

One of the most potent medicines of all is the sound of RĀM. Those of you in the field of medicine will of course be wondering how a sound (like RĀM) can be a healing medicine. Well, here are some of the qualities of the sound of RĀM: active goodness; positive energy; goodwill; courage; compassion; helpfulness; service to all; intelligence; wisdom; bliss; peace; constructive activity; the presence of God; Enlightenment; perfection; fearlessness; physical, mental and spiritual strength; righteousness.

The Power of Sound

To discover the reality behind the magic sound of RĀM, you have to understand something of the Primordial Language of Sound (also called the Sacred Language or the Divine Language). The ancient clairvoyants—I do not mean the modern psychic clairvoyants but the ancient clairvoyants with spiritual, or interdimensional, vision—discovered that the Universe is actually made out of *sound-atoms*. When they went into

Cosmic Consciousness or other higher states of consciousness and they arrived at the Source of Creation, they discovered a tremendous energy-field that in various languages came to be called "God as Sound" in various languages: *The Word* in English, *Logos* in Greek, *Nāda* in Sanskrit and *Verbum* in Latin. They discovered that the whole Manifestation, the whole Universal Reality, comes from a mighty Sea of Sound that is the Sound of God or, if you like, the Name of God.

The Ancients also discovered that within this tremendous, all-potent Sound there are seventy-two Seed Syllables, powerful Sound-Vibrations that produce every possibility of manifestation, ability and development imaginable by the human mind and beyond. These make up the Primordial Language of Sound, and one of these sounds is RĀM, which is particularly powerful and beneficial to the human species on this planet.

Remember that RĀM is more than just the sound you make when you say it. The physical sound is just a microscopic atom of RĀM. RĀM is a stream of the Sound that comes from the universal reverberation of the creative process and descends through the planes, becoming the Bright Light-Vibration of Nirvāṇa, the Pure Light-Vibration of the Buddhic dimensions, the Sounding-Light Vibration of the causal dimensions, the subtle Sound-Vibrations of the Mental and Astral Worlds and finally the physical sound of the physical world.

So how does this relate to healing? The sound of RĀM sets up a rhythmic vibration on whichever level you use it. When you use it on the physical level (when you intone it aloud), it sets up a rhythmic vibration in your physical body that harmonizes the atomic structure of the body and gives it physical health. When you take the sound of RĀM inside (when you intone it mentally), it sets up a rhythmic vibration in the etheric body that evens out the disjointed etheric (Prāṇic) currents, your own life-force, so your etheric body becomes healthy. As you take the sound further inside by internal repetition and reach the Astral Plane, it evens out the vibration of your astral body, so your negative emotional vibrations—depression, hate, anger, violence, self-pity—are neutralized. When you go further inside and reach the Mental Plane, all your negative thoughts are also neutralized as your mental body begins to vibrate more harmoniously. And then finally on an even higher level, when you can start working with it internally on the causal level (the Soul level), it will harmonize your causal body and therefore stop the release of negative karma.

So the sound of RĀM is the most amazing, all-purpose medicine ever invented, and it is applicable to everybody, regardless of religion or background, because it works with the Science of Sound, by Sound-Vibration.

This is also *preventative* medicine. If you intone and meditate on RĀM regularly, it will help your nature adjust itself to Cosmic Law because it produces a state of harmony in whatever realm it is being used in. It puts your causal body in harmony with the Causal World, your mental body with the Mind World, and so on down to your physical body. But if you are one of those perfect specimens who are always in total health physically, emotionally and mentally, then RĀM is preventative, by maintaining you in that state of harmony and keeping you from attracting negative, disease-producing factors in the first place.

The Warrior Mantra of Health

RĀM is the Warrior Mantra of Health and in order to work with it you need two things. The first is the knowledge of what it is and how it works, and the second is the conveyance of its energy by a Teacher through the process of Initiation. You can get many benefits from working with the Warrior Mantra on your own, but to register it and get the power of its full potential it is best to get the energy conveyance from a Teacher, or Guru. That way, you receive the internal Sound structure that you need in order for the process to work for you. Knowing that a certain medicine works against coughs will not cure your cough; you actually have to take the medicine. In the same way, knowing that the

RĀM Sound has healing powers will not help you unless that energy, that healing vibration, is conveyed to you.

I am just telling you this because some of you may become enthusiastic and go home and try to get everybody to heal themselves by saying RĀM instead of taking their pills. It won't work because the Mantra Energy has not been conveyed to them. That energy is a subtle reality, in fact, it is the all-reality behind it, and as I said, it has to be conveyed through the regular method, which is technically called *Initiation*. But Initiation does not mean that you have to dress strangely or adopt some strange ritual like throwing salt behind your head. Initiation means that you receive the vibration pattern of the mantra you are working with from the Teacher on the inner levels.

Mantras were the craze in the sixties and seventies. Everybody had a mantra and was always asking if you had one and who your Guru was. It was the in-thing to have a mantra. But in the mass consciousness there was no understanding of the science behind it, the reality behind it. If you receive a Sound-Vibration (mantra) through the normal spiritual process of Initiation, it becomes a power in your life—a devastatingly awesome power. And when you really tune into that Sound-Vibration through systematic practice, you will begin to feel its power. In the case of RĀM, the more you feel its power, the more its reality will strike you, and the more you will be able to heal yourself and keep yourself in perfect health.

RĀM and the Law of Harmony

At this stage I want to impress on you that all diseases are wrong vibrations, whether they are wrong vibrations in your physical body, etheric body, astral body, mental body or causal body. *Wrong vibrations cause disease.* Only that which is working in harmony with the Cosmos produces health or is in the state of health, beauty, truth and order.

So when we have any kind of a disease it is simply a disharmony in the part that is ill. If your physical body is ill, you must have done something physically that produced disharmony. If you are emotionally sick, then you must have done something emotionally that produced disharmony. And if you have a mental illness, you must have done something mentally that was not in harmony with the Cosmic Law.

This also includes your karma, because you must have done something disharmonious previously to precipitate the karma you have now. The magic, or the beauty, of RĀM is that it produces harmony inside you, and the more harmony it produces inside you, the more it neutralizes the negative state or situation you are in. And when your whole being is in a state of harmony, not just your immediate personality expression, you will be in harmony with the Cosmos itself.

Most people are living out of tune with themselves and have accepted that life is a state of disharmony. Very few people think about why life on this planet is such a mess; they just accept that it's messy and there is nothing they can do about it, except to blame the government or God. The mass consciousness does not realize that the planetary situation need not be as it is, that it is caused by billions of human beings producing disharmony on every level, in their thoughts, feelings and physical actions.

The Law of Harmony is the Natural Law or Primordial Law within Creation itself. In Sanskrit it is called Dharma and in Hebrew Torah. But it has nothing to do with the teachings of Buddha or with Jewish Scripture. *None of the religious teachings are the Law.* The Law of Harmony maintains every plane of existence according to a certain harmonic

---

Some Angelic Hierarchies, like the Cherubim and Seraphim, have always followed the Natural Law and as a result have never known a moment of suffering—and they have lived for billions of years! No mental suffering, no emotional suffering, no physical pain, no guilt consciousness, no output of disharmonious waves—because they have managed to keep in tune with the Primordial Law within Creation. They do not know what it is like to be in a lawless condition and therefore only know bliss, creativity and harmony.

structure and order; otherwise there would be chaos. I'm talking about an absolute cosmic law, a tremendous vibration that arranges the atoms of the inner and outer realms into a certain order and activity.

That same law also exists within you and it will keep you in perfect health always, if you follow it from the time you are born until you die. Humans would have no mental, emotional or physical illnesses, because the Law of Life is harmonious, orderly and perfect. But because of our wrong thinking, wrong feeling and wrong action, we are not in tune with that law.

By *Natural Law* I do not mean just the law of how the grass and trees grow. That is only the minutest part of the Natural Law. The Natural Law manifests in the inner dimensions all the way to Nirvāṇa and beyond, right to the Throne of God. It is produced by the very highest aspect of God, and Cosmic Intelligence directs this law into Creation, which functions according to it.

My point is that there is an absolute law that is perfect and good, a perfect state or condition in the Universe, and if you remain in that you will never experience suffering. But if you break it, you will suffer.

Now, suppose we acknowledge that we are in a state of suffering, then the next thing is, what can we do about it? You can use the sound of RĀM to harmonize your internal bodies so that you do not have to suffer. You need to practise it sufficiently to start experiencing its inner dimensions and how it is in tune with the Inner Law. It is a choice you can make intelligently and wilfully, but you have to remember that there is another cosmic law and that is the Law of Effort.

You cannot live in depression and self-pity for fifty years of your life and then sit down and intone RĀM for five minutes and expect to become God-Realized instantaneously. It won't happen, for the simple reason that over fifty years you have created a massive negative vibration in your inner bodies that cannot be easily neutralized. RĀM is powerful but in the initial stages you're not reaching its true power. So you have to start at the bottom of the ladder and use it day in and day out until it has enough chance to start working and getting rid of the negative vibrations inside you.

Of the seventy-two Seed Vibrations, or Seed Syllables, in the Sacred Language, RĀM is a particularly good one because it is what I call an *active harmonic vibration*, which means that it will not draw your consciousness away from the world. If you use, say, ŌM, which is another Seed Syllable, the ŌM Vibration will take you away from worldly consciousness; it is a good sound for a sannyāsin, sādhu or monk, somebody who has renounced the world and does not need to engage in life, because it is a straight path from the Physical World to the Causal World and beyond. It pulls your consciousness up and out of worldly conditions.

But the beauty of the RĀM Vibration is that it enables you to be fully worldly conscious and fully divinely conscious both at the same time. This vibration is like a huge wave that goes down to the depths of matter and up to the heights of Spirit. I call it the great Universal Vibration of Light, the very energy of Life itself.

As you use the RĀM Sound, your life-wave will increase, your health and vitality will increase and therefore your ability to fight disease will increase, and your Enlightenment potential will increase. If you are a monk, you should use ŌM because you don't need to be engaged in interaction with the world. But if you are in the world, which we are— the Warrior Path is a way of action—then you should use RĀM, which opens up everything from healing powers to psychic powers to divine abilities to all knowledge.

RĀM: the Warrior Power

Now we will begin the practical instruction for developing the Warrior Power. What do we mean by the Warrior Power? First of all, you have probably heard of folk heroes like Bonnie and Clyde or Che Guevara. Most folk heroes and national heroes were people who killed for the sake of killing or for political motives. Such heroes were not true Warriors and never had anything to do with the Spiritual Warrior Path. The Warrior Path is a secret path and relatively few people have ever been on it, so forget about the heroes of your country being representations of Warriors; they are not.

I'm talking about another class of entity here, the true Warrior. The great Warriors were the kings and rulers of ancient civilizations such as those of Japan, China, Egypt and Babylonia. They were leaders of huge armies but their function was to rule and guide their nation to prosperity, which has nothing to do with going into battle. That is not what the Warrior Path is about. The great Warriors were always dynamic leaders who influenced the course of history. Slowly, that breed of people died out, and with them died the Warrior Path. Even two thousand years ago, people had forgotten all about it.

The majestic Warriors of ancient times had supernatural powers to change human consciousness, and thereby change human society as well. And that supernatural power of the Warrior is embodied in the mantra RĀM, which, as I said, is a sound-structure from the *Primordial Language of Sound*, the ancient language of Atlantis that arose many hundreds of thousands of years ago, long before the Greek and Roman civilizations, before the ancient Egyptian, Chinese and Indian civilizations. It is the primary language of Mankind and was preserved in Sanskrit and other ancient languages.

RĀM is not a word, although later generations gave it the meaning of "God". (All the names of God in Hebrew, Chinese, Sanskrit, Tibetan,

Egyptian, Greek, Roman and Arabic came from the Primordial Language of Atlantis.) But the word RĀM has no meaning; it is a powerful sound-structure that gives the Warrior his or her supernatural power, a power that can be developed through that sound-structure.

RĀM is the Warrior-Vibration given to the ancient Warriors of all nations. It is a Universal Sound-Vibration, a pulsation in the Infinite Mind of God that structures all of Creation according to a pattern. It is the *disciplined* order of the Cosmic Mind, the disciplinary vibration of the Cosmos. And that is why it was adopted by the ancient Warriors for developing the Warrior skills—tremendous discipline and cohesion, tremendous skill in action, tremendous power to do good and benefit all of Creation.

There have been many martial arts schools throughout history— Japanese and Chinese martial arts schools, the Knights of the Round Table during the Middle Ages, the Knights Templar, Greek and Roman martial art schools, and so forth—but all the true martial arts schools had a spiritual dimension, functioning as *spiritual* training grounds focused on inner development before they started outer skills training.

In the ancient music schools of India, for instance, you practised meditation for many years before you actually learned to play an instrument. You spent many years tuning into the Cosmic Sound, until the Guru decided that you were ready to learn the physical instrument and use it to express the Cosmic Sound. It was the same in the ancient Spiritual Warrior Schools, where you practised spiritual techniques for many years, controlling your mind, controlling your breathing, tuning into the Soul within you, tuning into the Universal Soul. And when you completed that spiritual training, then you were taught the physical skills of the Warrior. The physical skills came at the end, not at the beginning of your training.

Nowadays, this whole spiritual science has been lost: people study music without knowing anything about the spiritual nature of Sound;

or they go straight to dance classes without any spiritual preparation; or they go straight into learning the fighting skills of Kung Fu or Karate without the spiritual foundation.

In the Warrior School, we start with the spiritual foundation: the power of the Warrior, the power of RĀM, a real energy stream that, when it is awakened inside you, makes you feel invincible. As you get in touch with the incredible power of the RĀM Vibration, you will understand, *internally*, what your true function is and what you are supposed to be doing in this lifetime.

Remember that this is an ancient vibration existing in the Mind of God *before* Creation. It is that which gave Creation its structure and purpose, that which made the Plan and is fulfilling it. So when you are tuning into the sound RĀM, you are tuning into the Divine Mind, which sees the Plan and will make it manifest on Earth. We *can* manifest the Divine Plan—as individuals, as groups and as a planetary human society. Through us, the Energy of the Divine Plan takes shape in physical form.

How to Intone RĀM

First we intone the Ā (AH) sound, then RĀ (RAH) and then RĀM (RAHM), which is the foundation of the Warrior power inside you.

To sense where the RĀM sound comes from in the Infinite Mind, you have to be able to sense internal Sound. So when you intone the Ā sound, listen to the sound you are making but try to feel *beyond* the sound you are making physically; the human physical sound is not the real Ā sound. See if you can hear the Universal Sound-Vibration of Ā that is reverberating in Creation all the time, the Universal Ā Sound that is part of the planetary structure and is vibrating all around us.

From the pure Ā sound came the many syllables of the Divine Language, which was mastered by the ancient Atlanteans long before there was Hebrew, Sanskrit or Chinese. Hundreds of thousands of years ago there was a superior race called the Atlantean race, and they were called the *Scientists of the Invisible.* They were the scientists of the day but they did not invent gadgets like mobile phones; they invented ways of transforming themselves through the power of Sound and Light. They knew about the inner dimensions and had powers that are unimaginable today. They transformed the planet in their early days, before their civilization degenerated and they turned to using black magic.

The next sound we will work with is RĀ. In the Infinite Mind, every sound is a dynamic *potency*, a sea of massive dynamic electromagnetic waves, and RĀ is the explosive sound that brings things into Manifestation. It is a powerful syllable from the ancient Primordial Language of Mankind, the primary root sound of the Warrior power—the power to *do*, the power to *become*, the power to accomplish any miracle or feat that you need to, the power to change the world.

When you are able to intone this sound on the Soul level, you will then be able to perform miracles. That is how Jesus performed His miracles. In the Bible it says that Jesus "cried out in a loud voice" (Matthew 27: 46), which is the ignorant scripture writer's way of saying that He used a powerful Divine Name or Mantric Sound as a healing technique. It did not mean that He cried out in agony; He was not crying at all; He was intoning a powerful mantra. The scripture writers, of course, would

---

Once you are established in the energy-field of RĀM, the Warrior will awaken within you spontaneously, without any martial arts training. You will be a Warrior because you understand the power of the Warrior within you. Then, any other subsequent training will simply be a modulation of that power, or an expression of it. And then you will understand what the great ancient Warriors were about.

It is an incredible science, one you can only understand once you have completed some part of the Spiritual Warrior Path. You will be completely renewed; your whole life will shift to a completely different level. You will realize that in everything you do, God is acting through you. A Warrior makes a simple sword movement and changes the planet. It is impossible to understand until you actually experience it.

not know that because they had not mastered the understanding of what Jesus was about (which was way above the worldly human consciousness); they did not know that Jesus used the power of Sound, the power of the Divine Name, to perform His miracles.

The next sound, RĀM, is used internally—it is *the* Internal Power—but we first sound it physically, aloud, so that you get accustomed to working with Sound-Vibration. In most Mystery Schools and Spiritual Schools, a chant or invocation is first sounded physically and then mentally. When you intone RĀM it is different than the other two invocations of Ā and RĀ because the open vowel sound is closed with the consonant *M*, which is a humming sound when it is intoned aloud. This means that you are calling on the Universal Mind of God but you only want to work with a certain measure or a certain quality of the Universal Light-Vibration.

With this exercise you can learn the technique of mustering energy and then letting it go. When you intone RĀM, feel that you are producing energy (RĀ) and then letting it go (M). All the Warrior techniques are important in life; even this one Warrior Principle will teach you a dynamic lesson that can be applied in real life. Suppose you suddenly become angry about something. Normally, you would grumble about it for days on end or even for years. But when anger arises inside you as a Warrior, you get angry—scream and do whatever you have to—and then let it go. The sooner you let it go, the sooner you establish your inner harmony.

True Warriors are Cosmic-Conscious but they cannot use that state of consciousness all the time, because they would burn out. Imagine having a high-frequency energy inside you like RĀM, which is the great sound-structure of the Mind of God. If you were using it all the time you would simply burn out. Many sādhus of India get this power but they hold on to it and their brains fizzle out, and they are not able to act or function properly in the world. So the technique of the Warrior is to open up and get the energy needed for a particular task at that moment, and then release it and get on with life.

You must understand that letting go is actually *easy* to do; the difficult part is holding on to the negative emotion. That is what everybody likes to do. Everybody likes to be in a bad mood because it gives them something to do and makes their lives worth living. We are human and have emotions, and there is nothing wrong with having emotions. What is wrong is the endless holding on to them, the stupid grudges that could have been forgotten years ago.

The Warrior doesn't do that. The Warrior acts and it's done, then on to the next thing: action-release, action-release. Every moment the mind is pure and clear and ready for the next action. That is the mind of the Warrior. Energy comes, works; energy goes, disappears. It is as simple as that.

When you are in a battle situation, in a life-and-death situation, what saves you is the ability to muster up energy and then release it. In other words, when you are a Warrior, you do not carry your furniture with you; you do not go into battle with a grand piano on your shoulders. As a Warrior, you act spontaneously in the moment, with no background or burdens. If you fail to do so you have lost the battle even before you start. What saves you in a real battle situation is the ability to muster up energy and then release it. Then the energy comes in, you act and you are done, ready for the next thing. This is part of the Secret Art of the Warrior.

This technique will teach you that you can create energy, or rather get in touch with energy when you want to. But it has even deeper implications, because later on you will learn how to receive the Energy from within. It can make your life a hundred percent different. If you practise this technique you will realize that you have an infinite source of energy inside you. RĀM is your source of energy. It is an aspect of the Divine Vibration, the primordial vibration of the Sound of the Universe, so whenever you feel you need energy in your life for a purpose, just sit down and repeat this mantra for twenty minutes. You will have the energy you need for your purpose because you have tuned in to the all-accomplishing power of the Divine Mind, the power of the Warrior to accomplish anything at will.

Practice

~

Intoning RĀM

First, practise sounding the pure Ā sound, prolonged, physically (aloud) and then mentally (internally).[4]

Pronounce the sound brightly and clearly, because as you pronounce it physically so will you intone it mentally. If the physical sound is not bright and clear, then the mental sound will be dull and ineffective.

Next, practise the RĀ sound, physically and then mentally. Feel the RĀ sound as an *opener, initiator* or *commencer* of energies. It *opens you up* from within yourself into the Energy-Field.

Next, practise the RĀM sound, first physically and then mentally. Here the Ā sound is long but not prolonged (only for 2 or 3 counts). Feel the opening up of energies with the RĀ sound, and let them go with the M sound. With the RĀ you generate energy and with the M you relax or let go of the energy. (Tension and relaxation, action and letting go of action—this principle is important in daily life.) ⚔

Intoning RĀM internally for twenty minutes or so every day will not only prevent you from having negative emotions but also protect you against those of others. That is because regular meditation on RĀM will create what we call a *Shield of Light* inside you. What this means is that as you practise the RĀM technique and build the Shield of Light inside you, you will feel fewer and fewer negative energies—your own as well as other people's—because the brightness and positivity of the RĀM Vibration will drive them out. As you repeat the RĀM sound, the vibration moves out in concentric circles of Light that push away and block any negativity around you. Once you are in that clear space, you can make the right action.

4. An audio file demonstrating the intonation of this mantra can be found at http://www.thefhl.org/mantrarepetition/.

~ 5 ~

THE WARRIOR CONTROLS
THE NEGATIVE EMOTIONS

The Spiritual Path requires some sort of effort on your part, things you have to do willingly and consciously. Whether it's Yoga, Tibetan or Zen Buddhism, Christian Mysticism or Jewish Kabbalah, there is no path where effort is not required. This is important because the New Age tendency is for *easy* spirituality. There are books written on how to master the Tarot system in ten lessons or attain Enlightenment in five minutes—which is of course total nonsense. Unfortunately, people like the idea of becoming enlightened without having to work at it, but it is a delusion, a cruel and dangerous one. Every Spiritual Path requires discipline and hard work. There is no escape from it. And anybody who promises that it is an easy thing has no clue about the Spiritual Path.

Now, discipline is a part of the Warrior Path also. By *discipline* I do not mean the gloomy Christian idea of discipline: that you can't go dancing because it is of the devil or you can't eat chocolate cake because it is of the devil. This, too, is just nonsense. And *discipline* is not what the Indian sādhus do who stand on one leg until the other leg withers away or who contort their bodies for years until they are totally useless. That is not discipline either, just another form of stupidity.

By *discipline* I mean that you structure your life in such a way that it makes sense towards your spiritual ideal, that you organize your time and energy in such a way that you will be able to perform the spiritual work necessary to accomplish your goal. That is true discipline; it is intelligent and coherent and has understanding and purpose.

Part of the discipline of every true Spiritual Path is that you are required to work on your emotions. First, of course, you have to have emotions. I am not joking. Some people nowadays are so intellectual, so focused on the activity of their brain cells, that they do not actually feel emotions. They work out everything in their computer brains, like how they should react in certain situations, because they think emotions are just functions of the mind. They do not know that we have an emotional body and a mental body and that the two are completely separate from each other.

This is a tragedy, of course, but it does not concern us here. Most people have emotions and dealing with them is a supreme challenge on the Spiritual Path, whether it is an Eastern or Western Path. Whatever spiritual attainment you want, you must have *some* control over your emotions. I do not say complete control but some control.

The Warrior Path is the best and clearest example of this. In the olden days you had to fight with physical weapons. Nowadays you just shoot each other; there's no art in it at all. Anybody can shoot anybody; there's little skill required. But in the olden days the Warrior really had to be *aware*; it was a matter of life and death. In the midst of a battle you couldn't daydream, and if you lost control of your emotions, if you suddenly became angry and allowed the emotion to sweep over you, you would immediately lose your balance and you would be finished in no time. The Art of the Warrior is the supreme example of being in the moment one hundred percent, because if you are not, if you lose yourself for one second, you are finished.

This is a Warrior Principle and it can be applied in daily life because it is a practical example of the right way of living. When this principle of battle is transcribed into the battle of life (because life is literally a battle situation) it becomes: *If you lose emotional control, you have lost the battle.*

The real Warriors were warriors twenty-four hours a day and they lived as if they were in battle conditions every second of every day. They had to be full on, awake, aware, with their emotions under control and everything in their existence flowing coherently. It was an amazing spiritual discipline—unfortunately gone out of fashion these days—the toughest and the best of all the spiritual schools on the planet: the Spiritual Warrior School. It demanded total commitment and the results were miraculous.

In the early days, the Spiritual Warriors used to meditate for months on end before they went into battle. In battles like the great battles of Kurukṣetra, which involved many nations, the generals of the armies did not just start fighting and slashing about. No, they went into profound states of meditation because they wanted to tune into what the cosmic destiny behind the battle was, what the outcome *should* be. There is a good example of this in the first chapter of the BHAGAVAD-GĪTĀ, which is the story of Arjuna, one of the great Warriors of his time, and his Master, Kṛṣṇa.

The Bhagavad-Gītā opens on the eve of a major war with hundreds of thousands of soldiers on each side. In those days, war was fought in a gentlemanly manner; they didn't just drop bombs on each other. It was planned out and the enemy was notified months in advance, and then both sides set up and settled into their respective camps. There were exchanges and discussions even after the actual battle date had been fixed. In the Bhagavad-Gītā story, it was the time before the battle was about to start and Arjuna was in his chariot together with Kṛṣṇa.

Although a great Warrior, Arjuna still had imperfections in terms of the Warrior Consciousness, in terms of the cosmic nature of the Warrior. He had been well trained and had done many spiritual practices but was not yet a Master Warrior. But he had his Master beside him, who was Kṛṣṇa. They were in the midst of hundreds of thousands of soldiers—horsemen, charioteers, foot soldiers—all drawn out in battle lines.

In those days, the leaders were in the front line of their armies, leading the charge, not controlling the armies from behind a bunker. So Arjuna was also in the front line on his side, and when he looked at the sea of faces on the other side, he recognized some of his own relatives and previous Teachers from whom he had learned the skills of life and Yoga—meditation, breathing techniques and the whole Spiritual Path.

The presence of these great Teachers and well-known Masters in the opposite camp puzzled Arjuna. He was not quite in Cosmic Consciousness, only on the verge, and he realized that he could not fully understand the scene in front of him. He knew there was some destiny happening but could not quite figure out what that destiny was.

So he turned to Kṛṣna and said that he could not fight and kill those respected Masters and great heroes on the other side. It was then that Kṛṣna gave him a quick lesson in the ultimate meaning of Warriorship. He said: "This has all been preordained. Just look into the Mind of God. The battle has already been fought. We are merely going through the motions. The people who are meant to die are already dead; the people who are meant to live are alive; the battle has already taken place."

The rest of the Bhagavad-Gītā is about Kṛṣna teaching Arjuna how to look into the Mind of God and accept his destiny as a Warrior and fulfil it. A lot of people who are not on the Warrior Path cannot understand the Bhagavad-Gītā—because it is a book for Warriors. It is not for people who sit around in caves contemplating their navels. It is a book for people who are active in life, people who are participating in the process of life.

So that was the first lesson that Kṛṣna taught Arjuna: to look at his emotions. He was having doubts about fighting against his relatives and the famous Teachers and Sages on the other side. But Kṛṣna took him in a new direction, into the Mind of God, to see the Cosmic Reality, the Divine Plan behind it all. Once that great vision opened inside him and he saw the Divine Plan that Humankind and the planet were undergoing, it was no problem for Arjuna to go into battle.

This is relevant for you because the first lesson to learn in the Art of the Warrior is to look at your emotions. You cannot undertake a project in life if you are doubting yourself or doubting the purpose and plan behind the project. So we first have to look at our emotional state, why we are reacting as we are. Once we learn to observe our emotional reactions, the next stage is to do something about them.

For example, once you realize that somebody is attacking you emotionally, just stand back and observe the person and try to see where he is coming from and what is behind the situation. You may sense that that person is upset because he lost his job or something happened to him. You realize that the situation has nothing to do with you, and then, in

---

Of course, the basic idea is that there is a *plan* that you must seek out. In the Middle Ages, many countries in Europe had knights. They were trained warriors who fought battles, but fighting was not the point of being a knight. The point was to find Enlightenment, to find the mystery behind all the conflict, the human suffering, the human problems, the battles between kingdoms. They wanted to know: What is the Plan? Is there a divine meaning behind it all? Then they would be able to fight correctly, for the right reason and the right cause—the progress of human evolution on the planet.

Many battles are going on today to destroy the crystallized emotions and situations in the world; otherwise the planetary life-force will get choked and suffocate. When there are crystallized religions with millions of people thinking in archaic ways, who are back in the Dark Ages in how they do things, their combined vibration actually blocks the breathing mechanism of the planet. These conditions have to be remedied or eliminated so that the planet can breathe and human evolution can move ahead. And because Humanity is not able to do it intelligently, it has to be done through the Warrior System, through war. There is no other way because people do not realize how they are holding back planetary evolution with their wrong thinking.

So not all the wars you see are useless; behind some of them there is a picture you cannot see. And the politicians cannot see it either because they are just puppets on strings. Behind them there are forces and agencies that know what is really happening.

that calmness, you can respond in such a positive way that it is helpful for that person.

Once you have stood back, a sense of compassion arises within you and you can deal with the situation correctly, because merely standing back does not solve the problem; it's just a preparatory stage, like the two armies standing and waiting for the bugle call before they could fight. But once the sense of compassion arises in you, the solution will be immediately apparent and you will know the right way to deal with the situation (which will turn out to be radically different than if you had responded with the normal emotional reaction). Because compassion is universal—it embraces you and everyone else—you can accept your part, whether you have to play the part of the good guy or the bad guy.

The Warrior can meet any situation with confidence, without worrying about the results. Part of Arjuna's problem was that he was worried about results. He wondered what would happen to him if he killed a relative or a great Teacher or Master, how that would rebound on him. He was aware of the Laws of Reincarnation and Karma, so he was worried about his karma. He was not yet a Master Warrior, which is beyond the stage of the Yogī or Saint. Master Warriors see the plan of life, the destiny of individuals, families, groups and nations. They see that destiny and then play their part in it—not as an intellectual choice of what they should or should not do; they see it brightly and clearly inside themselves, their part in the great cosmic drama. ✗

~ 6 ~

THE WARRIOR AND
THE LIFE-FORCE

First of all, the average person has a certain amount of life-energy, or life-force, which is uniquely designed to maintain the physical body. That amount of life-force is actually very small. It may be likened to a car in idle, when the engine is just turning over and the car is staying in one spot. It is using up energy, but it's not actually going anywhere. Similarly, the life-force of the average human being is just maintaining the person, just humming away and keeping them alive—and that is all it does. It is the lowest possible expression of the Life-Force.

So those of you who are dreaming of great conquests and building great empires won't be able to realize your dreams unless you have enough life-energy behind them. This is why many dreamers fail: they have ambitions and dreams but they do not know the esoteric side of it, that unless you have the corresponding life-force you will not be able to achieve your dreams. That is why an understanding of the life-force is important.

Most people do not know that around us there is a tremendous life-force, an ocean of life-energy. Just like a fish lives *in* the ocean, *from* the ocean and *within* the ocean, we live in, from and within this energy-field. This great ocean of life-energy is a radiant, vibrating *power* that gives life to every living thing, that makes the ants move, the birds fly, the bumble bees sting you, the flowers grow. It is the One Life-Force that permeates all Creation, all the Seven Great Planes of Being from the subatomic particles of the Physical World to Nirvāṇa and beyond.

The Ancients realized that human beings, by nature, are limited in life-force. Why? Because our connection to the Universal Life-Force is limited. They also knew that every entity in Creation has as much of that life-force as he or she or it can get in touch with, and the secret knowledge of the Ancients was how to get in touch with the Universal Life-Force, which is the Breath of God, the very Life of God, and draw more life-energy into their systems. And I don't mean just physical life-force but also emotional life-force, mental life-force and the life of the Soul—one's total beingness.

The Science of Using the Life-Force

The ancient Warriors were focused on how to discover the life-force and use it. In China, there were two great warrior schools: the Shaolin Monastery and the Wudan Monastery. In the Shaolin School they used the life-force to strengthen the power of the physical body. In the Wudan School they developed miraculous powers like flying through the air by tapping into the subtle psychic regions of the life-force.

In India the yogīs used the life-force for many purposes: to levitate, to perform miracles, to heal. And the ancient Hebrew Kabbalists used the same life-force, calling on the names of God, because to them a divine

---

Christians portray God as an old man sitting on a throne in heaven and they pray to him and call him Jehovah, which is fine as a mental idea but does not convey the truth. God is everywhere: a boundless energy-field of Infinite Intelligence and Consciousness, an omnific power that contains all possible things that can happen in the Universe through all beings, all intelligences and all hierarchies. Whether it is a lord of a galaxy, an archangel, a human being or a plant, animal or stone—everything feeds off that tremendous, omnific energy-field.

power was an expression of a name of God. In the Tibetan Bonpo arts and in Chinese Taoism, and in the Mystery Schools of all the ancient races, they were after the same secret: how to expand their life-force and be able to do more, express themselves more, live more and be more; how to use the life-force to evolve and progress spiritually.

Nowadays it is obvious that the average person is not progressing at all. People are born with a certain amount of life-energy and they live with that energy until they die. They are not taught in school or any-where else that they can actually increase their life-force—on all levels. I'm not talking about physical life only: I'm talking about the life of your mind, to make your mind illumined; the life of your emotions, to feel the cosmic harmony around you; the life of your Soul, to become more radiant and divine and god-like.

So this knowledge was prevalent all over the ancient world and people were practising techniques aimed at developing aspects of this tremendous Life-Power. And then came the Piscean Age. During the last 2,160 years people forgot about that science because they were focused on internal illumination, escaping from the lower worlds, the physical, psychic and mental dimensions, into the purely spiritual heights of the Buddhic Plane and the Nirvāṇic Plane, where miraculous powers are not necessary. Since the emphasis was on escaping, naturally the science of using the life-force in this lower Creation was forgotten.

But now in this Aquarian Age, which is the complete opposite of the Piscean Age, the science of using the life-force is going to be revived. And we are starting that revival. It will be a science again in this age, which is practical and down-to-earth, and it will develop the body, the mind, the emotions, the total personality. It will be taught to increasingly larger numbers of people until it becomes a major science about how to extend the life-force and how to invoke the Divinity *in manifestation*, not in abstraction. In the Buddhic World or the Nirvāṇic World you meet God-Transcendent, the Transcendental Deity; but when you bring the Life-Force down to the personality level, you meet God-Immanent, God-in-Incarnation, the aspect of God that is right here with us.

This knowledge will increasingly come to be rediscovered over the next one or two hundred years, and people working in Haṭha Yoga, Tai Chi and other esoteric exercise systems will especially understand that it is not the physical exercises that are important; the real goal is to awaken the life-force and to be able to use it. For what? For self-evolution, for evolving yourself intelligently and consciously from point A to point B.

In other words, this will become a science of self-evolution, and as part of that, the evolution of Humanity, because nobody is an island, as you know. If a person attains a skill or a degree of mastery over anything in life, they make that possibility available to all of Humankind.

For example, if you take a kitten away from its mother and other cats, it will still lick its fur and sharpen its claws and behave like a cat as if it had undergone training for years. It will know how to catch a mouse, how to do everything an adult cat does, without any instruction. What this shows is that within the subconscious mind of the cat, the whole plan of being a cat is already programmed, because other cats did those things before.

The lesson here for human beings is that when a person discovers something or learns to do something, that knowledge gets transferred to the human subconscious mind and becomes common to the human family. That is to say, whatever humans have done in the past is already within your subconscious mind—even something you have never done before—but it has to be awakened.

Human Potential Development

So all the knowledge of the Ancients is already in your subconscious mind. All the miraculous powers they achieved are already programmed inside you and are therefore accessible to you. We grow by the knowledge of the Ancients; we grow by the wisdom of the Wise; we grow by the enlightenment of the Enlightened. The Divine Powers, the powers of the god-like beings, are already programmed inside us; the possibility of divine evolution for the human species is already here. All we have to do is unveil those powers, or bring them out of ourselves.

So how do we bring out that possibility?

The first step is to realize that you are a fish in an infinite ocean of energy and that up to now you have been alive in proportion to how much you could breathe in, or use, that energy. The next step is to go a bit further and recognize that you do not have to stay on the same level as when you were born, that there are ways to increase that life-force inside you so that your life-wave becomes larger, your ability to be becomes larger.

Suppose there is a tiny fish that wants to become a whale. There's a problem of evolution there, of course, because the little fish cannot become a whale; it has to wait for the next cycle of Evolution. This is true in the Mineral Kingdom, the Vegetable Kingdom and the Animal Kingdom but not in the Human Kingdom. In fact, the whole purpose of human evolution is to become more.

At this time I have to remind you that we are not apes. The apes are limited to a certain evolutionary level and they must stay there and they will. But we humans are in another category, on another evolutionary level, and we have a choice to become more than what we have attained by natural evolution. If you want to follow the natural evolutionary pattern over millions of years, you will be perfected, that is, Mother Nature will force you to evolve by the time the natural evolutionary span expires. But you have to have infinite patience for that; you have to incarnate another hundred thousand times and do the same old silly stuff, each time making a microscopic movement forward.

But because we are humans we can move up to a higher level *consciously*—by right understanding, right practices, right behaviour and the right mode of being. We have that choice by birthright as human beings belonging to the Human Kingdom.

There is another thing to understand, that the hundreds of millions of people are evolving along what I call the mass consciousness, or world consciousness, level of Evolution. They keep plodding along until somebody tells them that they don't have to be like that all their life, that they can actually become more and develop their human potential. But we have to understand what they mean by *human potential*. Nowadays there is a big movement amongst the new agers toward all kinds of human potential development, by which they mean developing one's personal power for money, for name, for fame, to be able to control other people. Their so-called personal development courses aim to do just that, with no spiritual understanding whatsoever. They do not understand that the human being is a spiritual being, that the personality is part of a larger reality and is not the *only* reality.

By *human potential development* I mean the development of the total reality that you are—Spirit, Soul, mind, emotions, body. And the total reality that you are can be developed by increasingly absorbing the Life-Force and increasingly becoming more like the Life-Force. This is the secret science that was known to the ancient Chinese, Kabbalists, Sūfī Masters, the ancient Jewish Prophets. All the highly evolved people in the East, West, North and South understood and practised this science, and they achieved success according to their ability to understand and practise—right understanding and right practice.

First we have to recognize that there is this Life-Power within us and around us and secondly we have to be able to use it. We are like the fish in the ocean. The fish breathe in oxygen from the ocean, which is their life-force, but they cannot direct the ocean or make any impression on it. That is how it is for us on the normal human level: we are living in an ocean of energy, breathing in the Prāṇa, Chi or vitality in the ocean, but we are not actually doing anything to the ocean; we do not make an impression on the ocean whatsoever. To actually make an impression you have to have understanding and techniques that will allow you to impress that ocean so that it responds to your command, your will, your idea, your inspiration.

Whether you are a Yogī or a Warrior or a Kabbalist or a Tibetan Lama makes no difference; the Universal Life-Force is the same for everyone, but it is used for different purposes. You can use it for Enlightenment or for becoming a Warrior; you can use it to levitate or to get profound wisdom. But once you understand that the Power is One, then you have every possible way of evolution open to you, because you know that that Power can be used for anything you want. And *there* is the danger: because people on the Other Side also use the same Power.

The White Magicians use the Power for performing miracles for unselfish reasons, for healing or to further human evolution, but the Black Magician use the same miraculous Power for selfish, negative and destructive ends. In the *Star Wars* movies they call it the *Force*, and some characters use it for good, some for bad. George Lucas, the creator of the Star Wars series, had studied the Esoteric Science and the use of the Force, so he made these movies as teaching stories, to make people more aware that there are other possibilities in the Cosmos besides the humdrum of daily living.

So with the Power comes also the responsibility to understand how to use it correctly. For example, suppose you have awakened some of this Power inside you and you get angry and yell at someone. Well, your anger is much more powerful than it would normally be because you have that Power working inside you, so it hits the other person with a larger force than you actually want. If you are in a bad mood, therefore, you will influence a large amount of people around you, and they will feel bad because of the higher energies working inside you. Your life-wave is larger and influences your environment in a larger way.

I will give you an example of what it means to have a larger life-wave. This has happened to me many times: when I'm travelling on a train and watching the countryside go by, sometimes there's somebody on a road quite far away and I look at them and immediately they turn around and look back at me. It's a simple thing, but that look carries the energy of my life-wave and it touches them through their psychic mechanism and they immediately respond by looking back at me. This shows why Warriors try to develop an extended life-force, a larger life-wave. They have to be able to sense in all directions simultaneously; they have to know when something is coming from the back or the front or around the corner, or wherever.

These are simple illustrations of the reality of this Life-Force, and the more you are able to draw from it, the larger it becomes inside you and the more responsibility you have for how it impacts others. As your life-force increases, therefore, you also have to develop more sensibility. That is just how it is; it is part of working with a larger reality.

The Secret of the Life-Force

The Way of the Spiritual Warrior is the Secret Way, and only a few Warriors who were specially initiated knew the secret at any given time, those who were specially initiated. Unfortunately, it is a total life circumstance—to become everything, to become life itself—and it cannot be explained or attained in one easy lesson.

Before you can become a real Spiritual Warrior you first have to understand this basic principle: *you and the Cosmos are one.* In the olden days when you trained to be a soldier they didn't tell you that you and the Cosmos are one. All they gave you were good techniques for killing people and for avoiding being killed; there was no cosmology in it whatsoever. When you study martial arts, a whole series of complicated movements are given to you, but without connecting them to the Cosmos or anything. It is the same in ballet or gymnastics: you learn a set of movements and practise them until you memorize them, but there is no connection to the Cosmos.

But the Way of the Spiritual Warrior is a different art: it starts with cosmology, understanding that you and Nature are one, that every movement you do is connected to the Cosmos. You might say that you and the Cosmos are not one because you have a separate body and the trees are separate from you. But the space between you and the trees is an illusion: it is actually full. It is full of Prāṇa, vital energy, the Life-Force, or the Holy Spirit. The Holy Spirit is right here, inside you and outside of you. You are breathing it in, the trees are breathing it in, the sky is breathing it in. It is an all-pervading energy-field.

When you practise a Warrior sword technique, therefore, you are moving your sword through the air but you are actually cutting a pathway through the Prāṇa, or the Life-Force. So you practise until you *feel* the energy moving as you swing your sword. This is where the idea of Tai Chi came from. In Tai Chi you learn to feel the Energy; you can actually feel it with your etheric body. When you move the sword, your palm starts warming up because you are pushing Prāṇa, and you immediately feel a tingling sensation in your arm as the sword contacts that energy.

The simplest movements are the best and you practise them over and over again, not as a practice but as an experience. You can practise a movement just to develop certain muscles—that's what you would do in a sport—but if you did that with a Warrior exercise, you would be completely missing the point. You don't practise to develop muscles—you don't even think of your physical body; you think of the energy flow and feel the movement of the energy.

It is better to practise one movement completely until you feel that your whole being is moving in the Cosmos, that you and the Cosmos are working simultaneously as one. And if you cannot feel it you have to practise that movement until you can feel it, because you can never become a Spiritual Warrior without being one with the Cosmos.

Another important thing is to be aware of the cutting edge of the sword, because that is what cuts the Life-Force, and learning to shape the invisible life-force into certain energy patterns is what gives you power. After a while you will feel the power coming through you, and your sword will become a flaming sword, quite literally; you will see sparks of energy moving through it. Then you know that you are in tune with the Cosmos.

Now, to be in tune with the Cosmos you do not have to be a muscle-bound athlete; you just have to be yourself. Some of the best martial artists in China were small women, but they wielded a devastating force because it was not physical strength they worked with, but the Life-Force, which is present everywhere, an all-powerful, infinite energy source. So you don't have to go to a gym and build up your arms and legs to do this Work. That is the beauty of it: everybody can become a Warrior exactly as they are.

Strengthening the Life-Force through the Divine Name

Being alive presumes that you must have a life-force to keep you alive, and the occult teaching is that your potential in life is in exact correspondence to how alive you are, no more and no less.

First you must recognize that the life you live on a day-to-day basis is just a fragment of a fragment of Life, that you are not living life fully. Jesus said, "I have come to bring life, and more life" (John 10: 10). Of course, the scholars have all sorts of interpretations for what Jesus meant, but what He meant has nothing to do with any intellectual explanation. Jesus always said what He meant. He came to bring more *life*—life-force, life-energy. To the average Christian nowadays that means nothing, but to the early disciples it had a meaning: Jesus taught them how to increase their life-force through the power of the Divine Name. He was not speaking symbolically or philosophically. He meant that He came to bring people more life, that He would show them how to have more life.

The Life-Force *is* the Divine Name. The Chinese call it CHI and in Sanskrit it is called PRĀṆA, PRAKRITI or ŚAKTI. In Christianity it is called *God as the Creator*. But regardless of our point of view, what we call *life*—the power of existence, the power to be—is the Divine Name, the Name of God.

Again, you have to understand that the Name of God is not a name, in the sense of a name somebody decided to call God. Christians, Jews and Muslims think the Name of God is what *they* call Him—Jehovah, Lord, Allah. But those are words *symbolizing* the Name of God. They are just symbols and have nothing to do with the real Name of God.

The Name of God is a universal electromagnetic Light-field and every entity in Space and Time breathes in this vast Energy-Field. By *electromagnetic* I do not mean the scientific sense of the word, which refers to a low-frequency vibration that is just a small aspect of the Universal Energy-Field, but the cosmic sense of the word—a vast field of Energy that we have no words for in human language. It is not just energy but total Intelligence, total Consciousness, total Bliss, total Power, everything that anything in Creation can ever become from the beginning of time to the end of time. It is the limitless Universal Life-Force—the Name of God.

Every entity, whether it is a human, animal, plant, angel or a god or goddess, is alive and moving and being and growing and becoming because it is drawing energy from the Universal Energy-Field, the Name of God. And once you understand that this tremendous Power is inside you and all around you—everywhere in Universal Space, between the stars and between the atoms—then you will begin to understand what is actually available to you in terms of your own evolution, your own growth, your own power of becoming more and being able to do more.

Practice

~

Invocation: Eheyehe Adonai Elohim Chim

This is a Hebrew mantra, an ancient sound-structure of the primordial Hebrew language, which has nothing to do with the modern spoken language. The ancient Hebrew language was a language of Fire, meaning that the primary sound-structures of the language activated the Fire Principle inside you, which is the Holy Spirit, the Breath of Life. Of course, these ancient structures have to be sounded in the proper way. You can look at or read a Sanskrit or Hebrew mantra in a book but it would just give you mental ideas. The power of the language is in the sound itself, that which connects you to the Universal Life-Force.

And that is what this mantra will do: teach you how to connect to the Universal Life-Force, how to increase your life-force and become more able to gather the life-force and use it in day-to-day living.

In ancient Hebrew, Eheyehe means "I AM", that is to say, the Universal I AM, that which is the central conscious reality of the Universe— and which is also you, because you are a fragment of the whole. Expressed in a different way, there is the I AM within you, that which makes you *you*, and there is the I AM in the Cosmos, the Infinite Intelligence within the Cosmos. Adonai is normally translated "Lord" or "God" but it also means a "focal point". So Eheyehe is like the circle, the All-Inclusive Reality, and Adonai is the point within the circle, the focal point of Reality. Elohim means "all powers, all divine faculties, all possibilities to be unfolded in the Universe". On the cosmic level the word Elohim indicates every possible manifestation in Creation, and on the personality level it indicates every possible power, energy and attribute within you that you are capable of manifesting. Chim is the "Life-Force" or "Life".

So the mantra means: "I AM the Lord God of all living things, the Life-Force." It is a mantric formula meaning that *you* are the Lord God within, you are all the powers embodied in your life-force. But on the cosmic level it means that the Great Universal I AM, or the Bright Reality, is the Lord, or the Manifesting Power, of all possible evolutions, states, conditions and energies; that is, you are saying that the Divine Being manifests all the powers, which are Life itself. The key word is CHIM, the one Life of all. As the Divine Being is limitless, Life is limitless, and in as much as you draw that Power inside you, you also become limitless.

Invocation

Stand up straight and invoke the mantra aloud in a clear voice several times, giving each word four syllables as follows:

E-HE-YE-HE / A-DO-NA-I / E-LO-HI-IM / CHI-I-I-IM

Then, sit in your favourite meditation position or in a cross-legged position and repeat the mantra mentally, pausing between each repetition.[5]

Notes

You can also intone just the first word of the mantra, E-HE-YE-HE, rhythmically repeating the word for a few minutes. When you do this, the E sound and YE sound activate your Throat Chakra and the two HE sounds stimulate your Heart Chakra, so the mantric energy circulates between these two chakras in a rhythmic fashion.

Try to open up your heart area when you say HE in order to connect your breath to the Life-Breath. Because it stimulates the Heart area, the HE sound will increase the vitality of your physical, etheric and psychic bodies, and so on. Your whole inner being becomes more vibrant with the life-force because the Heart is the central point of your inner and outer structures. And as you know, the heart beats only because of the life-force. Scientists say that the heart works because of muscles and

---

5. An audio file demonstrating the intonation of this mantra can be found at www.thefhl.org/mantrarepetition.

nerves, but take away the life-force and that explanation is meaningless; the heart just goes kaput. *It is the life-force that moves the heart.* Full stop.

~

An invocation differs from mantra chanting: in mantra chanting the power is in the multiple sounds and in the melody, rhythm and harmony; in an invocation, the power is in its simplicity—the simple utterance of the sound is where the power comes from, not in melody, rhythm or a complex sound-structure. That is why we do not put a tune to an invocation. By the way, when the sound is complicated it's Female; when it is simple it's Male. Each has its own reality, its own power. Energy directed in a simple, straightforward manner is powerful, and energy built up in a beautiful, complex way is also powerful. It is just the difference between how the Male and Female energies work: they are each powerful in their own way when they are used correctly.

~

You invoke this mantra standing up because you are invoking the total Life-Force, and it is easier for the life-force to work through your whole body if you are standing up. You sit in a cross-legged position to purposefully block the life-force and keep it inside you. When you stand up, the whole idea is to expand and experience the life-force in large measure.

~

There is a beautiful saying of the Ancients that is true for this mantra and all mantric formulas in the ancient Sacred Languages:

> There comes a day when the Sounds sing by themselves. Then you know that you are God.

This shows the highest stage of spiritual development, when the Universal Power is beginning to express itself through you and you become an instrument of the Universal Power. ✷

~ 7 ~

THE WARRIOR BREATHES
THE SUBTLE AIR

Meditation is the number one necessity for the Spiritual Warrior. And breathing is number two. Those of you who have been practising Haṭha Yoga, of course, have heard about the importance of breathing and have done a lot of breathing exercises. And those of you who are in the field of martial arts are also aware of the breath. In all forms of physical activity, breathing is important. So I want to tell you about the value of breathing from the esoteric standpoint, in the context of the Spiritual Warrior Path.

The Art and Science of Breathing

We started breathing in Lemuria, the great human evolutionary epoch before the Age of Atlantis. In the early part of the Lemurian Age, when we first started adapting to physical bodies, we had to consciously breathe. In the Atlantean days the breathing process was further refined and we had breathing techniques for controlling substances and other people's minds, for gaining powers, for all kinds of purposes.

There was a vast science of breathing in the Age of Atlantis, but after the destruction of the Atlantean civilization, which took thousands of years, that science was lost. And if you look at the last six thousand years of recorded history, which is really only yesterday in the history of the planet, you see that people have been breathing automatically, unconsciously; that is, the average person does not think that there is any significance in breathing at all. They just breathe because they breathe, with no intelligence or understanding behind it.

In actuality, the Breath—what in India is called PRĀṆA, in Hebrew RUACH (RUHA), in Chinese CHI or what the Greek initiates called PNEUMA and the ancient Romans called SPIRITUS—is an aspect of the Deity Itself. It is a cosmic force, a colossal energy within the mind of the Deity Itself.

Everything, on a large scale and small scale, breathes: you breathe in and out, the planet breathes in and out, the Solar System breathes in and out, the Milky Way breathes in and out and the whole Universe breathes in and out. The Breath of God, the Breath of the Absolute, what the Ancients called the *Great Breath,* is a terrific *power,* a tremendous *energy* that creates Life and maintains the Life-Force of the Universe. This Great Breath of the Deity breathes in and out through all of Creation, on ever larger and ever smaller scales, and carries in it the Life-Energy that sustains all life.

In the physical body you have to learn to breathe consciously, to be aware of breathing. In the higher planes you do not have to—breathing is just automatic—but here you have to be aware of it because your breathing changes according to what you are doing, what you are feeling and what you are thinking. Have you ever noticed that when you get angry or become afraid or are under stress, your physical breathing will change? You might go into a state of shock or start hyperventilating.

Everything that happens to you affects your breathing, whether you like it or not and whether you are aware of it or not. A change of mood, a change of thought or a change of activity directly impinges on your breath, which is your life-force. Your breath process is actually the life process inside you (which is where you are connected to the life-force of the Cosmos), and it is important to understand this, otherwise you will never develop the magical powers of the Spiritual Warrior. A Spiritual Warrior can use the *Science of Breathing* to develop amazing skills and for many purposes. But it all starts with being aware that your breathing process changes when a change takes place inside you.

This is what people who do sports have never understood. Why do you think people do extreme sports? To change their breathing rate. And why do they want to change their breathing rate? Because it gives them extrasensory perception, a feeling of power, timelessness, fearlessness; it gives them an immense surge of energy. In other words, they are trying to do Yoga, but in the wrong way; they are trying to walk the Warrior Path, but in a completely silly way. When people do something extreme to get a kick out of it, it is because they know that there is a bigger reality behind it and they somehow want to get in touch with that reality.

You could say that they are unconsciously trying to alter their breath so that they can have a mystical experience. Even regular athletes, like marathon runners, say that there comes a point when they know that their breath goes into a completely different level and they feel transcendent, like they're floating on air and feeling blissed out. Even people who have never been interested in spirituality will have these experiences. Why? Not because they were running a marathon or whatever sport they were doing; that didn't mean anything. The specific sport they did was just a technique, a way to get beyond the normal breathing rate.

The Warrior knows this and the Warrior has scientific breathing methods, precise ways to work with a particular weapon or body movement, structured ways of altering the breath rhythm for specific purposes. Breathing is a science and an art, which is no longer known to the masses.

Now, let's establish another factor: your breath is part of the planetary breath, part of the planetary life-force, because your breath *is* the life-force. By *breath* I do not mean your physical breath only, the taking in of oxygen; that is the "skin" of the Breath. Just like you have skin, flesh and bone, the physical breath is only the skin part of the Breath; behind it is the flesh, the subtle expression of the Breath, and behind that is the bone, the subtlest expression of the Breath. That is to say, there is the outer breath (the physical breath), the inner breath (also called the psychic breath or subtle breath) and the subtlest breath (which can only be experienced in higher states of consciousness), and they are all the same life-force (Prāṇa) moving inside you, a continuum of subtler and subtler regions that you can actually experience.

Nowadays, people are starting to understand a bit about breathing and maybe learning how to breathe for relaxation or to relieve stress. But that is a primitive way of using the Breath, which is as large as Life itself, because it is not the physical breath that is important; what is important is getting to the next layer of the Breath and beyond that to the subtlest part of the Breath. The ancient Warriors learned how to do that by practising all kinds of breathing techniques—Connecting Breathing, Energizing Breathing, Penetrating Breathing, Strengthening Breathing, and so on.

One of the earliest breathing methods is called Connecting Breathing because its purpose is to connect you to the Source within you. Yogīs, Mystics, Sūfīs and Masters from all the great spiritual traditions have a basic drive: to connect to the Source within. You may call it Self-Realization or finding your true Self, who you really are. This technique enables you to penetrate deeper and deeper until you connect to the source from where your consciousness arises.

As you do the Connecting Breathing technique and penetrate into the deeper side of the Breath, you will be able to sense the *life* in objects. When you look at a flower, you will penetrate the life-force of that flower and realize that it is a *living being*, and sense its beautiful, gentle vibration and its purpose, meaning and intelligence. You will sense the life-force even in inanimate objects, because everything in existence has an internal reality, no matter how inanimate it appears to be. Even a stone is alive. In fact, stones are very much alive. That's why people collect them: they feel that there is something in them, that they radiate some energy—which they do.

I'm trying to say that all of Nature is alive with intelligence. *Even a sword.* The sword has always been a special weapon, used in Warrior Schools in many countries since time immemorial. One of the sayings of the great Masters of the Warrior Schools was that the sword was the Heart, or the Soul, of the Warrior. When you first hear that your sword is your Heart or Soul it does not mean anything to you. But once you have meditated and gone through the spiritual training of a Warrior, you realize that, yes, your Soul, your Heart, expresses itself in your weapon. Quite literally. Your weapon becomes an extension of *you*, your Soul, your Heart—"Heart" meaning the essence of your *inner* being.

Connecting to the Natural Environment

A Warrior can breathe in Power and breathe out Power, drawing the breath in from the Cosmos and pushing it out as a thought, feeling or action. How you use the Breath of God, or the Cosmic Breath, is up to you; whether you are a devotee or a Warrior or whatever, you can use that same tremendous Power mentally, emotionally or physically. And this is important to understand: there is only one Life Breath for all

---

In ancient times the weapon of a Warrior was respected; another Warrior would not dare touch it or go near it because it was special and unique to that person. The weapons of great Warriors were always treasured, handed down like sacred objects from generation to generation, like the sword of King Arthur. And this is why in the olden days a sword was handmade specifically for a purpose. The sword maker knew what the requirements of a particular Warrior were and infused them into the sword. And then when the Warrior used it and infused his or her life-energy into it, the sword was energized and made powerful; it became magical. And this all has to do with Breathing, with the interconnectedness of your life with the life around you on the planet and with the Cosmic Life.

of us. When you become a Warrior you will feel the Life-Breath of all the entities around you—animals, plants, trees—and the Life-Breath of planet Earth. And when you become sensitive to the Life-Breath you will notice that it flows in different ways in different places, so you will know that some places are better for your work than others.

Those of you who have been meditating for many years know that it is easy to meditate in some places and impossible in other places, and that sometimes it is easy to meditate and at other times it is not. This has to do with the life-force within you and how it is connected to the life-force of your environment. As part of the Warrior training you need to find a spot to do your spiritual practices—breathing practice, sound work, meditation. Obviously, a dense materialistic environment where everybody's thoughts are on the material level will have a low vibration that is not good for practising meditation.

There are two kinds of vibration: the vibration produced by a human being, the human aura, and the vibration of Nature itself—the natural vibration (which includes the invisible dimensions) produced by the planetary surface at a particular place and time. If there are no human beings there, then there is only the vibration of Nature; but if there are people living there, then the environment will be infused with their particular life-force. That is why spiritual seekers have always wanted to get away from human beings and go into deserts and mountains to avoid the human vibration and be in a natural environment.

But even that is not perfect because not every natural environment is conducive to humans. In some places we will feel welcome and in some places we won't. The simple reason for this is that human beings have been destructive to Nature for millions of years, so Nature is suspicious of any human encroachment. All human beings will be welcome in any kingdom of Nature when we have a harmless vibration. Even the most antagonistic parts of Nature will welcome you if your vibration is in harmony with the Cosmos, that is, you are radiating out positive vibrations.

It's only because so many human beings throw out violent and negative vibrations into the environment that they are not welcome. For Nature, it is purely a matter of self-defence.

The ancient Māori had respect for Nature. When they needed wood for a canoe or a house, they used Karakias, ritual chants, asking the tree spirit to forgive them and give them the wood they needed. They had an esoteric knowledge that human beings have an impact on Nature and we need Nature's cooperation for our activities—because it is the right thing to do. But nowadays, of course, they go in with chainsaws and cut down trees to make chopsticks or newspapers, no longer respecting Nature, no longer asking Nature for permission. It's just wholesale slaughter.

People do not understand that trees are living beings, just as alive as you or anybody else. Have you ever entered into the psychic aura of a tree and felt its inner being? If you have you would know that a tree is much bigger than what you see, which is only the physical body of the tree. Imagine those giant trees in big forests—enormously tall and a thousand years old—the actual size of their being is ten times larger, above and below the ground. That is because the physical body of any object is its smallest part. Your physical body is the smallest, most constricted part of your being. Your astral body is bigger, your mental body is yet bigger and your causal body (your Soul nature) is even bigger. It is the same for a tree or an animal or any object. So if the physical part is large, you can imagine the real size of that entity.

Buddha spent forty years practising meditation in all kinds of places before finding a banyan tree, an ancient, majestic, highly intelligent tree. He attained Enlightenment under that tree because the tree actually helped him; the tree spirit understood what the Buddha was trying to do, that He was on the last leg of His spiritual training, and the tree helped steady Him. (A tree is a steadying force, standing immobile for thousands of years.) Because of the aid of that tree, Buddha went through to Nirvāṇa and beyond.

Practice

~

RŪ-HĀ Connecting Breathing

RŪ and HĀ are syllables of the Primordial Language of Sound, and they are connected to the breathing process.[6] The RŪ sound draws you inward and the HĀ sound draws you outward, so you are breathing in the Universe and breathing out your self. Normally, what people do is breathe in the Universe and keep it to themselves. Most people just live for themselves. They have a limited life-wave that circulates around themselves—how *they* feel, what *they* do, what *they* think. They live in a little world. This breathing technique will teach you to *breathe in* the large world outside of you and then *breathe out* your small self into the large world.

The RŪ-HĀ Connecting Breathing technique is one of the many breathing techniques the Warrior uses. This particular technique connects you deeper and deeper inside—to your astral nature, your mental nature, your Soul nature—and further and further outside, eventually to the Cosmos. When you can do this, an amazing, miraculous transformation takes place—you become large, you become the Cosmos, the Cosmic Will in action.

This depends, of course, on your level of Attainment. You can become the agent of your Soul power, or you can become an agent for the Spiritual Hierarchy, or you become an agent for the Cosmos. This technique will shatter the conception you have of yourself, that you are not just a small entity but a cosmic being, and it will help you begin to expand into that greater reality.

---

6. For the correct pronunciation of these syllables and those in the other meditation exercises in this book, see the Sanskrit Pronunciation Guide at the back of the book.

The technique itself is simple: As you breathe in, mentally say RŪ, and as you breathe out, mentally say HĀ. Do not manipulate your breath or count your breath or use beads; just breathe naturally, in and out, and let your breath flow by itself. It may speed up or slow down; it doesn't matter.

Once you start connecting, this practice will teach you how to breathe for every occasion, and once you master this technique, you will be able to connect to your environment, wherever you are—in a forest or a busy city. You will know how to tune into the environment you are in. You will be able to be at home anywhere and everywhere, at all times. The Warrior is *at home* in the midst of a battle. When you are sent into a battle you have to be at home; it is a matter of life and death. If you're not, you are lost. This is a powerful technique that enables you to feel comfortable no matter what situation you are in.

Remember, this is not an intellectual exercise, so try not to think of anything. Simply breathe in RŪ and breathe out HĀ and let the breath flow in and out naturally.

Notes

The Sanskrit word for *connection* is YOGA, which also means "union, at-one-ment, joining". So this is a connecting breathing technique of Yoga, except that it was not invented in India but in Atlantean times 800,000 years ago.

~

When you do this meditation correctly your mind disappears and does not function at all. If your mind is still functioning, it means that you are either not doing it correctly or you need to practise more because your mind is stronger than the Breath-Current. In actuality, the Breath-Current is stronger than the mind; *the mind obeys the breath*. But because the normal person is not used to using the Breath-Current—they are only used to using the mind, which runs nonstop twenty-four hours a day—the mind appears to be the stronger. But once you start using the Breath-Current you will realize that it is much stronger, and much more true to life, than the mind. Then the mind just dissolves. Once the Breath-Current is established inside you it becomes all-powerful and you begin to experience an expansion of consciousness and all kinds of experiences.

In the East, in China, Tibet and India, they were aware of the fact that the breath is stronger than the mind, and that is why they developed breathing techniques. This was also well known in the West, in the ancient Greek and Roman Mystery Schools and in Egypt, Babylonia and Persia. In the ancient world it was known everywhere that the breath was stronger than the mind. It is only in our so-called modern scientific society that nobody takes any notice of the breath at all, or gives it any meaning in ordinary life. They do not teach you at school that your breath is something you can work with to attain Higher Consciousness. That does not exist even as an idea.

~

During this meditation you may have physical reactions like your heartbeat speeding up or feeling that you might get sick. These are the physical body's reactions that occur when you are going beyond the body's normal limits. When you are doing Yoga or spiritual practices, you can often go beyond the established rhythm and nature of your physical body, so naturally there is a reaction. You should just acknowledge such reactions and just carry on. Meditation is not going to hurt you but you have to be aware that you may have physical reactions. It's not a big deal; it's not a real sickness.

Sometimes you can have a panic attack, feeling like you are going to die or have already died. This too is just a natural physical body reaction because you are going beyond its limits. This happens because of the reaction of what we call the *body consciousness* or the *body elemental*. There is an elemental that keeps your body together, in its shape, otherwise the millions of atoms and cells that form your body would be going in different directions.

When you meditate, you sometimes expand beyond the body's limits until there naturally comes a stage when the body elemental gets frightened that you will go so far away that its purpose is finished, that it has no reason to be. Then it starts panicking and you have the symptoms of a panic attack, feeling that you are going to die. All you need to do is calm the body elemental down by sending a telepathic message that you are not going to die, that everything is fine, you're just going away for a while.

~

You may experience the breath as a cold or hot current during this meditation, which means you are experiencing reality. I'll explain: In Christianity, as you know, God is always male—God the Father is male, Christ the Son is male and God the Holy Spirit is male. But actually, the Holy Spirit is a curious part of God because it is simultaneously male and female, and this is what you are experiencing. You experience the masculine and feminine aspects as a hot current and a cold current, respectively.

But in the teachings of the Eastern Mystery Schools, the ŚAKTI teaching, it is the other way around. Most of the Śakti Schools say that Śakti is feminine, and only feminine. So Christians think of the Spirit as being only male and Hindus, only female, and both of them are missing the other side. In actuality, the Spirit is both male and female, and you can experience all the dualities—positive and negative, active and passive, hot and cold—when you are fully developed in this technique.

~

This one technique, if you work at it with sincerity and perseverance, will take you to levels of consciousness where you can actually sense fluctuations in planetary life, solar systemic life or even in the great cosmic tides of the Galaxy. You can sense when something is wrong or things are not in tune with Cosmic Harmony.

This is depicted in one of the Star Wars movies where Luke Skywalker gets angry and kills a few subhuman creatures, but then his Teacher, who was on another planet in another part of the Galaxy, sensed that there was a change in the vibrational structure of the Cosmos and tuned in to Luke. It might sound like science fiction but it is real, because the basic pattern of the Cosmos is harmony, and if a system or a species or a creature goes out of that harmony, you can feel it—if, as I said, you are evolved enough *inside*.

Harmonious Breath, Harmonious Life

The Ancients knew that there is more to your breathing than taking in air so that your physical body can exist. As I mentioned previously, the Breath has many subtle layers and the Warrior connects to the inner layers of the Breath by utilizing the Science of Breath, which teaches that you have an invisible energy-field around you that connects you to the invisible part of the Cosmos, and your breath directly connects you to that invisible part of the Cosmos.

On a practical level, the rule is:

If your breathing is chaotic, your life is chaotic. If your breathing is even, your life is even.

This is the ancient Spiritual Warrior rule: If your breathing is even, harmonious and gentle, your life is even, harmonious and gentle. If your breathing is chaotic, your life is chaotic. If you read about the warlords of ancient times, in China, Japan and other countries, as well as the warlords of today, you notice that they are all fired up and out of control. Their lives are exactly like their breathing: chaotic. Yet to be true Warriors we must be in harmony with ourselves and the whole Cosmos. To achieve that, our breathing process must be harmonious.

Have you noticed an interesting thing about movement in modern society? Those who have studied ancient forms of movement like Indian

Yoga or the Chinese system of Tai Chi may have noticed that in the past people were taught to move gracefully, which was simply a product of graceful breathing, or harmonious breathing. But if you look at the modern music of today, like rap, or modern painting, sculpture or the performing arts, what do you notice about it? It is jerky and tense and chaotic—which shows that there is tension in the breathing and tension in the mind. The external production is only a reflection of what is inside. When you sing an angry melody, it's because you have anger within you. When you sing a harmonious melody, it's because your mind is harmonious. What comes out of you is not accidental, not something that just happens; it is because of what you are.

I recently went to see a modern dance performance and I found it absolutely unbelievable. Every movement of the dancers was totally jerky, as if they were puppets and their arms and legs were on strings being pulled in all directions. As I was watching I thought, "If your body moves in such a jerky way your mind moves in the same way. And what about your life-force? How can you express life beautifully and harmoniously when your mind is totally jerky?"

This is important because if you want to be a Spiritual Warrior you cannot have an unintegrated mind, you cannot have an unintegrated breathing process, because your life will be unintegrated. This is something the Ancients understood profoundly. In the ancient Warrior Schools, when the young boys became angry they would be sent into the desert or the mountains or a forest to spend some time by themselves. They had to calm themselves down by tuning into Nature, feeling the life within a rock or a tree, feeling the life within the forest. Calming down involved learning to breathe in harmony with Nature.

Breathing is much more than what you think it is. It is a serious thing, one of the most serious things you can do in your life. Once you learn to breathe correctly, it will change your day-to-day life. You will deal with people, situations and events differently, for it will be a matter of making choices not with your mind but with your inner attunement with the Life flowing in and around you all the time.

That training in the art of tuning in and harmonizing yourself is vital, not just for your sake but for the sake of society also. The ancient Warriors had to make choices that affected thousands of people, sometimes whole tribes or nations. They could not make correct choices if they were frustrated and angry and their minds were working overtime. A Warrior's mind is like a lake, steady and clear, and in that steadiness and clear sightedness the Warrior can see and make the right movement. This applies to the battlefield as well as one's whole life.

Obviously, when you go into a fight, if your mind is working erratically your movements will be erratic and you will get hit. But if your mind is steady and calm, simply observing, aware, then the right energies will be flowing through you and the right movements will follow. Your hand, your arm, everything will move in the right direction without strain, for the simple reason that you are tuned in. Tuning in is the key to being a Warrior and tuning in deeper is the key to being a Spiritual Warrior.

To be a Spiritual Warrior is an unbelievable state because everything will flow the right way for you, everything will be just as it should be. The whole Universe opens up towards you and you will do the right thing.

Practice

~

HŌNG-SAU Harmonizing Breathing Technique

The HŌNG-SAU breathing exercise will integrate you and make your breath flow smoothly—and therefore make your mind flow smoothly. This will give you a sense of incredible bliss inside. The warrior films that are popular nowadays seem to show that a warrior is a serious kind of person, almost grim. Well, yes, some warriors can be serious and grim, but you can actually be a happy warrior. Can you imagine that? You can actually be a warrior full of joy and bliss.

The warriors who are always serious are not trained in the internal techniques of conforming with the harmonies of life, because when you conform with the Universal Harmony in and around you, you actually relax and let go, and you enjoy life as it comes. You are full of joy, peace and harmony because you feel the Life move inside you and outside you; you feel the "within-ness" of all things.

To give you some esoteric understanding of the Science of Breath, you must understand that the physical air you breathe only sustains your physical body. There is an internal breath that sustains your emotions and another, more internal breath that sustains your mind. The HŌNG-SAU breathing exercise moves from the outer breathing process to the inner. It calms the body, calms the emotions, calms the mind.

HŌNG and SAU are sounds, or syllables, from the Primordial Language of Mankind. There was a time, hundreds of thousands of years ago, during the days of Atlantis, when there was only one language for all Humanity, a language of pure Sound-Vibrations. Some languages nowadays reflect, or have a connection with, the ancient language of Atlantis—ancient Sanskrit, Hebrew, Latin, Arabic and Greek, among others. These languages are sacred for the simple reason that within their internal structure there are remnants of the primordial Sound-

Vibrations of the original language of Atlantis, when every sound was a magic formula that had a meaning and an effect on the consciousness of the person who spoke it.

The technique is this: Just sit and breathe in and out calmly. Feel the breath coming into your nostrils, down into your lungs, into your tummy and back to your lungs and out through your nose. And mentally say "HŌNG" as you breathe in and "SAU" as you breathe out. These are the sounds of the breath inside you, not your physical breath (whose sounds in the ancient primordial language are HA and SA). HŌNG and SAU are the sounds of the internal psychic breath.

Throughout the exercise breathe naturally, without forcing or doing anything to your breathing. Watch your breath and try to enter deeper into it and go beyond the physical breath until you enter the finer regions of the Breath, where you will discover amazing things. Once you can breathe internally, you will start to become luminous, begin to feel yourself becoming light and fine, as if you were made out of a light substance or other very fine structure. What is more, you will sense an internal harmony, a feeling of being healed and balanced that will be reflected in your outer life.

Notes

There are several ways to practise this meditation: You can sit down in any posture—on your heels, cross-legged or in a chair—and meditate for twenty minutes or half an hour once or twice a day, or whenever you have time. Or you can go out into Nature and sit under a tree or on a rock by the sea and meditate steadily for a long time.

You will get many benefits from this exercise: your health will improve, your mind and emotions will improve. You will go deeper and deeper into internal harmony until you begin to feel the harmony in the Cosmos around you, because these syllables are links to the Cosmic Harmony.

~

This is one of the Warrior techniques and it will radically change you. It will spiritualize you. You will begin to feel transcendent, translucent, that you are made of a fine substance or fine consciousness. It will actually make you lighter, quite literally, so you can leap through the air. Why do you think the Kung Fu fighters in the movies can fly through the air? The Chinese had this secret, of course, because the Chinese language is one of the Sacred Languages that have the Primordial Syllables.

As a result of this meditation your physical body will become less dense in terms of *vibration*. Normally the atoms of the physical body vibrate at a particular rate, but after doing this meditation for two or three months your body will begin to vibrate faster. You will have exactly the same shape but your atomic structure will vibrate faster—which means your body will be lighter and you will move more gracefully, more easily, so that when you leap your body just flies, because you are already light inside.

~

One of the practical aspects of this exercise is that it will help you in your day-to-day life. Spiritual Warriorship is a philosophy of life; a religion of life; a science of life; an art of life. How do you apply it? Suppose you have a difficult decision to make or you have to meet a difficult person or situation, or suppose you are angry with somebody or something is troubling you and your mind is full of worry. When you worry, your vibration becomes dense, you become heavier and more solid. Any negative emotion—anger, violence, worry, fear—will make you dense. This meditation has the opposite effect.

So if you use it apart from your normal meditation time, when you are worried or agitated about something, it will calm you down. Your mind will be an ocean of calmness and you will be in harmony with yourself and the Cosmos. Then, when you meet that difficult situation or person, there will be a totally different outcome.

Normally, meeting a difficult situation in a troubled state of mind in itself causes trouble. Why do you think people fight? One person has a troubled mind and the other person responds with a troubled mind. You have two troubled minds together so there is tension and fighting. If everybody had a calm mind there would be no tension, no fighting, no wars. Everybody would agree all the time and do things together.

You cannot expect the other person to be like you, so you have to change yourself. If you put yourself in a state of harmony and then work from that state, it will not matter what the other person does or says. So far as you are concerned the situation is already solved, the situation is already in harmony, and you just act from that level of consciousness.

~

Suppose you are having a fight with your partner. He or she may be ranting and raving at you, but you, having established harmony within yourself, stay calm. And because you are not responding, because you are standing in your own light, the light of your inner being, the other person will either not want to have anything to do with you or they will also calm down—either way you will have averted a conflict.

You can make so much more of human relationships when you approach them in this way. Try it out and see for yourself how it works. You can disarm the most annoyed person but you have to establish yourself in that state of harmony. It is not just a thought. You can't go up to an angry person and say, "I am harmonious." That won't work. You actually have to be in the state of harmony. It will radiate out from you and the other person will pick it up. They will feel the Warrior within you and the whole situation will be defused. ✗

~ 8 ~

THE INTEGRITY
OF THE WARRIOR

One of the important aspects of being a Warrior is to know what stage you are at, in your own state of reality. You cannot master the next technique until you have mastered the current technique. This is a Warrior Principle and an important lesson in life: *You cannot go to the next stage—properly—unless you master the stage you are in now.*

For example, in old-fashioned schools you had to pass an examination; if you did not pass you had to repeat the same grade next year, because you were not able to do the next level of teaching. In life, this means you have not mastered the life situation you are in and cannot go on to the next situation. This is why the world is in such a mess, why human relations are such a mess, why everything about human life is such a mess. People are always moving on to the next thing without having perfected the thing they are in. In life, people go through many changes without understanding a fraction of what they are going through, and therefore their whole life-streams are in a mess.

So this is a Warrior Principle that you need to apply in life. Look at your life in terms of your relationships, in terms of the way you understand life, in terms of the way you deal with life's problems. Have you mastered your present situation? If you haven't, then when you move on to the next stage it will be a mess, and when you move on to the stage after that, it will be a bigger mess. If your life is out of control, you can never become a Spiritual Warrior.

So you must be comfortable with yourself and with the situation you are in. If you are restless in the situation you are in it means that you have not mastered that situation; you want to get out of it and get onto the next situation, which of course will not be mastered either. This does not mean that you have to be perfect in every aspect of your life. No. You have to know where you are at because everybody is at a different stage.

The important thing is that you have to be sufficiently integrated within yourself that you at least know what your situation is—what your weaknesses are and what your strengths are; what your positive activities are and what your negative activities are; how your life-stream made you as you are now and how it will affect your future. Only when you know where you are at have you achieved a sufficient level of intelligence to start doing the next thing.

This is the problem with the education system: you learn about *things*, not about yourself. You learn all kinds of facts about things: their colour, size, shape, length, breadth and what have you—all kinds of stuff that has nothing to do with *you* and your life. But when are you taught about yourself, your thought processes, feeling processes, your relationship to others and to your environment? When are you taught about how consciousness works in you and in other people or how the Universal Consciousness works in Nature? This is what is missing in education. Of

---

A Warrior has to be aware at every moment how he or she feels, thinks, acts and receives life. Remember this is not about being perfect. There is no such thing! Everybody makes mistakes. Jesus did, Buddha did, Kṛṣna did. But the difference is that people like them are aware of their mistakes. They are aware of when the energy flows strong inside them and when it flows weak, when their mind is bright and when it is not so bright. They are aware of what goes on inside and outside of themselves. This is the Art of the Warrior. This is knowing your immediate situation.

course, there are Christian schools where you learn the Old Testament stories, but that is not real spiritual education. You just learn about mythologies and memorize who did what, when and to whom—nothing about *you*!

Meditation *and* Action

The Shaolin School and the Wudang School in China were true Warrior Schools. You started when you were four, five or six years of age. First you became a baby Warrior, then a junior Warrior, senior Warrior and finally a Master Warrior. As you grew physically, so you grew spiritually. You were a Master Warrior not because you were old but because you had acquired wisdom through many years of instruction and practice; you had completed and mastered the science of Warriorship.

This science was based on meditation and action. Not meditation *or* action. Meditation *and* action. Many people on the Spiritual Path think: meditation only. This is because many of them had several past lives of being sādhus, sannyāsins or renunciates in India, or Christian monks in the Middle Ages, and they were born in this lifetime with the conviction that the Spiritual Path consists only of meditating and somehow trying to get to Nirvāṇa, or the Kingdom of God. But in the ancient Warrior Schools the Path of Action was simultaneous with the Path of Meditation. You meditated, you did breathing techniques, sound techniques, and then you did your physical training. You did that every day, year in and year out, systematically, until you became the perfect Warrior.

In the olden days the Warrior Schools were live-in schools, like the ashrams of India and Tibet. The Teacher was in residence and the pupils lived there also. The teaching was twofold: the Teacher taught by words and by being there, living together with the pupils day to day. The Teacher provided an example of how to live, but again, this does not mean that the Teacher had to be perfect. No one has ever been perfect on this planet and no one can be at this stage of our evolution. When a mistake was made, therefore, the Teacher acknowledged it and rectified it, setting a good example of humility to the pupils.

The pupils knew that the Teacher was human, that it was possible for him to think an off-key thought or feel an off-key emotion, but they also knew that the Teacher was superhuman. And the pupils appreciated both the humanness of the Teacher and the supernatural nature of the Teacher, and they had to work with both. If the Teacher had a lousy personality, they had to deal with the tremendous power, integrity and intelligence of the Teacher on the spiritual level, and at the same time his lousy personality. This was part of the learning process of the disciple. When they grew up and became Teachers they would also have a human side and a divine side, and their pupils would have to deal with them, because every Teacher has a human side.

You also have a human side and a supernatural side, and those two have to merge. The only people who try to separate them are the Indian yogīs and others who spend all their lifetime in contemplation. They want to abstract themselves from the physical world and live only in their divine nature, with the complete negation of their human nature. That is the way of the sādhu or the sannyāsin but it is not the Way of the Warrior.

The Way of the Warrior is to live with both the human and the divine nature. Prior to six thousand years ago it was the Way for all Humanity, the normal understanding of what we are supposed to be doing in life: fusing the normal and the supernormal inside us. Then it was forgotten and people separated material life and spiritual life, quitting the material life to live a spiritual life. But that is not the Way and never has been, and this will be especially true from now on.

So the Warrior skills give you a great reward: how to be human and superhuman at the same time. You can learn this principle through various practices, including training with a weapon, but you can also learn it in how you act in every situation, because a Warrior is a Warrior twenty-four hours a day, not only on the battlefield, and he or she applies this principle in daily life, moment by moment. When to be passive and apply feminine energy, when to be active and apply masculine energy, and when to bring in supernatural power—it is all part of the Warrior training. When you become a Master Warrior you will be able to do all these things simultaneously, knowing what is the right application of force in all situations. For the wrong application of force, even for just a fraction of a second, can be devastating.

But remember that this is a gradual process of transformation. As you apply your training in your day-to-day life, the intelligence or wisdom behind it grows inside you gradually. And then one day you will wake up and know that you are a Warrior. Then, whatever weapon you choose becomes an extension of your Soul. If you are a true Warrior, your weapon is actually you.

It is similar to being a true artist or musician: your instrument becomes you. I am talking about people who are artists by feeling and sensitivity, rather than by mental effort. You can be an artist by learning

---

The Confidence of the Warrior

As a Warrior, you first master your weapon and that gives you confidence. When you become a Spiritual Warrior you have that same confidence *without* your weapon. Your confidence is so strong and bright inside you that you are ready to tackle any situation in life without your weapon. You are confident because *you are confident*. You know that you will win no matter what happens. Even if they cut your head off you will still win.

A Warrior knows his or her moment of glory in life, and it does not mean winning a battle. It is winning on moral strength. The ultimate battle of the Warrior is not a physical battle but a battle of strength inside, a battle within the Warrior consciousness. As a Spiritual Warrior, you know when you have won the battle, no matter what happens on the outside. And that confidence, that knowledge that you have already won the battle before you even start can only be developed through internal practices, by getting in touch with your Self, the Source within you.

the techniques of playing an instrument on a mental level and developing great technical skills. That is not art and your instrument does not express you. If you are a real musician, your whole being—your emotional nature, your heart and soul—pours out through your instrument. The instrument becomes you and when you play it, it has its own life, its own reality, and it becomes part of your Soul expression.

It is the same for a true Warrior—the weapon of the Warrior is an expression of their Soul; it has power and energy in it. When you are dealing with a real weapon, therefore, it is important that you remain calm. If you act out of anger, fear or any kind of negative emotion, your movements will not be precise and a skilful warrior will beat you straight away. No fear. No anger. No self-doubt. No aggression. Otherwise you have lost the battle before you start.

This lesson from the Warrior School can be applied in life: you must not have fear in life; you must not have anger in life; you must not have aggressive tendencies in life; and you must not have self-doubt. If you can do that, your whole life will move onto a positive keel and you can only attract positive energy, positive situations and positive results. ✻

Do not forget that Jesus was from the line of King David, which was part of the Warrior Class of ancient Israel. Buddha came from the Kṣatriya Class, the Warrior Class of India. Kṛṣna and Rama were also from the Warrior Class. Lao Tzu, the Pharaohs of Egypt—all the great Teachers who changed the world were members of the Warrior Class. That in itself is a huge lesson; they were not just abstract contemplators who decided to go into transcendental states and stay there. They were active people. Everyone who ever changed world consciousness belonged to the Warrior Class.

This is why I say: You have no idea what it means to belong to the Warrior School and become a Warrior. You cannot appreciate the tremendous significance of it. It is a great honour, an inestimable privilege.

THE FOUNDATION
OF THE WORLD

The *Foundation of the World* is an important subject if you want to attain Cosmic Consciousness. The word for *foundation* in Sanskrit is Mūlādhāra—Mūla means "root, source or foundation"; Adhāra also means "basic, basis or foundation". So Mūlādhāra has a double meaning of "foundation, root or basic substratum". Also, the Mūlādhāra Chakra is commonly called the Base Chakra.

Everything has a north pole and a south pole—an atom, a human being, a planet, an angel, a solar system, a galaxy and even the whole Universe itself. What we call the North Pole and the South Pole of the planet are actually invisible energy radiation fields, tremendous vibrant fields of energy with opposite polarities. In a human, the Crown Chakra is the North Pole and the Base Chakra is the South Pole. In the Cosmos, the Physical World is the South Pole and the Nirvāṇic World is the North Pole. (The terms the *Kingdom* and the *Kingdom of God* are found throughout the ancient Jewish-Christian literature, including the New Testament and the Old Testament. The *Kingdom* refers to the world, the South Pole, and the *Kingdom of God* refers to Nirvāṇa, the North Pole.)

You have to understand this before you can develop Cosmic Consciousness because you cannot move from Self-Realization (the first stage of Enlightenment) directly into Cosmic Consciousness (the second stage of Enlightenment). Many Yogīs remain on the level of Self-Realization, thinking they have achieved the highest, whereas they have reached only the first stage of Enlightenment. In fact, attaining Cosmic Consciousness requires more than just reaching the top, the North Pole, and staying there.

Cosmic Consciousness is essentially about acquiring a *cosmic sense* through the union of the Base Chakra and the Crown Chakra, the North Pole and the South Pole. This involves the correct functioning of your whole energy-field, from North to South, that is, the harmonious functioning of all the various energy centres and life currents inside you. Only then can you attain Cosmic Consciousness.

This is an understanding that you have to apply first and foremost in your daily life, because any extreme activity will prevent you from attaining Cosmic Consciousness.

In the world today there are many fitness freaks who think of nothing else but their body and every milligram of substance they eat and every microsecond of exercise they do. They have an overactive Base Chakra, just like the people who are into extreme sports and are always looking for something to challenge their physical bodies to the extreme limit.

Cosmic Consciousness is defined in the Lexicon (Volume 4) of my book *Heavens & Hells of the Mind* (Sounding-Light Publishing, 2007) as follows:

The term Cosmic Consciousness can be understood in two ways:

• The condition of absorption into the exalted Consciousness of Nirvāṇa, the Kingdom of God (ĀTMA-VIDYĀ).

• The integration of the Buddhic Consciousness (Pure Consciousness, TURĪYA) into the states below. In this exalted condition, therefore, the objective consciousness, the subjective mind (dream states) and the dreamless-sleep state have fused perfectly into the Transcendental State of Pure Consciousness. One is simultaneously aware of the four states of Consciousness, from Buddhi downwards, while functioning in the waking state in the physical body. This state is known as TURĪYĀTĪTA-AVASTHĀ, "beyond the Fourth State".

This Base Chakra activity is increasing, thanks to the Aquarian Age, and because the Base Chakra of the Earth is being stimulated by cosmic energies and forces.[7] These energies influence all of Nature, including human beings, so more and more people have overactive Base Chakras, which makes them physical and dense in vibration and blocks their possibility of awareness of the North Pole, the Crown Chakra. If you are a materialist, for example, if you think about life in terms of money or gain, you have a strong Base Chakra and because of that you cannot sense the subtle energies of the higher realities.

At the other extreme there are the people who are always spaced out, who are always up in the clouds and do not relate to physical conditions very well. They have a hard time doing what needs to be done in this physical dimension. Their problem is that they have very little Base Chakra activity and too much North Pole activity.

Your view of the world depends on the state of your Base Chakra. Your experience of life, the way your physical body works, how you relate to other people, how you relate to the Cosmos—they are all about your Base Chakra. If it is malfunctioning, therefore, it is not possible for you to become a Warrior, or attain Cosmic Consciousness, in the first place.

The Base Chakra represents Earth, meaning "Earth" in a cosmic sense, that is, Matter. And here is the mystery, because the Base Chakra is also called the *Foundation*. In the New Testament, Jesus refers to "the kingdom prepared for you from the foundation of the world" (Matthew 25: 34). That "foundation of the world" is cosmic. Everything in the Physical World, the Astral World and the Mental World is made out of Matter, and Matter is the *foundation* of the Universe—the basic substance, the basic essence out of which all things are made, out of which all manifest things are possible.

---

7. This is discussed in more detail in: Imre Vallyon, *Planetary Transformation: A Personal Guide to Embracing Planetary Change* (Sounding-Light Publishing, 2010), 15–23.

Everything has a gravitational field and the Base Chakra is the gravitational field that attaches you to the planet Earth, the Earth's gravitational field (in the same way that your Crown Chakra attaches you to the gravitational field of the Spirit). If you could see chakras clairvoyantly, you would see that the Base Chakra is facing down towards the centre of the Earth (and the Crown Chakra is facing up). This means that the task of the Base Chakra is to enable you to live on this planet, not only in the physical dimension but also on the astral, mental and even the causal dimensions. Without the pull of the Base Chakra you would not be able to function in those dimensions.

Incidentally, for those of you who are science fiction fans and dream about travelling to outer space, I would suggest that you not do it, because you would get into a huge stew. Every planet has its own gravitational field with a north and south pole, and your physical body is made to respond to the gravitational field of this planet; your astral body (your emotional body) is made to respond to the astral gravitational field (the astral body) of this planet; and your mind body is made to respond to the mental gravitational field (mental body) of this planet—not of Pluto, Jupiter or Saturn and certainly not of some other planet outside the Solar System. All the planets have their specific energy-fields, and you cannot change your energy-field unless you are a highly evolved human being.

The Base Chakra is about realism—seeing, hearing and feeling things as they really are; grasping the environment as it really is and not how you imagine or wish it to be. For a Warrior, the realism of the Base Chakra is essential. A Warrior needs to act with the right proportion of Base Chakra, to do the right thing at the right time in the right way for the right result. No dreaming about it or imagining or exaggerating it; just exactly how it is. This is why the Zen monks focus on the correct alignment of the Base Chakra, and this is why they say, "Before Enlightenment I chopped wood; after Enlightenment I chopped wood."

Now, coming back to the important point: to the Ancients, the *foundation* was something you had to have a right relationship to before you could liberate yourself from the human condition. That is, your foundation, your Base Chakra, must be well balanced and functioning how nature intended before you are able to neutralize the influence of Matter and reach Cosmic Consciousness.

If your Base Chakra is not active, you will become like the Yogīs in India who are in Samādhi, or Trance, and are incapable of looking after their own physical body, let alone doing something for anybody else. They are focused on the Crown Chakra, where all their life-force goes, so the Base Chakra is undeveloped and they are therefore disconnected from *this* world. They are actually malfunctioning spiritual beings, because to be properly functioning you have to be able to relate to this world. Do you think the Buddha was a malfunctioning being? Do you think that Jesus Christ was a malfunctioning being? His Base Chakra was solid and fully active and at the same time His Crown Chakra was fully active, too. He had Cosmic Consciousness: He was together with his Father in Heaven while His feet were firmly planted on Earth. He was not a total basket case; He was the ideal Warrior.

If you read the New Testament you will notice that Jesus had human emotions. You could say, "If He was a man of God, why did He have human emotions?" It was *precisely because He was a man of God* that He had human emotions. He went to a temple, and in those days everybody did business there, changing money and selling this and buying that, so Jesus became angry with them, got a whip and started hitting people left and right, saying that the temple was the house of God, not a business exchange. He went wild because He saw that what was happening was not the right thing. He was a Warrior, one hundred percent.

Another time Jesus was sitting on a mountaintop overlooking Jerusalem and started crying, "How many times have I tried to bring you together, to inspire you to turn towards God, and you would not" (Luke

13: 34). He had tried to teach and save Jerusalem many times, and the result He got was basically nil, so He was frustrated with the people and was actually overcome by that human emotion. But that shows that although He was illumined, united with his Father in Heaven, He was still concerned about day-to-day life on Earth. And that is a true Warrior, because in Him the North Pole and the South Pole—the Kingdom (this physical dimension, physical life) and the Kingdom of God (the Nirvāṇic Consciousness) were functioning simultaneously.

There is nothing wrong with this world per se, but what is wrong is that people are either totally spaced out and cannot relate to the world or they relate to the world so much that they cannot relate to the Spirit. In the Bhagavad-Gītā it is said of Kṛṣṇa that "He comes at every age to rectify Dharma", which means that a Divine Avatāra comes in each age to put the dharma of the world right because, obviously, people mess it up all the time. And that is what the Warrior does: rectifies wrongs by whatever means, because that is the duty of the Warrior. But to do that, the Warrior has to have a properly functioning Base Chakra.

As I said, our planet is malfunctioning at the moment because it is being bombarded with cosmic energies that are being absorbed through its Base Chakra. This is why science and technology—the improvement of physical life and physical conditions—are suddenly such big things. In every aspect of physical life we have made more progress in the last 150 years than in the last 150 *thousand* years.

Everybody is concerned with the welfare of their physical bodies and their physical life, getting more and more involved in the physical dimension, which in one sense is good, but things are getting out of balance and people are getting more disconnected from the North Pole and feeling less obliged to do anything spiritual. Many countries are so well off materially that people can't be bothered seeking spiritual things. Why should they, because everything is fine, right? They have all their goodies, so why worry about God or the Spirit or the Soul? That's the danger of it, the downside of the situation. People are enjoying better material lives while the poor Soul inside them is starving to death.

The Way of the Warrior is not to be out of balance like that. The Way of the Warrior is to walk in the Light with your feet solidly on the ground. So the process of grounding yourself, grounding your Base Chakra in the world, is important. When you stabilize your Base Chakra you can live a normal human life—"normal" meaning how you were originally intended to live on this planet. Originally we were meant to function as representatives of the Spiritual Hierarchy, representatives of the Divine Plan. Human beings actually have a mission to fulfil. Most people do not know this. They think their mission is to go to work and watch their favourite TV programmes, but actually humans have a bigger mission than that.

A part of the problem for the Ancients was that they said the world was evil, that it was the work of the devil. And of course there are still people who think that the world is the work of the devil. But the world is not the work of the devil because there is no devil. The world works according to its own law; matter can only do certain things in certain ways. It is not the devil. This world cannot be Nirvāṇa, ever. But this world has lots of nice things—nice trees, for instance—which Nirvāṇa does not have.

What we call Spirit is really Matter, and what we call Matter is really Spirit. So this division between North and South is an illusion; it exists only in our minds.

There is a massive field of Energy that vibrates extremely rapidly at the top (what we call Spirit) and extremely slowly at the bottom (what we call Matter). This does not mean that there is an entity called Spirit and an entity called Matter—there is no such thing; God is one. It means that there are degrees of vibration. What we call Matter is a slow-moving Spirit. Everything in Creation starts from Nirvāṇa, which means that the Nirvāṇic Light is called Spirit and this Physical Plane, Earth, is called Matter. But actually everything is Matter and Spirit, just different frequencies, vibrations or wavelengths. This Earth is Nirvāṇa and Nirvāṇa is this Earth, in different wavelengths of Energy.

The Law of the World is called Dharma, or the destiny of the world. This world has its dharma, in the same way as human beings have their dharma, and as the Moon, the Solar System and the Milky Way have their dharma. Everything has a dharma to fulfil, and as human beings living on this Earth we have to discover what our dharma is, what we are supposed to do, and if we can fulfil it we will help Mother Earth fulfil her destiny.

The human being is a Cross—feet on the ground and head in the clouds (in Nirvāṇa), with everything else in between. We should be able to embrace the Astral World, the Mental World, the Causal World and the Buddhic World in one massive Sea of Consciousness, able to direct our attention to any part of manifested Creation. That is the ideal human being in the Mind of God. Of course, most people have not reached that ideal yet, but that is what our Spiritual Warrior School is trying to do. ✗

~ 10 ~

THE LAW
OF YOUR BEING

When I was young I had a Chinese Kung Fu Master, and what impressed me about him was that he was like a cat. You know how cats are: They can lie down on any odd-shaped thing and be completely comfortable, and when they move they don't shake or jerk but move stealthily, with perfect coordination. When they are hunting a mouse or a bird, they will sit still for hours on end, just watching, and then pounce at just the right moment.

I used to watch this Kung Fu Master, amazed that a human being could be so much like a cat—that grace in every movement and that patient stillness of a cat. And then I thought that there was something almost supernatural about him. He did not behave like a normal human, who is always kind of jagged and vibrating in all directions, uncoordinated in actions, thoughts and feelings. And what is more, I sensed that his coordination was not mentally controlled but spontaneous and one hundred percent natural.

As I learned from him in those days I began to get a sense of where he was coming from. So I tuned into the source of that kind of spontaneous being and realized an interesting principle, which I'm going to tell you about. I call it the Law of Your Being, because there is no other word for it. I could call it *being like a cat*, but, of course, it is much more than that.

To explain the Law of Your Being, which I subsequently explored, you should know that there is the reality you employ in this world—the superficial reality, or the way you have been told or brought up to behave by custom, tradition, religion and society—and there is another kind of reality inside you, the real reality, which is the Law of Your Being.

First of all, realize that everything you do is according to how you have been taught to behave; it has nothing to do with the Law of Your Being. Children in one country are taught not to burp after dinner because it's bad manners, but in another country they are allowed to burp after dinner because it's good manners. There are many customs all around the world, one stranger than the other, and people are brought up in them. They are also brought up with a religious view, what to believe in and how things are and how they are not. Then there are family traditions, which could be any nonsense whatsoever. So people are saturated with what they have been taught and faithfully replicate it. Naturally, they do the same thing to their children, so that one generation after the other does what they are told by their parents.

My old Kung Fu Teacher was different; he did not believe in a written tradition, although many spiritual schools in India, China and the Middle East, including martial arts schools, had written laws, or what they called scripture. He was a great teacher, a great consciousness, and he said that scripture would divert you away from yourself. Of course, in the beginning it was difficult to comprehend what he meant, but he kept saying, "Practise and then you will know."

This idea of "practise and then you will know" runs counter to scripture, because scripture conditions your mind, and it gives you a clue regarding the way to be, which may be difficult for the normal person nowadays to understand. But in being yourself, not how you have been taught to be, you discover what you really are and the infinite potential within you, which is far superior to anything you have been trained or conditioned to do.

I'm just trying to put the idea into your mind that there is a way to be that is not how society expects you to be. Society expects you to follow a tradition, as I said, but when you do that, you stay on the level of worldly consciousness, how worldly people think and act. And because the worldly consciousness is extremely materialistic, which means it is dense, your consciousness remains dense and you cannot be a liberated human being on this planet. Put simply, to attain Liberation you must renounce the *way you think*, that is, your normal worldly consciousness.

Renouncing the way normal society thinks does not mean that you have to become a revolutionary and overthrow the government. As you know, thousands of governments have come and gone and society's problems remain. That is another delusion. Freedom lies in something else.

So if you want to attain Liberation in this lifetime, one of the first qualifications is to be yourself, who you *really* are, not who society made you to be. First of all there is identification with nationality: you say you are a Dutchman, a German, a Frenchman, an Italian, a Briton, a Hungarian. Then, there is identification with religion: you say you are a Christian, Muslim, Buddhist. And there is identification with all kinds of class distinctions that, if you believe in them, immediately reduce your potential. A person who is termed an outcast in India has to do things like clean toilets and bury corpses. So if your parents tell you that you are an outcast and you believe them, that is what you are going to do in your life. There are millions of outcasts in India living in slavery to a stupid idea—all because they are termed outcasts by their religion and their society and they believe it.

Before you can be yourself you have to stand up to all your conditioning. If you've seen the movie *Crouching Tiger, Hidden Dragon*, you might remember that at the end of the movie the young hero comes back into the heroine's life. If the ending had been done according to society's standards, according to worldly consciousness, the young couple should have gotten married and lived happily ever after. But instead, what happened? The young hero asks the girl to come with him and the girl says no and jumps off a bridge and floats away into Eternity.

That is the way of the Spiritual Warrior, which is nothing like what society expects you to do. That girl was a Master Warrior and she realized that the spontaneous flow of time is only a fragment of Eternity and the real flow of life is in Eternity itself, which is on a different dimensional level. She went right into that dimensional level and was therefore no longer bound by society's customs and rules.

To discover that principle, the Spiritual Warriors went out into the desert, the mountains, the valleys, away from society, and spent time by themselves. When you spend time by yourself you discover that your life-force has nothing to do with the conditioning of society whatsoever. You move away from the normal idea of just learning fighting techniques, the normal expectations of what you are supposed to be doing, to a stage beyond—the stage that my Kung Fu teacher showed me a long time ago, the stage where you discover *who you are.*

Only when you begin to discover who you are, and not what you have been taught, do you become a genuine revolutionary, a person who can convey Eternity in the place, time, culture, and tradition you are in. You can be in China, Russia, Holland—anywhere; it does not matter. You are flowing with the eternal Law of Your Being, which is how Eternity expresses itself there and then. Then you are a Master Warrior, a vastly different state than that of a conditioned warrior.

Previously, all your training was about learning to do this form and that form, techniques learned through the mind, memorized and precisely executed until you became an expert swordsman. But as a Master Warrior you are focused inside and move according to an inner direction, not a direction of the mind but according to another kind of consciousness within. You move in ways that are not learned, not what you are conditioned to do, but in ways that you actually *are*, according to the Law of Your Being. It is a completely different reality.

The important thing, therefore, is to know that you have been conditioned and that conditioning is a superficial reality that works in the world for worldly purposes, but it is not what you really are. What you really are is infinitely larger and your potential is beyond your wildest imagination. You can discover that through Stillness and other ways of the Warrior. And once you establish yourself in the Law of Your Being, you lift yourself up to another plateau of reality. You are a human being but you relate to life on an unimaginably different level.

I'm trying to say that there is a level of consciousness completely different from the normal conditioning processes of the world, and what is more, that there is a way to attain it. It's one thing to realize the possibility that you can live in a timeless, immortal state of consciousness; it's another thing to actually get there.

Here we need an important quality: *determination*; because it is only through determination that you can get to that state. Somebody can tell you about the wonders of being human, the infinite possibilities inside you, and you can say, "Yes, that's really nice, but I don't have time now. I'll think about it after I retire, when I have more time." That person lacks determination and will therefore not get to that level of consciousness in this lifetime or in any lifetime, until he has determination.

To bring it down to a more ordinary level, some people decide that they are going to be a doctor, lawyer or a dentist because they can earn lots of money, so they go to university and study until they become one. Others might have another ideal, say, helping people. But whatever view of life you have, whether you want to earn money or help people, you still need the same quality: determination. If you want to be a ballet dancer or a musician, you have to practise hours and hours a day, year in and year out, with absolute determination. Yogīs in India sit in their caves and meditate fourteen hours a day, year in and year out, with absolute determination to attain Enlightenment. You cannot succeed in life unless you have *determination*.

Determination is an energy stream inside you coming from your Higher Self, the Soul, the Immortal Principle within you. It is a real energy, as real as electricity or steam or atomic energy. It is not a thought. In fact, the energy comes first; the thought about success comes afterwards. First you have the energy and that motivates you to think the vision. That energy is the power inside you driving you on to your vision, like a fire inside you that drives you to plod on day in and day out, year in and year out, until you attain your goal.

As I said, this determination energy comes from the Soul realm, not from your mind. Your mind is actually the thing that obstructs your determination, that will stop you from succeeding, for the simple reason that it will find excuses. It is not the mind that is determined; it is the mind that is your enemy. In any aspect of life, no matter what field you are in—spiritual or material—success depends on how much determination you have. *But that comes from your Soul Energy.*

Remember, I'm not talking about having to become a monk or nun and join the silent orders of a Roman Catholic monastery, or having to become a sādhu in India. That has nothing to do with determination at all. I'm talking about a magical power of your Soul. If you say, "I'm going to attain Enlightenment in this lifetime" and really mean it, then your Soul will begin to rearrange your whole life-stream for that purpose, and that purpose will work itself out in miraculous ways in your daily life.

It is the Soul that will work out the miraculous occurrences of your daily life, not your mind. You will just feel that you have to do this or that with a clear, precise knowing. You won't have to logically or rationally work it out; your Soul will rearrange every circumstance and every moment of your life to fit in with your determination.

So the first thing is to determine that in *this* lifetime you will attain Enlightenment. And then, if that determination is really strong, the power of your Soul will work miracles in your life to get you there. Nothing can obstruct it. The fact that you have a job and a family is no obstruction; the fact that you are poor is not an obstruction (it may be better for you); the fact that you are rich is not an obstruction (though it could be harder for you). All the things people identify with in the world have no relevance to the Enlightenment process at all. The external life you live is not where it comes from or ends; your external life has nothing to do with it. It has to do with the immanence of the Soul within you, whether the bright, shining Self within you is active in your life. That is what leads to Enlightenment.

Moreover, it does not matter where you are or what you are doing. You can be in the midst of battle and attain Enlightenment. As the arrows are flying and you are ducking them, in that moment you can attain Enlightenment. There was a famous Kabbalist who attained Enlightenment while he was sitting on the toilet. He was thinking about Malkuth (the Physical Plane) and all its functions and in that moment he got it: the Divine is in every aspect of the Physical Plane. Enlightenment is determined by the state of your being, so you do not have to restrict your existence in any special way to attain it. You just have to be what you are—live the Law of Your Being—and it will come.

~

This is an exercise you can practise on the Law of your Being. It is really an attitude to life itself. Sit in your meditation position and read the following paragraph many times. Try to develop this attitude in your life, firstly while you are sitting quietly and later on while you are doing other things.

> The way to your Being is not a matter of distance, nor of time. It always is. Although we speak of a *way* or a *journey*, it is really not going anywhere. It is being inwardly still, silent, receptive, being bright and awake inside. *You* are the Way, the Truth and the Life. To realize your Being, or Self-Nature, you have to turn your attention within rather than outside. You have to cultivate the *Silence that just is*. This is the way to your Being. ✗

~ 11 ~

BRAHMA-MURTHA
TIME WITH GOD

The difficulty with the modern age is that people have access to too much information, so they can pick up many ideas from many different sources about all kinds of spiritual processes and techniques, like meditation, breathing exercises, chanting and mantras. They spend a short time doing one thing and then a week later they are doing something else, and the overall result is that they don't get very far.

This is a drawback of the modern information age. In ancient times, information was only given from the point of view of practical application, not as something to be stored in your brain. In those days learning was something else: you learned to *be* something, to *become* something and make full use of it. Nowadays it is impossible to make full use of all the information you have. You are bombarded with information, but the fact that you have so much information can be a hindrance because you are not inclined to put any of it into practice, or if you do, very little.

This is the age of gadgets, which is deceptive because everything is given to you. Somebody worked hard to invent something and it's given to you. So you take it for granted that next week there will be a new gadget and the following week another, and you need do nothing about it whatsoever. This is where materialism spoils the minds of people; they do not see the need to make any effort because everything is just given to them.

Well, in the spiritual field, the teaching is given to you, the method is given to you, the knowledge is given to you, but if you do not put them into practice you will get nowhere. In the spiritual field—and in the Way of the Spirit itself—you cannot reap the benefit of others. You cannot wait while somebody else works hard and attains a higher state of consciousness, and then you get there, too. You will not get there. *Your* effort is important; in fact, it is the only thing that is important in your life. And this must really be understood. In the spiritual field you have to do it yourself. This is still the Law.

You cannot say that you do not have time to practise because you're too busy running your business or family. Some techniques, like the Warrior technique of *from Action into Stillness, from Stillness into Action*, can be applied in the midst of your business activities, before or after a meeting, for example, which means that you can practise your spiritual path anytime in the twenty-four hours of a day. (If you are old enough, Soul-wise, you are on the Spiritual Path every night while you are asleep, because for a person who is Awake only the physical body sleeps; the rest of the person is doing inner work on the inner dimensions during the night.)

Most people think that they are doing the Spiritual Path by going to a retreat. Yes, that's true, but being on the Spiritual Path means being in the moment, in the here and now. That is the Way of the Warrior. If you do not have time to be in the here and now, well, where are you then?

Try to imagine that you are going to die any moment and have only the next five minutes to attain Enlightenment. This does not mean that you should start frantically repeating your favourite mantra. What you have to do is shift your attitude and wake up to the fact that time is actually precious in this process. Unfortunately, young people have no sense that life is very short. When you're young you don't feel the nearness of the end; you're buzzing around all day doing this, that and the other thing, and you think this busyness will go on forever. But as you get older you realize that rushing around being busy all day is not endless, because you are already sixty-five, seventy-five, eighty-five, and you know that the clock is ticking and you can hear the ticking getting louder.

It is not anyone's fault, just the imperfection of human nature, because the sense of the shortness of human life, the immanence of death, has not been given to human beings. If people were aware of it then they would be more concerned about their lives and their purpose in life: Who am I? How much have I accomplished? Am I fulfilling my destiny? Am I fulfilling my Soul purpose? Am I doing what I was really born for?

We are trying to inspire you to live every day as if it were your last, which means that you have to undergo a miraculous transformation inside yourself. I do not mean stuffing your brain with all kinds of information; that does not transform you. It is more like having to realize that there is a divine purpose in existence—a Divine Plan—and that

---

Time with God

Let every moment of your day be part of your spiritual path. Apart from knowing that you have a spiritual destiny and purpose, you must also periodically sit down and do a specific technique, a breathing technique or a mantra technique or whatever. You must dedicate some time, maybe ten minutes, half an hour or an hour, when you withdraw from any activity and say, "This is my time with God." This is a beautiful Sanskrit expression used by the Yogīs: BRAHMA-MURTHA, meaning "time with God". So set aside a certain part of the day for when you can be with God, and let nothing disturb your time with God.

I am sure that sometime within twenty-four hours you can dedicate five minutes to God. I mean, God is actually worthwhile to spend at least five minutes a day on. During that time you can practise the process or technique you feel the most inspired to do, what you are consciously aware will benefit you to get to the next stage. Your time with God is when you do a technique that will draw you closer to the Divine Presence, not because of the technique itself. The technique itself is not important. What is important is that you feel that using that technique you get closer to the Divine Presence. It is the idea of the Divine Presence that is important; the technique is just a means to connect you.

you are part of that purpose and must therefore live as an intelligent being with a function in the Divine Plan, not just somebody who rushes around with no plan or purpose.

In the busyness of life you must know that there is a path within it for you. In other words, you are your path and you create it out of your total consciousness, your total *beingness*. And you are unique. We all share similarities in ways of thinking, in ways of doing, in cultures and traditions, but within all that each one of us is still unique. In spite of all the outer appearances, your consciousness—your level of being, how far you have evolved in the great cosmic picture—is yours and yours alone.

Believing in Jesus Is Not Enough

You are totally responsible for your life, and you are totally responsible for your spiritual development. Unfortunately, besides the problems of too many gadgets and too much information, in the West there is another problem that came about due to the misunderstanding of the teachings of the Christ.

As you know, the earliest Christian Scriptures were written ninety years after the death of the Christ, that is, about three generations afterwards. Of course in those days they did not have video and audio recordings, and they did not even write down word by word what Jesus said. Usually manuscripts were written afterwards, like the story of Moses, which was written many generations after the death of Moses, not during his lifetime. And it was the same with the teachings of Buddha and Kṛṣṇa: they were written many generations afterwards, so nobody really knows precisely what they said.

The point I'm bringing up is that the later generation of Christian writers thought that what Christ said was that He died for our sins, and that believing in Him was sufficient for you to go to Heaven. Now, I'm sure He did not say that, because any Spiritual Teacher knows that you cannot get to Heaven, or any higher plane of consciousness, unless you work for it. A Teacher can teach you a technique, inspire you and help you, but without your work, *by the Law*, the absolute Law of Karma, you will *not* get there.

Christ would never have taught that for all future generations anybody who believed in Him would automatically ascend to Nirvāṇa. That idea would have been absolute nonsense to Him. What He probably said was that He would give the way—the techniques, the inspiration, the processes—but He would expect the disciples to put them into practice *then*, while He was alive, and after He was gone the principle of practice would still apply.

Whatever Spiritual Path you follow, whether it's Buddhist or Christian or the Warrior Path, does not matter: *you have to practise*. Without practice there is no attainment; even if you have generous Teachers giving their blood for you, you still have to do something about it yourself. You can be forgiven your sins—a Teacher can take bad karma away from you—and that is fine, but you still have to work for your Liberation.

Unfortunately, as I said, it is a sadly wrong teaching in the Western World that people believe they do not have to make any effort on the Spiritual Path because all they have to do is believe in Jesus Christ. That idea would break all the Spiritual Laws that ever existed from the beginning of Creation. You still have to work to get to Heaven, Nirvāṇa or whatever you like to call it.

You must therefore work out your own salvation or destiny in your own way. Going to spiritual retreats and workshops can help you, inspire you and give you momentum, but apart from that, you have to feel your own inspiration to do the work. If you want to be a prima ballerina, for example, you know that merely aspiring to be one will not get you there. You have to have an internal vision of what a ballerina is and orient your life to becoming that vision. Going to ballet classes will train your physical muscles, but it won't be enough. There has to be a radical shift inside you, in your attitude toward your life.

So you must see yourself as you truly are—a spiritual being, a Spiritual Warrior, an expression of the Divine—not what you apparently are—a computer technician or the head of a multinational company or whatever you identify with in the world. If you keep identifying only with the *image* you have in the world you will never make it, because that image is always limited, by circumstances, race, culture, religion, economical status. To become a spiritually enlightened person you have to have another image. You have to think of infinite possibilities inside you, infinite possibilities of forward movement in evolution.

With cultural, religious or social conditioning, you behave in the way you were told to behave by your parents, your culture, your religious authorities. That is extraordinarily limiting. It is like a mouse in a cage with a little wheel. The mouse runs and runs and the wheel goes round and round. If you were a mouse born in captivity and all you had was a cage and a wheel, then naturally you would run on the wheel and think you were living the great life. If you were born a free mouse in a field, however, you would be running in this direction and that direction, anywhere you wanted to. For you, running on a wheel would be the most boring thing ever invented. It would not be a life at all; it would be an utter *condemnation* of life.

Now, human beings are like that: they are running around in a little wheel and they think that that is their life, which is a complete delusion. Everybody is brought up in this religion, in this culture, in this society, in this tradition, in this education system. Do you realize that education systems come and go? The ancient Greeks had a completely different education system, so did the Persians and the Chinese. We think that today's education system is *the one* and will be until the end of time. It will not; it is just the education system created by the Western mind today. It will change.

I'm trying to say that the normal human being runs on a little wheel provided by parents, culture, society, religion, and so on. But you have to break out of that wheel. You have to realize that no, within you there is an infinite potential; you can run in any direction like the field mouse. You are *free*.

An enlightened human being is a free person. An enlightened human being has a tremendous freedom inside: freedom in feeling, freedom in action, freedom in thinking and, what is more important, freedom in *being*. And that freedom in being is totally indescribable. It has nothing to do with how you were brought up by your parents, what traditions you followed, what silly habits you picked up.

When you are a free person you realize that all these things human beings do are just trivialities which could be done in any number of ways; it is not important whether they are done one way or another. There are necessities you do because you are in a physical world, but inside, you are free. You can move in any dimension in Time and Space. The whole Universe is yours to explore, to be, to become. This is what the freed consciousness is: a bright, unlimited awareness of omniscience, omnipresence, omnipotence, of infinite fields of possibilities. ✗

PART TWO

~

THE SPIRITUAL WARRIOR SCHOOL

THE UNIVERSAL TEACHING

~ 12 ~

THE WARRIOR USES
THE CREATIVE WORD

The Science of Sound

One of the most important aspects of the Spiritual Warrior Path is the Science of Sound, or the Primordial Language of Sound. The people who received special instructions in all the great ancient traditions—initiated Hindu Swamis, initiated Kabbalists (not the common rabbis) in the ancient Hebrew system, initiated Chinese, Sūfis and Gnostics—were taught this Sacred Science. So where did this amazing science, which was completely known to the Atlanteans, come from?

The Atlantean races were taught the ancient Primordial Language of Sound by the angels, the Angelic Hierarchy. Remember that in those days the Atlanteans did not have an intellect, or an intellectual mind, as we have now. They thought in terms of *sound and light waves*—that is, Colour (Light) and Sound. That was also the ancient language of the Devas, or the angels, who still think and communicate by Colour and Sound, because they also have no logical minds. You might think that the Archangel Gabriel and the other angels are all rational beings or computer nerds, but they aren't. All the angelic species express themselves through Light-Vibration and Sound-Vibration.

That is because, in the Inner Worlds, Colour (Light) and Sound are the same thing: every sound produces a colour-wave and every colour produces a sound-wave. The two are not separate, except here in this physical world, where you can paint a colour without producing sound and you can make sound without producing a colour. From the astral dimensions to the causal dimensions and beyond, Colour and Sound are inseparable.

This is important to understand because the Light and Sound Language, the language of the Devas, was also the Primordial Language of early Humanity, the first races on the planet.

So what is this Primordial Language about?

When you go into higher states of consciousness, such as Superconsciousness, Cosmic Consciousness, Buddhic Consciousness or Nirvāṇic Consciousness, you will discover an amazing thing: the Universe is planned.

The beginning of time was trillions of years ago because this particular Creation is only one of a series of Creations. This whole vast Universe exists now and it will dissolve into the Unmanifest. Before this there was another Universe and before that another and before that another. You can only perceive these great epochs of Creation and Dissolution when you are in Nirvāṇic Consciousness or above. In Paranirvāṇa, where the Buddha is, one is able to perceive Ultimate Causes, Cosmic Realities and Absolute Consciousness. Once you begin to sense even a fragment

---

You have to understand that this is a *science*, meaning that when you understand the Science of the Primordial Sound Language you can experiment with it and get results. In a science, what you do produces certain results and you can test those results over and over again. If your theory is correct you should get the same results; if you start getting different results then there is something wrong with your theory. With the Colour and Sound Language the results are always the same. Certain sounds—like RĀM, for example—produce physical, astral, mental and causal vibrations. In the physical world you do not see the colour of RĀM, but on the astral and higher levels you can see the waves of Colour that it produces.

of that consciousness you realize that it is totally purposeful, intelligent and meaningful, that it has reasons for doing things, although the reasons are way beyond human comprehension.

On that infinite scale of Mind, in the Infinite Mind of the Deity, certain internal stresses or vibrations arise, because everything that is alive has to move. If there were no movement in the Mind of God, this Creation would not exist. Nothing that is stationary can make something happen; for something to happen, there must be movement. So originally, aeons and aeons ago, at the beginning of Creation, the Cosmic Mind fluctuated in a certain way and caused vast "ripples" within its Consciousness—the first movement towards Being, towards a new Creation, a new Universe, a great new epoch of movement forward in Evolution.

These ripples, or waves, of Light become denser and denser, forming the boundless Worlds of Light—the Nirvāṇic dimensions, then the Buddhic dimensions and eventually the Causal World. It is at this point where the human mind can first touch Reality: on the causal dimension, in Causal Consciousness, which we can also call Superconsciousness, a consciousness beyond the mind in which you are conscious of yourself as a Living Soul. This is where you first experience that everything that exists is pure Sound and Light Vibration, where you first connect to the great science of the ancient language, the Primordial Language of Sound.

Levels of Consciousness

Superconsciousness is the first level of Samādhi, or Self-Realization, realization of the Self (the Soul), which is superior to the other levels of your being—your thinking nature (rational mind), your feeling nature, your dream nature and your sleep nature. Self-Realization is only the beginning in terms of the perception of Higher Reality (although in many Yoga schools it is said to be the final goal). The next level is Cosmic Consciousness and above that there are various levels of God-Consciousness, in which you gain a deeper and deeper sense of the plan, direction and purpose of the Universe.

It is also in the Causal World that you see for the first time that the whole Universe below—the Heaven World, the Astral World and the Physical World—is also made out of pure Sound and Light Vibration, *as it is perceivable to a human being.* There are Buddhas, Avatāras and other cosmic Beings who perceive this further up in the Creation process, but for Humanity, the first time we can get in touch with the Higher Reality is in the causal dimensions. There you hear the Sounds that later became the Atlantean language, which later became the syllables of all the Sacred Languages of ancient Hebrew, ancient Greek, ancient Chinese, ancient Arabic, and so on. You can hear those Sounds in the Causal World like frequencies of Sound and Light, that is, *Sounding-Light*, because Sound and Light are one. You *see* and *hear* simultaneously.

And it is in the Causal World, in Causal Consciousness, that you understand where the Primordial Language of Sound comes from, where the Science of Mantra comes from and how the lower regions of Creation came about. You can actually hear the Song of the Planet, our Mother Earth, and the Songs (the musical frequencies) of Venus, Mars, Pluto, or the Song of the whole Solar System. You realize that every-thing—whether a Solar Logos or Planetary Logos, a solar system or a universe or a plant, tree, human or an angel—has a Song, a particular

---

The Logos

Knowledge of the Primordial Language of Sound was preserved in the ancient religions, like early Christianity, which borrowed it from the Greeks, who called Sounding-Light Vibration the *Logos*, the Word of God. "In the beginning was the Logos and the Logos was with God and the Logos was God" (John 1: 1). Everybody thinks that this is a Christian idea, taught by Christ, but if you read the New Testament you will see that He does not mention the Logos at all. The Christians borrowed this idea wholesale from the Greek Mystery Schools, which taught about God as Sound and Light thousands of years before Christianity. It was fine for the Christians to borrow that idea because it is a correct idea: God is Sound and God is Light.

frequency of the Sounding Primary Word. And then you realize that the whole Universe is caused and shaped and moulded and maintained by Sounding-Light Vibration.

Originally, during the prehistoric development of Humanity on this planet and the early days of Atlantis, humans could still access the Causal World in Causal Consciousness. I'm talking about the peak of development of the Atlantean civilization, which had a period of ascension and then a period of decline. The use of black magic and the sinking of the continent happened later, during the decline of their civilization.

The time of Atlantis was not six or eight thousand years ago. There is a Greek story about an island that sank about eight thousand years ago. The Greeks called it Atlantis and ever since then there have been legends about Atlantis. But the real Atlantis existed 800,000 years ago. It was a huge continent that broke up and parts of it sank into the ocean, and then hundreds of thousands of years later the other parts sank. The small island that sank eight thousand years ago was but just the final leftover part of the continent of Atlantis.

The early Atlantean races had Causal Consciousness and could correctly see and hear and respond to the Inner Worlds. They could see and hear the Sound and what it did in the Causal World, how it created the layers of the Astral World, how it formulated the Etheric-Physical World, and they could also see how physical objects came into existence and how they are maintained. That was the Golden Age, the Age of SATYA YUGA.

At present we have lost touch with the Inner Worlds, which was expressed symbolically in the Bible as being cast out of the Garden of Eden. Where do you think the Garden of Eden was? Do you think it was somewhere in the desert in Palestine or Israel? Definitely not. The Garden of Eden was the Causal World.

Remember that many of the Old Testament stories are symbolic and are not to be taken literally. They are teaching stories like the PURĀNAS of India. One of the teaching stories in the Old Testament is the story about Adam and Eve, who ate an apple, so God got angry and cast them out of Paradise. Since this is a teaching story, in the old days a real Teacher could explain what the story meant.

What it means is that Humanity lost touch with the Causal World because we were forced to descend below the causal dimensions by the force of Evolution, by the Will of God. Once we descended into the lower regions of the Mental Plane (the Heaven Worlds) we naturally lost our Causal Consciousness. And when we descended into the Astral World we lost our consciousness of the Heaven Worlds. When we descended into the etheric region of the Physical World (which was at the start of the Lemurian Age a few million years ago) we lost touch with the Astral World. And then when we finally took on these animal bodies, borrowed from the Animal Kingdom, we even lost touch with the etheric dimensions of the Physical World.

The Origins of Humankind

You can therefore see that being cast out of the Garden of Eden took aeons of time and a long series of *de*volutions—all planned by the Divine Mind, whose final objective for human evolution was to join Spirit and Matter, to embody the higher spiritual realities in the densest bodily form. That was the Primordial Archetypal Plan for Humanity in the Divine Mind, and that is why we had to lose touch with the previous dimensions in order to gain this (the physical) dimension.

Whether ascending or descending, you always have to lose one level of consciousness to gain the other. Before we could even come down to the Causal World we had to lose our Nirvāṇic Consciousness, our awareness of the Pure Spirit within us. To gain something below, you have to lose what was above. But the reverse is also true: to gain something above, you have to lose what is below. That is how the system is set up.

When the Spiritual Hierarchy discovered that human beings were gradually losing touch with the Higher Realities because they were increasingly focusing on the lower dimensions as part of their devolution, they invoked the Angelic Hierarchy to help humans stay in touch with the causal dimension, which, as I said, is the lowest spiritual dimension. That was when the angels taught individual human beings the Science of Sound, or the Science of Mantra Yoga, if you like, or the Primordial Language of Sound.

Later on, when Humanity descended into the Astral World, that science was taught less and less because people unfortunately became entangled in the Astral World and began to develop emotions, for the Astral World is a seething sea of emotions, from the basest negative emotions to the most exalted spiritual emotions. For them, astral consciousness became their normal consciousness and the Astral World their normal world. So when you were an Atlantean you lived in the seven sub-layers of the Astral World. You were aware of the physical dimensions, the mental dimensions and a bit of the causal dimensions, but your full consciousness was focused in the Astral World.

Then a new problem emerged: we developed a sense of separation. Before that, when we were still in the Garden of Eden, in Causal Consciousness, everybody felt one with everybody else. We were all Souls living in causal bodies in the Causal Worlds in a state of unity and harmony. There was no reason for us to have a sense of separation. But once we descended from the higher astral dimensions to the lower astral dimensions we began to develop a sense of isolation, a sense of ego, a sense of attaining things *for oneself alone*—a sense of selfish grasping.

Once the sense of selfish grasping arose, there came with it the problem of evil, for the simple reason that when you wanted to grasp something you often had to do it through force. That was when the Atlanteans developed the highest system of black magic ever invented. They could use real elemental beings and could create artificial elementals, and they fought psychic wars with each other using the Primordial Language of Sound.

When this happened the great Teachers of the time stopped teaching the Science of Sound except to initiated people, those who still remained on the right path. Later on, when Atlantis became so degenerated that it had to be sunk, the Science of Sound was abolished and was purposefully not taught. From then on, amongst all the ancient races, it was only taught on an individual basis, teacher to pupil; it was no longer taught publicly because of the danger of it being misused as it was in Atlantis.

The Science of Sound is about using this knowledge intelligently, for individual progress, for group progress and for the progress of Humanity. Remember, I'm still talking about the Warrior Path, because the Warriors have always used Sound. The ancient Atlanteans were great Warriors who used Sound and Light, the superior forces of Nature, to do what the Christ did: change physical conditions—such as stilling a stormy lake. First they mastered the Sound within themselves and saw how it works within and without, in the physical environment. Then they mastered the Sound on the astral level, seeing how it affected astral matter, and then on the mental dimensions, where they saw how the Sound works to structure mental matter. And finally they saw the Sound on the causal dimension, where it becomes the first layer of materiality.

(Above the Causal World—in the Buddhic dimension, the Nirvāṇic dimension and the Paranirvāṇic dimension—everything is pure Spirit, which means it is Light in its most refined nature. Only in the Causal

---

For those of you on the Spiritual Path, the existence of God should not be in doubt, but remember not to limit God to the Jewish, Christian, Muslim or Hindu idea. Those are *ideas* of God; they are not God. Ideas formulated by the intellect, the reasoning faculty of the human mind, are not even a fraction of a fraction of a fraction of Reality, because the human mind is incapable of seeing Reality correctly.

World does the Light becomes dense enough to be perceived as matter; above that, it is just Light with no sense of materiality in it.)

The Causal World is the critical stage because it is the halfway point between the material dimensions below, which have forms and shapes, and the spiritual dimensions above, which are formless. Below the Causal there are waves or energy modulations of Matter, or what appears to be substance having some sort of solidity. Above that there is no sense of solidity, just waves of Pure Intelligence. In the Monadic dimensions, or Paranirvāṇa, which is where Buddha reached in his last incarnation, the Spirit is perceived as Cosmic Intelligence. That is why Master Yogīs like Patañjali talk about the Deity as Consciousness, using words like *Pure Mind, Pure Consciousness, Pure Intelligence*, because on that level you cannot describe the Deity as Light. It is beyond that; it is just Pure Beingness.

The Symbolic Meaning of the Cross

Most religious symbols did not originate with their religions: The Star of David is not a Jewish symbol, the Swastika is not a Buddhist symbol and the Christian Cross is not a Christian symbol. They were borrowed from more ancient traditions. Great symbols like the Circle, the Triangle, the Square, the Cross, the Five-Pointed Star and the Six-Pointed Star are part of the Language of the Gods, the Ancient Primordial Language. They existed long before the religions adopted them.

The true nature of the human being is symbolized by the Cross. The top of the cross represents the Higher Worlds (the Buddhic, Nirvānic and Monadic Worlds) and the bottom part represents the Lower Worlds (the Mental, Astral and Physical Worlds). The human being embodies all the Planes of Being.

In the highest regions you have Absolute Intelligence, Absolute Consciousness, Pure Beingness; in the lowest regions you are limited to your physical body consciousness. This is an ancient mystery that can only be discovered in Causal Consciousness, where you see that you are divine and human, absolute and limited. Then you can understand the mystery of the Cross and you can ascend and descend on that Cross in your training.

So in the Causal World you know the true nature of things, and you know yourself as a Living Soul, halfway between Spirit and Matter. You realize that You are Spirit and Matter; that is, you realize that your physical body is the lowest point of your *self*, and the Pure Spirit, the Ātman, the Divinity within you, is the highest point of your *Self*. Above, you are the shining, absolute glory of the Monad, the Divine Spark; below, you are your personality in your physical body. As a Soul you are standing in between, right in the middle, and in that consciousness you see what you really are in Creation, in your true Fullness.

To be a Spiritual Warrior, therefore, you first have to reach Causal Consciousness and see your full grandeur and stature as a human being reaching up to Divinity and reaching down to the physical dimension. ⚔

~ 13 ~

THE POWER LANGUAGE
OF THE WARRIOR

I want to talk to you about the creative power of the Primordial Language of Sound. First of all, you need to understand that Sound is the
secret behind the entire Esoteric Science.

Primarily, the Ancients hid their knowledge in their written scriptures, and as you know, all the great religions since the beginning of
time have had scriptures. But what you may not know is that in ancient
times scriptures were always chanted aloud, sounded out physically. The
Old Testament was chanted by the ancient Jewish people in Aramaic,
Hebrew and Babylonian, and later on the New Testament was chanted
in Greek. It was the same in India, where the Vedic Scriptures were
chanted in Sanskrit and the later Buddhist Scriptures were chanted in
Pāli. And the Sikhs chanted their great scripture, the GURU GRANTH
SAHIB, which is an amalgamation of Sanskrit and Arabic.

In all the great spiritual traditions, when the people first received
that tradition it was encoded into a scripture and then chanted. Later,
this tradition of chanting scripture became lost. For example, the early
Christian scriptures were first translated into Greek and then into Latin,
so they were chanted in Greek and then later in Latin. Once they were
translated from Latin into English, German, French and other modern
languages, people ceased chanting the scriptures. Instead, people started

to read them for their stories, to get inspiration out of their meanings or instructions on how to live a pious life.

But scriptures have *something else* behind them; they were originally intended for something other than merely being read. In ancient times this was of course understood, which is why it was compulsory to recite the scriptures. (In Arab countries it is still compulsory to recite the Koran, although the secret knowledge of why they should be recited has been lost.) And this is the big secret: the scriptures are actually a source of *power*, because within the scriptures there is Sound, and within the Sound is the Secret Knowledge. In other words, every scripture contained the secret Science of the Primordial Sound Language.

Once Humanity translated those scriptures into the modern vernacular languages, the most important thing was lost: the sound, the Science of Sound contained in the original languages. All the great ancient races knew the Science of Sound, so when they chanted their scriptures they were actually using the hidden power of Sound. But with that single act of translating scriptures into modern languages, that great science was lost.

There were two main reasons for this: first of all, the scholars who translated those ancient scriptures did not know the secret Science of Sound behind the scriptures, and secondly, even if they had known it, the languages into which they were translated were unsuitable because they did not have the Science of Sound in them. Therefore, we lost a tremendous potential for human development when we lost the Science of Sound—like the loss of life, a primary, fundamental loss.

The Descending Sounding-Light Vibration

The Science of Sound starts with the Unmanifest. Those of you who have studied scriptures know that the whole of Creation came out of an unmanifest condition, which you may call the Transcendental God or the Transcendental Deity—*transcendental* meaning it is beyond the level of Creation. So the first reality is the Unmanifest Condition. This is not a philosophy, and if you go into meditation and reach a high level of Samādhi you will get a sense of the Unmanifest and know that it is just that: unmanifest, beyond the Creation states (the Physical Creation, Astral Creation, Mental Creation and Causal Creation) and beyond the spiritual realms above. It is ever the Unmanifest, beyond Creation, Evolution or Dissolution.

The Unmanifest
↓
Primordial Sounds on the Level of the Spirit
↓
Causal Sounds (Causal World)
↓
Sacred Primordial Language
↓
Physical Sounds

Now, suppose you are a great Seer and in meditation you are able to touch the various regions of Reality. The first sounds you will hear below the Unmanifest are the Primordial Sounds on the level of the Spirit. Unfortunately, in any language a word can be used in different ways. The word *spirit*, for example, is used by mediums, channeller and psychics, but what they are actually referring to is the Astral World (the so-called *spirit world*) and the entities in the Astral World (the so-called *spirits*)—people who have died and gone to the psychic dimensions. But that is not the Spirit that I'm talking about; I'm talking about a level much higher than that. The level of the Spirit is the Plane of Ātman, the Nirvāṇic condition. It is above the astral, mental and causal realms, and above the Buddhic, in the realm of Nirvāṇa. That is what the Spirit (capitalized) refers to in the Esoteric Science.

So the first sounds below the Unmanifest Condition are the Primordial Sounds on the level of the Spirit, which are seventy-two Seed

Sounds that are the source of human language. Later on they became known as *Seed Mantras*, or Bīja Mantras in Sanskrit. These sounds are not in a manifest condition, however, because the level of the Spirit to us is unmanifest, unreachable for the normal human consciousness. But if you have what I call *cosmic hearing*, you can hear them vibrating on the level of the Spirit—you can *see* and *hear* them vibrating, like Sounding-Light structures.

You have to be a highly advanced Yogī or Mystic to hear them, but they are not localized sounds. Buddha sitting in Nirvāṇa doesn't hear "ting-ting" and think, "That's sound number one. There's sound number two and now sound number three is coming up." It is not like that at all. Those sounds are vibrating through the whole Universe; the whole Cosmos is full of sound frequencies and rhythms. This is because the Seed Sounds, the Primordial Sounds on the level of Spirit, are how the Spirit itself *is*—its beingness, or how it functions. If you can hear them you know how the Divine functions on that level. It is as if you understand the thought processes of God, the vibrations of the Divine Mind itself, and in that state the reason for Creation to be is clear to you.

On the next level are the causal sounds in the Causal World, which is the start of Manifest Creation. Here, you can hear the Seventy-Two Seed Sounds as causal sounds, which are not like the Seed Sounds but more like musical notes. On this level you can see how Creation is coming into existence through Sound—which is the most amazing thing! You can see how the Universe is formed, how the Solar System is formed, how the planet is formed and, what is more, how you are formed.

You can understand yourself on a completely different level. You can know how your Soul vibrates—the musical notes, or the sound-structures, of your own Soul. You can hear yourself "singing"—coming into manifestation through the sounds that emanate from your being, your Soul-Nature. And you can also hear the sounds that emanate from the being of others. You can listen to the sounds of the planets, what in the ancient Greek Mystery Schools was called the *music of the spheres*. The Mystery School Teachers could listen to the various sounds made by the planets, not the physical sounds but the causal sounds of the Earth, the Moon, the Sun, Mercury, Mars, Venus and all the planets and all the stars.

The next level is the Sacred Primordial Language. The Primordial Sounds of the Spirit produce the causal sounds in the Causal World and these produce the Sacred Primordial Language, which is perhaps most important for Humanity because that is what brings about all the magical transformations in people's lives and plays a big part in the process of Enlightenment.

Remember, this is not a modern language like Italian, Dutch or Hungarian, and it is not even one of the ancient languages; it is a language

---

When you are in deep meditation and have reached the Causal World you will hear your own sounds and, what is more, you will begin to understand whether or not you are on the right track in your life, whether you are in tune or out of tune with the Cosmos, because your causal sounds will be warped if you are out of tune. You will hear the disharmony within your being. If you are sick—physically, emotionally or mentally—the causal sounds in your causal body will sound off-key. One part of you, which is still healthy, will produce a crystal clear sound; another part of you, which is no longer healthy, will produce a disharmony. The sound itself will tell you where the deformation is in the structure of your being and how to readjust yourself so that you are in harmony.

In the future, doctors and people in the healing fields will be able to listen to the auras of people and know what each sound in their being represents, and when a sound is off-key they will tell people exactly what is wrong with them and they will give them the correct mantras, the correct sequence of sounds that will fix the sound-vibration and re-establish their health—quite miraculously. What is more, the scientific community will also discover the value of Sound. At this stage they are concerned only about outer things, but within two or three hundred years they will have to accept the idea that there are other dimensions to reality besides the physical dimension, and that they can research those invisible dimensions in the same systematic way they research the outer dimensions now.

contained—actually, concealed—in the ancient languages. The Sacred Primordial Language is the sound-structure within the ancient languages, the sound patterns hidden in ancient languages such as Hebrew, Babylonian, Egyptian, Chinese, Arabic and Sanskrit, which is why they were chanted.

These sound patterns, which consist of vowels, consonants, semi-consonants, sibilants, and so on, are physically pronounced, which is the last stage of the process. If you work with these physical sounds they will take you back to the Sacred Primordial Language, and then you will discover a new universe, new possibilities inside you, because the Sacred Primordial Language is a part of the Universal Sound Language that is available to human consciousness. The Universal Sound Language is a vast sea from which the angels receive impulses, rhythms and vibrations that are perceivable to them; the animals receive vibrations that are perceivable to them; and humans receive certain vibrations that the human consciousness can register.

Sound and Reincarnation

Now we understand the importance of the physical sounds: that physical sounds are not just physical sounds but are actually a means of reconnecting you to the Sacred Primordial Language, which reconnects you to the causal sounds, which reconnect you to the level of the Spirit, which, if you are a highly advanced Yogī, takes you back to the original unmanifest source. It is a ladder that goes down and we can use it to go up.

This is a secret that can turn you into a White Magician, and you become a miracle worker for the benefit of Humanity, or a Black Magician, and you also become a miracle worker but on the wrong side. That is because the Primordial Sound Language is universal and does not discriminate. Your intention in using the language is what makes you a holy or unholy person. It's much like electricity: you can use electricity for good purposes, for light and heat, or you can use it for bad purposes, to electrocute somebody. The electricity itself is a neutral agency and it just does what it is directed to do. It has no intelligence to choose to light up a bulb and choose not to give somebody an electric shock. It does what it is supposed to do by its nature.

Similarly, the Primordial Sound Language is an infinite sea of Sound-Vibration, and the intelligence of the being using the language directs how that sound is to manifest. For example, you as a Living Soul in the Causal World are producing your own sounds, and this—your present personality—is your manifestation. If you reach a reasonably high development in your life, after you die you will reach the Causal World and be conscious of yourself as a Living Soul. Then you can hear the primordial sounds of your own life, and you can know where you are in your evolutionary scheme. It is at that moment that you decide what "sounds" (the kind of personality) you are going to manifest in your next lifetime.

Normally, to reach the Causal World after you die you have to be a spiritual person, a Yogī, a Mystic or a Saint. If you have earned the right to enter into the causal stream, you can experience your own beingness in relationship to the All-Beingness and then make adjustments, consciously making the right sounds so that you can obtain certain results in your next lifetime. When you produce those sounds, which are certain combinations of the Primordial Sound Language, they start attracting a

---

Only a consciously incarnating, intelligent human being will reach the Causal World after death, not the average person in the world. Hundreds of millions of people only go as far as the astral dimension, while some may briefly experience the Mental World (the Heaven World), and then they come back into incarnation. In fact, if they were densely materialistic all their life, they have no vibratory power in the astral dimensions and have to quickly incarnate back into a physical body, without even experiencing the full potential of the Astral World, let alone the Heaven World and the Causal World. That is another disadvantage of material consciousness: it drags the person back to the material world.

mental body to you that has the quality of those sounds. Then you start producing another wave of sounds, which are the Sacred Primordial Language on the level of the Astral World, attracting to yourself an astral body corresponding to those sounds.

Now, you are producing those sounds and coming into physical incarnation, but here on the physical level the process changes. You have your own vibratory frequency, the personality you want to manifest in your upcoming lifetime according to your Soul plan, but the problem is that you have to be born through a mother and a father. This is the big problem of the Human Kingdom—a colossally and occultly bad problem.

Unlike angels, who can sound their notes and keep to those notes all the time because they have no physical bodies, human beings can sound their notes and keep to those vibrations only down to the etheric body level. But they cannot do that with their physical body because the physical body depends on a father and mother. So when you are coming into physical incarnation you are trying to establish your own vibration like the one you established in your etheric, astral and mental bodies, but that vibration gets mingled up with the vibrations of your mother and father, producing a trinity of vibrations and throwing you off your original plan.

This is why everyone who comes into this world through a human mother and father has problems: even Saints and enlightened beings like the Buddha or the Christ have problematic lives in the physical world, having to adjust the pure vibration they originally intended to their worldly situation—which is something they can do but it is sometimes a struggle.

If we did not have physical bodies that we inherited from other people but could produce one like the bodies we produce in the inner dimensions—our own body with our own vibration—we would be like the angels, and there would be no diseases, no disharmony, no problems in this world. Unfortunately, human evolution on this planet was flawed right from the start. During the Lemurian Age, after we manifested our etheric bodies with the help of the Spiritual Hierarchy, there were no physical bodies available that would be suitable for human beings, so the Hierarchy used the next best thing—animal bodies.

We borrowed animal bodies from the Animal Kingdom and ever since then we have been functioning and working through animal bodies. So this physical body is an animal body, not really part of the human structure at all. (The scientists who say we descended from apes are about a quarter percent right: not that we descended from apes—we are human beings, not apes—but we certainly borrowed the bodies of animals so that we could manifest in the physical dimension, because otherwise we would not have been able to.)

This is one of the major fault lines in our evolution on this planet: that we cannot, as incarnating entities, create our own physical bodies in harmony with what we were intending internally. So, having come into incarnation, we then have to put up with the vibration of the world and the whole association with the physical body, and that is a continual battle against our true nature, or the true Self we want to manifest. This is why we have sicknesses and all kinds of problems.

The Ancients understood the situation; they knew that most humans were out of tune with their original plan, their Soul plan, and that living in physical bodies in the physical world was difficult for them. They also knew that the internal structure of the Universe was Sound. So they had the idea to use the Science of the Sacred Language, the Science of Sound, to give people the ability to try to be what they really wanted to be, to be more like the internal vision they had of themselves.

This science was based on this simple realization:

The physical body is not what you really are and your situation in the physical world is not what you really aspire to as a Living Soul who is cosmically evolving. But you can use the Science of Sound to change yourself and become who you really are.

The Key to Soul Evolution

The Science of the Primordial Language, which is just as real as the science of electricity or the science of locomotive power, can give you energy and power. All of the Seed Sounds have cosmic powers on the level of the Spirit and then they have power on the Causal, Astral and Physical as they come down through the various realms. If you practise these Seed Sounds they will help you physically, give you positive emotional vibrations and a luminous mind-structure, and they will create harmony in your life.

That alone is a priceless gift. But beyond that there is a much deeper dimension to it: as you use these sound-structures you will realize that what you are doing is also tuning into your own internal reality.

When you reach the Causal World and are in your Causal Consciousness listening to your own Soul, you can tune *down* and determine whether or not your life-stream is in tune with the plan of your Soul, and then you can modulate your life-stream accordingly. What is more, you can tune *up* and listen to the Primordial Song of the Spirit and know how much you as a Living Soul are in tune with the eternal Spirit, the dynamic reality we call the Godhead. Then you as a Living Soul can make internal adjustments to be more perfect in accordance with the Divine Plan in the Infinite Mind of God—which is what I call *Soul Evolution* or *Spiritual Evolution*.

Once you have established yourself in Soul-Consciousness and are able to work with it, then you start a completely new evolutionary phase: you begin to reach upwards towards the Spirit. You begin to hear the Song of the Spirit, Sound-Vibrations that are so perfect they make your Soul shake. Wishing you could produce that music, therefore, you begin to work on yourself, *internally*—a work within a work. You work on your essential Self, ever refining and tuning in, trying to reach that primordial sound, the Song of Creation. Then you are a Yogī, a Mystic or a Saint and start evolving on a different spiral of Evolution.

The Science of Sound, if you understand it and practise it, will radically change your whole life, but as I said, if you go further than that, one day you will wake up and know that you are a completely different person. This happens when, through your meditation and spiritual practices, you have reached a certain point of your Journey: you have touched the Causal Worlds, you have seen yourself as the Living Soul and you have seen where you are going in Eternity.

Suddenly you will realize that now your cosmic life and purpose have begun, that now you are a cosmic human being—a real Spiritual Warrior. Before that you were an ordinary human being belonging to a particular culture and nation, but now you belong to the Cosmos. You realize that your evolution has nothing to do with your personal self, which is only a fragment of your Self, and that your true reality is somewhere else, in other cosmic realities. ⚔

~ 14 ~

THE BIRTH OF
THE SPIRITUAL WARRIOR

The function of the Spiritual Path is to change you, but to change you towards what? Name and fame and material glory? No, the change is in another direction. If you have been on the Path for many years, you know that your inner reality is completely different than it was when you started the journey. You have actually made a journey *inside* and you know that you are different.

Try this out: look at old photographs of yourself when you first started on the Path and tune into your vibration, and then do the same with a recent photograph of yourself. You will be astounded at the difference! You have evolved, you have moved, you have changed. And this is precisely what the Spiritual Path is: a journey—a journey of change, evolution, progression, of forward movement.

The Journey to Perfection

The question is: If this is a journey, where is it a journey to? Obviously, every journey has a beginning and an end, some sort of a destination. So what is the destination of those of us journeying on the Spiritual Path? First of all you have to understand that we are not journeying towards an ultimate point of reference that is *outside*, in the physical dimension. I will give you a simple example. Scientists have been dreaming for ages about travelling through space in some kind of spacecraft, exploring the Solar System, the Galaxy or even the farthest reaches of the Universe. Well, with the present gadgets we have it would take an eternity to explore the Universe. It's a nice dream but that's where it will stay.

What they do not know, however, is that behind that dream there is a reality. That is because they are approaching the trip in the wrong way, trying to travel with gadgets and instruments made by a limited consciousness in a limited body. That is to say, you cannot travel a one-thousand-percent Universe with a one-percent vision of Reality. It does not work. One day scientists (and even science fiction writers) will understand that space travel is possible but in a completely different way than they imagine at the moment.

If it is not a journey through time and space, what is this other journey? This other journey is a journey *inside* yourself, in the realm of your consciousness, in the realm of your psyche, in the realm of your Soul, in the realm of your beingness. That is the real journey. It is a journey within, a journey in Self-Revelation, in understanding yourself on a much deeper level. In a word, it is a journey to *Perfection*.

But this perfection is nothing like what the human mind can comprehend. It is not the perfection of being the greatest musician or the cleverest politician or the most successful businessman. No worldly perfection can match even one-trillionth of what we mean by Perfection. If you achieve some worldly perfection it is relative and temporary and of no consequence to that other Perfection.

The Journey to Perfection starts, simply, with meditation. I'll use the previously described RŪ-HĀ Connecting Breathing meditation of the Warrior as an example to explain this process. With this technique we try to expand our consciousness and feel the Cosmos breathing in and out. We try to *connect* to the Great Breath, the Universal Breath, the Spirit within the Cosmos and within you. This is possible because the Spirit and the Breath are the same thing; your breathing is the Spirit.

During this breathing exercise you will feel that you are expanding inside and will begin to sense your connectedness to the planet, your first attempt at journeying in the Cosmos. You may sense that your breath is one with the breath-current, or life-current, of the Earth. You are already stretching your awareness to planetary proportions; you are travelling interdimensionally, expanding inward, without getting out of your chair.

As you continue to tune into the breath inside you and become more aware of that other greater Breath, the Holy Breath of the Spirit, you may then sense the Solar Systemic Breath, the great, vast currents of Solar Breath, and then finally the Cosmic Breath, the Breath of the Universal Spirit, which is like a tidal wave pervading the Universe.

Then your cosmic journey begins through planetary systems, solar systems, galaxies—*all inside you*—without moving from your spot, because what is moving is the Breath-Current of the Spirit inside you. And once you get to the level of Cosmic Perfection, where you and the Cosmos are one, you will be breathing in the life of the Deity as it is in Creation, and you will have Boundless Consciousness, Absolute Consciousness, which is the final point of your cosmic journey.

This process starts with you. First you are tuning in and connecting with your own auric field. Then, as you keep practising this breathing technique, your auric energy-field will start merging into the auric energy-fields in the environment and you will begin to sense the breathing of other entities both superior and inferior—plants, animals, human beings, angels and other hierarchies. You will begin to sense whether an animal is in tune with its archetype, or if a human being is in tune with his or her environment, or if the environment itself is in tune or not.

This is the first stage of your movement towards Cosmic Consciousness, because you are becoming aware of the world around you, but *not through your mind*, not because you are examining things and analysing them. Cosmic Consciousness, ultimately, is a cosmic feeling mechanism—not an emotional mechanism but an interior touch or sensation.

At the next stage, as your internal experience grows, you will increasingly come to sense other people's auras even on the other side of the planet, picking up on their thoughts or whether they are out of tune or sick or happy. This is still just using your own breath-current, but you would be changed even if you did not progress any further than that; you would already be a very different human being.

As you keep growing and moving towards Perfection—Pūrnā in Sanskrit—one day you will wake up and sense that there are two sides to you: one who lives *this* life, who goes to work every morning, laughs and cries, who is bound in time and space to this human condition on the planet Earth; but at the same time there is another part of you that is not this temporal manifestation, something timeless inside you, something existing on a completely different plane of being, a different reality. And *that* is also *you*.

This is where the real miraculous journey begins, because once you sense that there is That Other inside you, that vast, colossal being inside you, then you will increasingly tune into it, shifting your attention away from the personal sense of "I", the sense of personality, towards that greater being inside you. It is a gradual process that may take years, but you will feel that you are moving towards That Other because you know

---

Many years ago, when I was still a teenager, I woke up one night and sensed a tremendous Majesty inside me. It was like being in the presence of a king, not a worldly king but an awesome spiritual power, an awesome perfection that contained irresistible power, all knowledge and all possibilities. Once you have a vision of that Divine Being inside you and sense that it is somehow you, then at that moment your life changes. The rest of your life will be a striving to manifest the Perfection of that Divine Entity, or to establish a relationship with it. And you realize that there is only one thing you can do in your life: become a Spiritual Warrior, a Warrior for that Divine Being inside you.

That Other is boundless, full of Joy, full of Light—unlike the one who is down here, who has limitations, who gets sick, physically, emotionally and mentally.

So you will begin to lead what could be called a double life: *this* life and that other life inside you. In the New Testament, Saint Paul had reached this particular attainment in his spiritual life and, trying to explain it to the early Christians, he said, "I live, but not I; but Christ lives in me" (Galatians 2: 20). He was trying to explain that he was still Paul, still a disciple lecturing people, but it was not he but someone else—the Christ—who was doing everything. In Saint Paul's case, That Other was the Christ, but in the East it is called the Higher Self or the Divine Self within you, or the Buddha Nature, if you are a Buddhist. Every culture has a name for the Other Being inside you.

This is the moment when the Spiritual Warrior is actually born inside you, when you understand what the Spiritual Warrior Path is about, because you realize that your duty is to That Other inside you. It may take you days, months, years, lifetimes, depending on how you complete the process, but you know that somehow this little creature here has to serve that impossibly vast, impossibly perfect Reality, that somehow you have to use the limited instrument, your limited nature, in the service of that greater Being.

The Struggles on the Way

This is where the great battle begins inside you: the struggle of the Spiritual Warrior. First there is the struggle with the limited powers of your body, the limited powers of your emotions, the limited powers of your mind. You know that they cannot fulfil the majesty of that tremendous Power that wants to be expressed through you. You wonder how you could possibly serve that Other Being with the imperfection of your physical nature. So the recognition of your own limitations is one of your primordial battles.

Then there is the outside world. Obstacles are put in your way, maybe through your family or friends, and it can seem like the whole of life itself is opposing you, because to oppose is the normal reaction of the worldly consciousness.

But that is not the worst of it. As a Spiritual Warrior you realize that the real struggle is in the inner dimensions, in the Astral World, the Mental World and the Causal World. Saint Paul described this inner struggle in this way: "For our fight is not against kings and rulers of this world, but against invisible powers in high places" (Ephesians 6: 12). The rulers, the outside worldly powers, are only small cogs in the wheel, puppets in the hands of far vaster powers that they do not even know or understand. There are forces working for the liberation of Mankind and those working for the enslavement of Mankind, and you realize that as a Spiritual Warrior you have to fight for the side of Light against the side of Darkness.

Interestingly, this is portrayed in the Star Wars movies, in the idea that the Force has a good side and a dark side. These two great opposing forces do exist, and although they appear to be fiction in movies like *Star Wars* and *Star Trek*, they are absolutely real. There is one infinite Energy-Field in the Cosmos and some beings work with that Energy-Field towards ongoing evolution and progression, while others use the very same force to try to squash any evolution and progress in human society.

There are many religions—old religions—with many followers who oppose progress, who are working for the wrong side. They want to hold back the Light and keep people in the Dark Ages. And there are many worldly powers unconsciously working for the powers of Darkness, what Saint Paul called the "invisible powers in high places". As a Spiritual Warrior you understand this firsthand, and you know that you need to use your art of Warriorship on many layers. It is not only about physical fights but also about the struggle between the Forces of Light and the Forces of Darkness.

Unfortunately, the forces trying to hold back the forward evolutionary movement of the planet are winning, and they have been for a long time. Jesus said, "The harvest is plentiful, but the labourers are few" (Matthew 9: 37). Of course, when He said this to His disciples they thought that there weren't enough people to harvest the wheat so they needed to find more villagers to do the work. They could not comprehend that Jesus meant something totally different.

Jesus came with enlightened God-Consciousness and saw that the Forces of Darkness were enslaving the planet, and He also saw that there were too few people who had the Light inside them and could work through the power of the Light to liberate the planet. Even today, many Christians read what Jesus said and think that He was talking about physical things. They do not understand that little of what He said related to the physical world whatsoever, that with a consciousness like that of Jesus, everything, even the most trivial thing has a cosmic significance.

Even in Jesus' day, the harvesters—the enlightened Teachers and Masters struggling for the enlightenment of the planet—were few in number, while the opposing forces, the forces of materialism, were vast. By saying that the harvesters were few, Jesus was trying to encourage His disciples to become harvesters, to become enlightened so that they could help in the great Work.

So you have to become Warriors of the Light—Warriors *for* the Light—by understanding that the Divine Warrior is already shining within you, and that the limitations of your mind, body and emotions are just part of that struggle to liberate that other shining Self inside you so that you can become active in the world and join the great stream of liberators of the world.

It is not by accident that you are reading these words. It is because the shining Self within you wants you to read them and then wake up and become aware of its existence. Once you have seen the Self, you will have your destiny mapped out. You will know exactly what you have to do, no questions asked. There will never be the slightest doubt, not a moment when you lose your way and think you should do something else.

From the age of fifteen I knew I had to teach the Spiritual Knowledge, and that was it. I knew it was my destiny and I have never had a doubt about it. It will be the same for you, too. If you see that inner vision once, your destiny will be clear; you won't have to worry about what you should be doing with your life. You will just start working along that destiny and automatically assume that role, *regardless of your outer circumstances*. That is important, because you will still have to deal with your outer circumstances. In my case I had to get out of Hungary, which was under a fanatical communist dictatorship during the reign of Stalin. I had to get out because I knew that under that system it would be impossible for me to put my spiritual knowledge into practice.

Once you become a Spiritual Warrior you will have obstacles to overcome—which is part of your challenge as a Warrior. It might be painful, it might be difficult, it might cause you a lot of suffering, but you do it because that is what a warrior does. A Warrior fights, but remember also what a Warrior fights for. A Spiritual Warrior fights for the liberation of all Mankind, liberation from all kinds of limitations—physical, emotional, mental and spiritual. It is a life-and-death struggle.

The planet is sinking further and further down into such a level of materiality that even the conception of a non-material existence will be completely erased from human memory. Then the planet will become a dark planet, a *dark star*, in the occult language. (This is not impossible; the asteroids in the asteroid belt between Mars and Jupiter used to be a planet that became a dark star and blew apart a few million years ago.)

That is why these are critical times for the planet. I have said many times[8] that the next two or three hundred years will determine whether

8. Imre Vallyon, *Planetary Transformation*, (Sounding-Light Publishing, 2010); *The New Planetary Reality*, (Sounding-Light Publishing, 2012); and *The New Heaven and the New Earth*, (Sounding-Light Publishing, 2014).

this planet goes forward toward cosmic evolution or backwards into dense material consciousness. This is why the Path of the Spiritual Warrior is so important today. It is only when the Warrior awakens inside you that you begin to understand the colossal battle of cosmic forces.

In Nazi Germany, Hitler and his inner circle got in touch with real negative forces. There was a great king in Atlantean times in what is present-day Thule (now renamed Qaanaaq) in northern Greenland. He was on the Dark Side and wielded a tremendously destructive power, and because Hitler and his inner circle were practising black magic they managed to get in touch with that negative power, and then, of course, released it through their political system.

Remember, I'm not blaming the Germans or anybody. I'm talking about invisible occult forces that work through nations and people. It's not the problem of a particular nation but a planetary problem. In this case, the negative power came through Hitler and his immediate circle, but it could have come through someone else. The key point is, that power is so awesome that it can annihilate any spiritual awareness, and if it establishes itself on Earth it would kill out any spiritual sense in Humanity and the planet would become a materialistic planet.

What saved Mankind at that time was our Spiritual Hierarchy. During the Second World War it was clear to the Spiritual Hierarchy that the normal power of human beings working for the side of Light would not be sufficient to overcome the power of the Dark Side, and that unless some drastic measures were taken, that negative power would enslave the world. So they had to do something that they had never done before: they had to invoke hierarchies beyond those in charge of our evolutionary scheme—Solar Hierarchies—to come and rescue the planet.

This higher order of entities, or powers if you like, attacked the Forces of Darkness in the Astral World, in the Inner Worlds, and slowly shifted the balance towards the so-called allies' side. What the politicians did and the events that happened on the outer physical plane were only a reflection of what had already taken place in the inner dimensions. The inner situation had changed so the outer situation changed too. The allies finally won, not because they were so clever—on their own Germany and Japan would have controlled the world in a few years—but because the Hierarchy invoked Cosmic Powers.

I'm telling you this because I have actually seen that negative power. A few years ago I encountered it, not because I wanted to but because it tried to swamp my inner consciousness and throw me from the Spiritual Path altogether. At that time there was a moment when I realized that that force was absolutely overpowering, and no amount of outside help, like calling on the Christ or the Buddha, would be of use to me. I had to become the Spiritual Warrior myself, and that was when the Spiritual Warrior was really born within me. I realized that I was in a battle of life and death: I would either survive that overwhelming force on my own, relying on the Warrior within me, or get swamped by it. I managed to turn it back at that time, but I realized that that was my own little battle, and that the real battle was still to come, the battle for Mankind.

The Negative Power is still there. It has not been vanquished; it has just withdrawn itself. It is just as strong as ever and it will come back again, through another people, another country, as soon as the right conditions arise. That is why we must have a final battle with it, but not with just a few people, because it is a planetary battle. The battle must be fought by Mankind—every single human being standing as Spiritual Warriors like a solid wall of Light, shielded by the power of Light within themselves—who will withstand that Power and defeat it. Or the planet will fall. ✄

~ 15 ~

From Separated Consciousness to Unity Consciousness

The process of Enlightenment has very much to do with moving from separated consciousness to Unity Consciousness. In order to understand the process of moving from separated consciousness to Unity Consciousness, however, we first have to understand where separated consciousness came from.

The Origin of Separated Consciousness

Originally, there was a separation, or a pulsation, of atoms within the Divine Mind. Not physical atoms but what we call Monads. A Monad is a highly evolved Spiritual Atom, or Spiritual Being, in the Logos itself, and every human being was originally a Monad, a single, unified, indivisible being, a spark of the tremendous Cosmic Fire of the Divine Mind.

Then we became the threefold Spiritual Self, the Ātma-Buddhi-Manas, or the Triune Self. So the Monad, that one single, cohesive being, divided itself into a threefold entity that, although still in a state of Unity, had three different senses: a sense of Beingness, a sense of Unity and Wisdom, and a sense of Intelligence. Ātma is Pure Being, Buddhi is the Pure Love-Wisdom-Unity Vibration, and Manas is Intelligence, or the Mind that can perceive Itself (which later on would form our faculty of thinking).

So we divided from the One to the Three, and this process, which took aeons of time, was one step downwards in terms of devolution, or one step in the direction of the Creative Expression of the Deity. When we were still the Triune Self (Ātma-Buddhi-Manas) we could not perceive ourselves as different from anything else. We could sense three aspects of ourselves but our sense of Oneness was nevertheless complete and unbounded. Like a triangle within a circle, we were One in Three, or Three in One.

Then we descended further down, to the Causal World, which is the highest region of the Mental World, where we became Living Souls enclosed in causal bodies. This was when we experienced the first great separation, or loss of Unity Consciousness. When we became Living Souls—JĪVĀTMAN in Sanskrit—we lost our sense of Unity with all things and began to sense ourselves as "I". This is where the ego, the sense that "I am not the same as that", came into existence. Our sense of identity was not as strong as it is in the physical world, but we had a sense of knowing that "I am not those other Souls although we live in the same world."

The five-day period of the full moon is an important time for spiritual work. This is because the full moon in April is the celebration of the enlightenment of Jesus the Christ; the full moon in May is the celebration of the enlightenment of the Buddha; and the full moon in June is the celebration of the Spiritual Hierarchy, the hierarchy of all the human beings who have attained Enlightenment—Saints, Sages, Prophets and Masters.

During the full moon of June, therefore, we can feel the Spiritual Hierarchy as a Hierarchical Kingdom, rather than as individuals like the Christ or the Buddha. The presence of the total Hierarchy of Enlightened Souls—what the Christians used to call the Communion of Saints—is strong at this time. I'm not talking about the "saints" appointed by the Pope; most of them were not saints but politically expedient appointments. I mean the real Saints, those who attained higher states of consciousness. So this particular full moon period is the celebration of the enlightenment of the Human Being— that means *you*, if you want to get enlightened.

As I mentioned previously, this is the stage described in the Old Testament story of Adam and Eve eating the apple and getting cast out of Paradise. The real Garden of Eden was the Paradise State, the State of Unity, the Buddhic World, where we existed as the Triune Self. When we descended and became individualized Souls we were cut off from Buddhic Consciousness, the sense of overwhelming Oneness; we were no longer aware of the Buddhic World.

That is how the first sense of separation came about, but if we had been left on the Causal World we would still be close to the sense of Unity. Since then, however, we devolved one step further and became a personality. That is, you as a Living Soul (Jīvātman) living in your causal body in the Causal World took on a personality self, which includes a mental (mind) body, an astral (emotional) body, an etheric (vital) body and a physical body. These four bodies constitute your personality, and as a personality you are so far way from the sense of Unity that you are not aware of the fact that you are a Living Soul, absolutely unaware that you are a Triune Self and cannot even imagine that you are a Living Monad, One with the All.

On the personality level, therefore, we are really outcasts in the "outer darkness", which is a term that Jesus used as a symbol (Matthew 8: 12). The Monadic World is a world of Absolute Light, so compared with *that* world, this world is an absolute darkness, and we have been cast into that outer darkness, which is physical consciousness, or personality consciousness.

As we are now, in this personality consciousness, the sense of separation is total, and amazingly we have lived with the sense of separation as something real for many, many lifetimes. Since Lemuria and Atlantis, for hundreds of thousands of years, people have been incarnating with this separated sense of consciousness, or sense of the personal ego—the AHAṀKĀRA, which literally means "I am the doer. I am the one who accomplishes things". Whatever they did in life they had the sense that *they* were the ones doing it—unrelated to the Living Soul, unrelated to the Triune Self and unrelated to the Divine Monad—unaware of all the inner realities and with the false idea that the personality, with its puny powers and capacities, was doing everything.

This is what we call the Great Illusion, or MĀYĀ, meaning that people have been living under a sense of limitation, having accepted the idea that they are just a personality. Nowadays it is even worse, because for the last few hundred years people do not admit the existence of anything but the physical body. They do not even see the personality as a fourfold being; they do not see that the mind exists outside the physical body, that the emotional nature exists outside the physical body and that the etheric body exists outside the physical body. They think of themselves only as physical bodies, and when they die that's the end of it, they're finished—kaput—forever.

You could say that that is the utter degradation of consciousness. You can't sink any lower than that: plain physical-body consciousness and nothing else. And I'm not talking about one person who is unique; people by the hundreds of millions are like that. If you were to tell them that the mind is not the brain, that it is an energy-field surrounding the physical body, and within that there is an emotional energy-field, and within that there is an etheric energy-field of Prāṇa, vitality that you absorb from the planet, they would look at you and say, "What on earth are you talking about? This body is the real thing and that is all there is."

It is important to understand that most people are living with that consciousness. I have never had that consciousness in all my life. Even when I was a small child, I was aware of a larger reality and could never imagine what it would be like to be aware of yourself only as a physical body. Once I actually tried to see what it would feel like by tuning into somebody who was a confirmed materialist. So I tried to tune into that person as hard as I could to find out what was going on inside him and how he actually lived.

I tried to reason with the person, saying, "Aren't you afraid that when you die it will be the end of you? Can you imagine not existing for billions of years?" And he said, "Yeah" and he was quite serious. To me, that was so unbelievable because I would really be worried if somebody told me that after I died I would be nothing. I would go into a most incredible state of panic, because I just assume that life is a continuum and "I" will be forever. I cannot imagine just suddenly ending—chop, like that, and I'm finished forever. It is absolutely unimaginable, even as an exercise of the imagination.

But many people think this way and they are quite happy about it, which shows that their state of separation is completely and wonderfully perfect. You could say it is a miracle on its own. If there is a miracle in the Cosmos, this is it: one hundred percent materialistic consciousness. How is it possible for people to be conscious like that, or rather, unconscious like that?

Our devolution had already started in Atlantean days when our egotistical drives began to manifest, and with them came our acquisitive nature, wanting and grabbing things from others. Once you believe that you are separate from everybody else, then the sense of "I want this for myself" begins to arise. If you see something another person has, you want it because the only thing that is important is you.

When you are a Triune Self, you live in the Buddhic World in the pure, formless state of Mind, what the Buddhists call ŚŪNYATĀ, the empty form of Mind. You don't need something outside of you, for you are complete within yourself. You do not have the urge to get somebody else's possessions. But in Atlantean days human beings began to be acquisitive and selfish, using their emotions negatively and violently to grab other people's things, to have power over them, to control them, et cetera, et cetera—normal human behaviour. That was when the Spiritual Hierarchy was formed and the first Teaching was given to Mankind about the existence of Unity Consciousness, which is Absolute Harmony, Love,

Wisdom, Joy, Bliss and Togetherness, and that we should make an effort to regain it.

Ever since then we have had many Spiritual Teachers, from the Buddha to Moses to the Christ to Lao Tzu to the Prophets. All over the world Teachers were sent out to Humanity to remind people that their sense of isolation was actually a false reality, Māyā, a misperception of their consciousness.

The reason we have this misperception is because on the physical body level our attention is focused in the third-eye region of the body, so it does not permeate the physical body nor does it radiate outside of, or beyond, the physical body into the invisible dimensions. Therefore, the only thing we can perceive is whatever the physical body can give us through the faculties of seeing, hearing, touching, smelling, tasting. So nowadays that is the state of the mass consciousness, or worldly consciousness: only what can be perceived through the senses is real, and beyond that nothing exists.

The State of Unity Consciousness

So the idea is to shift the focus of your attention from the physical body and extend it so that you begin to sense things outside of your physical body—that is to say, outside of your physical body *internally*, toward the inner dimensions, using an interior faculty, an interior sense, which is vastly different from the worldly consciousness. Put simply, we have to move from separated consciousness to Unity Consciousness.

Technically, Unity Consciousness is Buddhic Consciousness, awareness of the Buddhic World, which is where we have the sense of Unity, the sense of being at one with all life, with all of Creation, at one with everything within and outside ourselves. You know yourself to be the real you, but at the same time you know that everybody else is the real them and you are all in the real world. In the Buddhic World you sense for the first time that you are in the presence of Reality, not Māyā, not something that will pass away or is subject to change; it is the first time you begin to sense boundless Reality.

In Buddhic Consciousness, moreover, you have a sense that you are one, complete, whole, that you do not lack anything whatsoever; more importantly, that you are also one with everybody else and neither do they lack anything whatsoever; and most importantly, that you are one with the whole Cosmic Reality and nothing whatsoever is lacking there, also.

So it is important for us to develop that consciousness and sense that we are complete. On the personality level, the basic nature of the ego is that it feels incomplete and always wants something more, and it always thinks that "something more" is outside of itself. Just look at little babies. Do you notice what they do first? They point their finger. When they do that it means, "I want that." Of course, at that time their mental faculty is not working, so they cannot say, "I want this and I want that." But nevertheless the "I want" principle, which is the sense of separateness, is there right from the baby stage.

This sense of separateness also exists to a certain extent on the Soul level. You as a Living Soul in the Causal World have a sense of "you" and a sense of something else "out there". Therefore you feel that you are limited and want to expand yourself "out there". Although as a Living Soul you are perfect, relatively speaking, compared with you as a personality, you still want to expand, to be more, to do more—which is the Ego consciousness of you the Living Soul.

In our separated state of consciousness on this planet, we always want more because we feel that we are limited. In the state of Buddhic Consciousness, however, that sense of desperately wanting more disappears because you realize that you are everything and everything is you; therefore the sense of grabbing parts of everything is not important to you. Suppose you are in Buddhic Consciousness now and you realize that somebody else is driving the latest car, which you would like to have. In your normal consciousness you would want it, but in Buddhic

Consciousness you simply know that they have it, and they are you. You already have it because they are you. Whatever you want somebody else has, but that somebody is you, therefore you do not need to have it.

Isn't that amazing? Buddhic Consciousness will transform your whole existence once you have even a glimpse of it. All this mad striving for things and all the stress in your life will disappear. If you want to be the Prime Minister of the Netherlands, for example, you know that you already are because there is a Prime Minister of the Netherlands. Whatever you have ever wanted to be, somebody already is and they are you, so you do not have to struggle towards it; you already are it. You do not need to make all the effort they did, because you already made the effort through them. This is the miracle of Unity Consciousness: you see things as they are and you are satisfied because everything in the world is you.

This does not mean that you will become a totally impractical person. There are two choices here: you can be one who lives in Unity Consciousness and still follows action, or one who lives in Unity Consciousness and gets totally blissed out and becomes one of the so-called *divine fools*. There are certain Indian and Sūfī saints who are so blissed out that they no longer relate to any outer events in the world whatsoever. That is not the healthy way. The healthy way is what is taught in the true Warrior Schools, the true Śakti Schools and all the true Yoga Schools.

Just because you have attained Buddhic Consciousness and have the sense of Unity does not mean that you are going to sit there and just smile all day and all night. Why? Because you realize that not only is it nice to be in the state of Unity, that you yourself lack nothing because you have everything, that your path is clear and you are saved, that you have established yourself where you are supposed to be; but you also realize that there are billions of beings who are not in that condition, and you feel a tremendous drive to help them attain that condition.

This is why Buddha's first statement after attaining Buddhic Consciousness, before He even started teaching about Nirvāṇa, was that there is suffering in the world. He didn't say, "I'm happy now so I can forget about everybody else." He realized that although He had reached the state of Unity, there were still huge problems for the separated selves, so He explained the reasons that there was suffering (due to the wrong ways of using energies) and the way that must be followed to get out of suffering.

When you are in the state of Unity, therefore, the first thing you do is realize that there is suffering in the world and get inspired to do something about it, rather than just enjoying SAMĀDHI by and for yourself. You become dynamically active and you want to extend your internal harmony and share it with others, because you realize that the Kingdom of God has to be established here on Earth. This means that every intelligent being who is capable of perceiving Buddhic Consciousness must attain it, and therefore the salvation process must be universal.

All our problems arise because we think from a separated consciousness, and that consciousness is not limited to individuals; it can be in a family, a group, a religion or a nation. A whole nation can think in a

---

It is interesting that the early Christians referred to the "universal salvation process" or the "universal work of the Christ", meaning the Cosmic Christ, the Second Logos of the Holy Trinity, the great Illimitable Light, the Intelligence that permeates all of Creation. That Light is calling the separated selves back to the state of Unity. In fact, that is its function; the Cosmic Christ, by Light-Vibration, stimulates the separated consciousness to become unified, to return to the Kingdom of God, or Unity Consciousness.

This is the energy that got the Muslim and Jewish Prophets of old into so much trouble. They had a flash of Unity Consciousness and then marched into the meeting-houses or parliaments of their countries and called the authorities silly old so-and-sos and told them what God wanted them to do, instead of the stupid things they were doing. And what reward did they get? They got their heads chopped off or were put into prison. They had no teaching ability (otherwise they would not have gone to the worldly authorities and told them they were stupid); they had only an inspiration to bring everything back to Unity.

separated way, that whatever it does is always right and whatever another country does is always wrong. Unfortunately, when we think that what we do is always right and what the other person does is always wrong, it means that there will always be conflict because the other person has the same view—what they are doing is right and what you are doing is wrong. When this happens on a large scale you end up with a global mess, which sums up the last few thousand years of human history: endless conflict, disharmony and antagonism, and war upon war upon war.

When you are in the state of Unity it is easy to see all this, and easy to see that if that sense of separation in human beings could be dissolved they would accept their differences, seeing the unity within the differences. They would no longer be driven to convert the other person to their own particular way of doing things or their way of being, because they would realize that the other person is also part of the Universal Whole. In the ocean there are fish that live at the bottom, other types of fish that live in the middle regions and fish that live in the top part of the ocean. If you have a holistic view of the ocean, you do not say that one fish is more important than another or one type of activity is more important than another; it is all just part of the activity of the ocean.

So it is in the state of Unity Consciousness: You see that all the massive activities of the Human Kingdom, the Animal Kingdom, the Vegetable Kingdom, the Elemental Kingdom and the Angelic Kingdom are all a part of a boundless, seething ocean of Reality, the Great Mother, MAHĀ-ŚAKTI. You see that all the kingdoms have their parts to play at their particular stage of evolutionary process and they are all fulfilling their particular dharma, or destiny. And you have no antagonism towards them.

I'm trying to explain that as long as the human species keeps the sense of personal ego, or self, we will have conflict on this planet *always*. Observe any conflict and you will always see one thing: one personality ego, or "I", working against another personality ego, or "I". When you are in a state of Unity, however, the personal self is the least important thing.

The Unity Consciousness of the Warrior

At a certain high level of the Warrior School, when you have that same sense of Unity that the Buddha had, when you are a Master Warrior and have attained the state of Buddhic Consciousness, you do not think in terms of destroying your enemy but are totally one with your enemy— and with the plan of the enemy. You know the enemy's plan and you are aware of your own plan, as well as all the related incidents past, present and future. And if you know that the plan of the enemy is the right plan—not yours—that it fits in better with the total Plan of Cosmic Harmony or Unity, then you sacrifice yourself. That is how great the sense of Unity becomes.

This is incomprehensible for the materialist. Why would you sacrifice yourself for somebody else? It is quite simple: because in a state of Unity you see that the other person has a better idea or a better dharma, one that will create better conditions for more people than you can. So you sacrifice yourself to that cause.

That is what Jesus did. Jesus chose to be crucified because it would help millions of people. He did not need to go through all the suffering He went through; He was already way above it, in Nirvānic Consciousness. But from His sense of Unity, in His All-Inclusive Mind, He saw that certain actions would make certain impressions on the human racial mind, and He was willing to go through the suffering to get those results. He was a Warrior giving His life for the greater cause.

To bring this into practice in our day-to-day living, the basic idea is for all of us on the Spiritual Path to achieve Unity Consciousness. This is where meditation is important because it shifts your consciousness away from your physical body consciousness and moves it internally until you penetrate into the astral consciousness and then into the mental, the causal and finally the Buddhic Consciousness, the state of Unity. It is a natural way of moving from a separated sense of self back to our original sense of Oneness. And we have to do that because Unity Consciousness does not come on its own. The only way it would come on its own is if you had already achieved it in a previous lifetime and recovered it in this lifetime. But normally people have to make an effort to recover the sense of Unity, and meditation is one of the most powerful, systematic techniques to regain the sense of Unity Consciousness.

Along with meditation we need a general understanding of how to deal with life itself. All conflicts arise because we try to impose ourselves on others and others try to impose themselves on us. But if you manage to glimpse that sense of Unity inside you and see a larger plan emerging, you will see that there are different ways of accomplishing the same thing in that larger context, and the stress of imposing yourself on the other person becomes diminished.

In practical life, therefore, what you need to do is stand back and assess things. Say to yourself, "Okay, my ego (or separated self) thinks this way and the other separated self thinks that way," and then look at the situation in a larger context. Sometimes you may be right, you know that you are definitely tuning in better because you have the greater sense of Unity. At other times you may see that the other person is right, so you sacrifice your way of doing things and go along with the other person.

In doing that, you will have learned an important lesson, because you will change the way you live, the way you relate to people, circumstances and situations. Then the principle of Unity will not be just a philosophy but a part of your day-to-day life. Otherwise it will just be a theoretical idea: you think that the other person might be right or you might be right, but it's all in your mind. It is not the real thing. The real thing happens when you touch the other person and embrace the larger reality, and get a sense of rightness from the larger reality. This is why it is so important to meditate and develop Unity Consciousness, and live your life from that sense of Unity.

This does not mean that you have to become gloomy and think that you always have to sacrifice yourself, saying, "Poor me! I have to let him win the argument again because I'm so self-sacrificing." In actuality, you will find that the state of Unity Consciousness is not gloomy at all but incredibly joyous. You always feel happy, knowing that in the end it doesn't matter which way things go. You realize that whether you win or the other person wins actually has no relevance. As long as the Plan is going ahead, as long as the Mind of God is doing the Work, that is all that matters. We are so small compared to the Infinite Mind, so whether we do something this way or that way, in the wide sweep of the Infinite Mind it amounts to nothing anyhow; it is so trivial.

You therefore reduce most of the stress in your life, knowing that you do not need to convince anybody, flowing along the way of least resistance. The easiest way is the way of least resistance, the way of least effort, because it is the most natural way within the Cosmic Reality itself. Then you will become lighter and happier in life. You will not be afraid of people, nor will you want to push yourself onto people. You will just accept things as they are, with a genuine sense of being an integrated person inside and outside, knowing that you are where you should be. Not where you want to be, where you could be or where you might be, but where you actually, really *are*.

~ 16 ~

THE THREEFOLD TRAINING
OF THE SPIRITUAL WARRIOR

Nowadays the word *warrior* is not understood because it is identified with the word *soldier*. That is not what the ancient word
warrior meant. There are many armies in the world today, millions of
people in police departments and security services, and in the army, navy
and air force, but they are not Warriors. Not one of them is a Warrior,
unless he or she has been trained in the Warrior School, which may be
possible. But it has to be clear that Warriorship has nothing to do with
belonging to the military.

Basically, the true Warrior training is threefold. First there is the
integration of your personality, your body, emotions and mind and your
personal ego, the sense of being a person. That has to be integrated because normally most people are disintegrated, that is, not functioning
as a healthy living unit. As people in the field of psychology, psychiatry
and the healing professions will tell you, many people have emotions
running wild and thoughts that are out of control, and most people are
not functioning as harmonious entities.

In the olden days, when there were true Warriors, this problem did
not exist because society was not as stressful as it is nowadays. Six thousand years ago, most people had the normal consciousness of the day
and there was not as much pressure on people to perform as there is

in this particular age. In those days, having an integrated personality was rather normal, not the unusual thing. Today it is unusual to find somebody who is really integrated; everyone has psychological problems to some extent or other.

So the first stage of the Spiritual Warrior training is to harmonize your personality: your body in harmony with your emotions, your emotions in harmony with your mind, and your body, mind and emotions in harmony with your sense of I am-ness, the personal sense of "I", the sense of ego. This is not the spiritual "I", the spiritual Ego, but the normal human ego, the normal sense of "I" that you identify with. So the first stage of the Warrior training is to bring the several parts of you together under the "I am" within you, that which makes you a particular personality.

In the olden days, when the teacher felt that you were ready, then you started stage two, what we call the stage of *withdrawal*. In this stage you started moving inside yourself with various internal meditation and breathing techniques, the aim of which was to link your personality with you as a Living Soul, that is, the *other* I Am within you, the eternal I Am Principle within you.

So the second stage of the Spiritual Warrior training is to withdraw your awareness slowly inside yourself, deeper and deeper, until you make a connection with yourself as a Living Soul and recognize that you are a living, immortal *spiritual being*, omniscient, omnipotent and omnipresent. Nowadays that would be called the stage of Yoga or Union—Union

---

The Living Soul—the Immortal Principle that you are and that keeps reincarnating life after life—has never actually been in incarnation at all. You as a Living Soul have never been on this Earth; the lowest level you exist on is the Causal World and you have never descended below it. You perform a trick and make a personality, and that personality is supposed to represent you the Soul on this Earth. But when you die and go back to being a Soul you realize that your personality was just a fragment of a fragment of what you really are.

with your Higher Self, or Self-Realization. This is where most Spiritual Paths would end; Self-Realization would be the end product in the Way of Yoga, the Way of Mysticism, the Way of Sūfism, the Way of Zen and the Way of Taoism. In the Warrior School, however, this is only the second stage.

Once your personality is integrated with you as a Living Soul—that is, you are living in two realities simultaneously, you are a personal self able to think, feel and act in the world but at the same time are totally aware of yourself as an eternal, transcendental being—then the Soul-integrated personality forms a single unit and the Spiritual Warrior is born.

In the way of the monks and nuns, you become the Soul through meditation and devotion, but as I said, you negate the personality; you just want to be the Soul, always in Ecstasy, in Samādhi. In the Way of the Warrior, however, you become the Soul and the Soul becomes the personality and that powerful union becomes the Spiritual Warrior. You not only master your own existential problems but also begin to tackle the problems of the world, the conditions of human society, so that you help to liberate Mankind from the restricting planetary conditions.

Then the third stage begins. In Mysticism this stage is called *Deification*, or you may call it Union with God or Union with the Divine Principle within you and within the Cosmos. When you have united the Soul with the personality and they are functioning as an integrated, holistic unit, then there comes a further push inward to reach the Transcendental Divinity within you (and within everything), as well as an outward movement to reach into the physical dimension. You are simultaneously moving in two directions: deeper inside towards the point of Divinity inside you and further outside into the physical environment.

So this is the stage of *activity—divine activity*. You perceive what needs to be done in the particular environment you happen to find yourself in, and then you do it. You become an agent for the Divine, literally, an agent for the Spiritual Hierarchy, the Hierarchy of Light; you move with the influx of divine energies moving through the inner and outer dimensions of Creation.

But this is not "you", not the personal "I", and it is not even your Soul; you have gone beyond that. It is your Soul-person mechanism acting as an agent for the Divine Will—and *that* is the Master Warrior, a Warrior of Light who stands in the Light, works with the Light, fights for the Light and *is* the Light.

The Ideal of the Hero

In the Warrior School a Master Warrior was also called a Hero, but not as understood by the world. There have been lots of heroes in the world. The Greeks had their heroes, the Romans had their heroes, every culture has its heroes. But those are not Spiritual Warriors; they are simply people who fought and won many battles for their country. They were skilled at fighting, they were good soldiers, but they had no spiritual content. What makes a Spiritual Warrior is the Divine Principle awake and shining brightly within.

So a real Hero is a spiritual being of a high stature, a Master, an Avatāra, one who embodies the Divine Will and expresses it to reshape society at a particular time and place.

Part of the revelation for the New Age, or you could say part of the teaching of the Spiritual Hierarchy for the New Age, is to re-establish the ancient ideal of the Hero, what we human beings are supposed to be on this planet, because first you have to establish an ideal before people can start working towards it. At the moment we have no ideals, we have no clue who we are and what we are supposed to be doing on this planet.

Children are not given ideals. For example, surveys in Europe and North America have found that children and teenagers, when asked who the heroes are that they look up to and try to imitate, usually pick sports stars, pop singers or Hollywood actors and actresses. This is a reflection of society, that people today, especially young people, have no real understanding of what a hero is and have no ideals to look up to. They look up to the wrong people because nobody teaches them that there are greater ideals than being sports stars.

In the past, at least, we had Jesus the Christ, Buddha, Kṛṣṇa, Lao Tzu, Moses, Mohammed—great religious figures who represented greater concepts of heroes than film stars or pop singers, because they had a spiritual stature, a spiritual dignity; that which is completely missing in today's so-called heroes. If you have no other ideal, a religious figure is good; you can tune into them and want to become like them.

The problem with religious ideals, however, is that they are abstract and transcendental; they draw your attention up to other worlds, like Heaven or the Kingdom of God or Nirvāṇa or Tao. Everybody knows that the Buddha attained Enlightenment and is in Paranirvāṇa, and that is fine. But Paranirvāṇa is an awfully long way away. And everybody knows that Christ is in Heaven sitting next to the Father, but that is also far away. You cannot have an ideal that is "out there" somewhere; you have to have an ideal that is here and now, otherwise you are trying to imitate something that you cannot grasp. The true Heroes of old brought Reality *here*, they brought the Absolute into the moment, the here and now.

The ideal of the Hero is inside us. We have actually been created with that ideal inside us. Many religious traditions say that in your Heart—in the innermost chamber of your Heart Chakra—there is an image of you as a Divine Embodiment, the true Hero that you are. This is taught by the Buddhists and in the Upanishads, the Bhagavad-Gītā and other major scriptures. So the perfect Ideal that you want to become already exists within you. This is why the function of the Warrior School was, still is and always will be to awaken that Ideal inside you, on the mind (understanding) level, on the emotional (feeling) level and on the physical (practical) level; to bring about the Ideal that is possible for each pupil at his or her particular time.

Remember, the Ideal is only what is possible in the here and now. The past and the future are not relevant for the Warrior; only the moment is relevant. What you are able to do in this moment is your Ideal. In the past, when monks and renunciates underwent their religious training, they always looked towards the future. They meditated, prayed and chanted, thinking that they would attain Buddhahood or Christhood sometime in the future, that they would become like Rāma, Kṛṣṇa or Lao Tzu *in the future*. They had a plan and worked and worked and then sometime in the future, in one life or another, they would become their Ideal. Which is good; that is one way of doing it.

But the Warrior Ideal is here and now, what you can accomplish in the moment. This is the true science of the Warrior, and it may begin with a little act, just moving a finger *with awareness*. Later on you can do a more complex movement, still with awareness. Later on you can make an even more complex movement, still with awareness, and later on you can expand your mind to embrace infinity—all in the here and now. As you get better at tuning into the here and now, your accomplishment gets more and more perfect, until you stand as the Master Warrior yourself. Then, when you make a movement, when you simply draw your sword, the Universe flows through that movement, right then and there.

The Master Warrior training starts after you have completed the threefold Warrior training and you can work in Higher Consciousness and at the same time function physically, emotionally and mentally like a normal person. That is when the real Journey begins, because there is much training to be done to become a Master Warrior. Why? Because when you are a Master Warrior you are liable to face much more complicated issues than when you were a student.

For example, martial arts movies like *Hero*, *Crouching Tiger, Hidden Dragon*, and *House of Flying Daggers* portray Warriors who have been in the Warrior School and have perfected their training but are at the stage of *beginning* their mastership training; that is, they still have problems to work through, problems that arise from the complex nature of Dharma, or Destiny—your destiny, other people's destiny, the country's destiny, the planetary destiny. When you are a beginning Master Warrior you will sense the destiny of the moment, know the possibilities this way and that way, but you are still not sure what the right action is—the right action, that is, according to the Divine Plan.

It takes further training of a very high frequency, training in the state of Superconsciousness, to manoeuvre through the tremendous influx of energies and destinies of people and of the planet and know your contribution to the particular destiny of your group or your nation. As a Master Warrior you have to be so tuned in that you know precisely the right action, moment by moment.

As I mentioned earlier, we are all warriors by nature because this planet is a school for warriors. If you look back in our history, since the

---

The Three Pillars of a Perfect Society

Basically, there are three great types of human beings: the Warrior, the Sage and the King, and together they form the three pillars of a perfect society. The Warrior brings Spiritual Willpower. The Sage brings profound Wisdom. And the King, or the Administrator or Ruler, brings Intelligence, intelligently understanding how society can be structured so that it is perfect.

Such a society functions harmoniously because the people at the top are tuned in to what they should be tuned in to: Reality, the basis of Manifestation, Infinite Wisdom. If those at the top are out of tune, then you have chaos. That is what we see today (and have for thousands of years). The politicians are out of tune, there are no wise teachers and the warriors just kill each other.

When these three pillars are standing, there is the possibility for perfect human living, when everybody does the right thing and relates correctly to one another. There were moments in history when those three came together and they created great nations, great civilizations that lasted until the three pillars collapsed. Those civilizations then vanished like dust, because society rises and falls on the presence or absence of the Warrior, the Sage and the King.

time of Atlantis and Lemuria there has been relentless warfare on the planet. So long as human beings have existed they have been at war with each other. It is a unique planet, a unique planet of war.

This means that there is a *misapplication* of reality by the human mind; that there is a chronic *illness* in society, a warping of the *ideal* of the Spiritual Warrior, a warping of the original ideal of Humanity. We were meant to be Spiritual Warriors, all of us, the whole of Humankind, but because people are not involved in the spiritual side of life, because they do not have the Spiritual Principle functioning inside them, they express themselves on the material side of life, so they fight each other all the time. That is the Warrior Spirit gone wrong; that is the soldier spirit.

Once the Spiritual Principle within is awakened in all of Humanity, the wars will end; they will be replaced by what we call Spiritual Warriorship, the art of working with the Forces of Light. Then we will no longer be physical warriors but Light Warriors. ⚔

HOW WE PROGRESS
IN SPIRITUAL LIFE

I t is important to understand the principle of *How We Progress in Spiritual Life*, because then you will know what you have to do to make your spiritual life more effective.

First, let's start with the idea that there is *progress* in spiritual life, which most people do not know; you do not reach the goal instantaneously. Disciples tend to think that once they've signed up for the spiritual life it's all done and they are practically in Nirvāṇa already. In fact, there are some teachers in the West who teach the idea that all you have to do is sit at their feet and you will become enlightened. This is a bad teaching and it is untrue. The spiritual way of life is progressive and you do not "get there" after listening to one sermon.

To give you an analogy from the world, the education system starts with kindergarten. After kindergarten, you go to school for eight or nine years and at the end of that period you get a diploma that shows that you are an educated person. Of course, then you realize that a diploma means nothing and, if you want to have a good job and a prosperous life, you have to go to university. So you study hard for another five or six years to get a university degree.

In spiritual life it is the same: what you experience and learn as a student gives you an entrance into the field of Spirituality, but you have not yet made the grade. You have meditation experiences regularly and you are steadily gaining knowledge and starting to get a sense of your direction. You have decided that you *are* living a spiritual life, but nevertheless your internal commitment at this stage is only about fifty percent; you are steady on the Path but still in the early pilgrimage stage.

Coming back to my analogy from the world, you have your university degree and to your amazement you still can't find a job. You think: I did my part, I worked hard, so I should be rewarded for my hard work. To your great consternation, however, it is not so. You have to struggle and line up for job interviews and get rejected, in spite of your degree.

A similar crisis point is reached in the life of the spiritual disciple. You have reached the point where you can meditate with confidence and you understand some spiritual principles and even try to live by them, but it is still apparently not enough. You get no recognition from the Spiritual World at all. It seems that nobody cares whether you are succeeding or not. You are expecting a great Master to come and knock on your door and tell you how wonderful you are, but nobody turns up.

My point is that spiritual life is just as difficult and harsh, and as much of a struggle, as material life. Many disciples get frustrated and begin to wonder what is wrong with spiritual life and even question if it is real. The spiritual way of life is parallel to the material way of life, just on a higher level. Nobody gives you a pat on your shoulder. You might think that if you are a Spiritual Master you will get lots of acknowledgement in the Inner Worlds, but you don't—because that would just build up your ego. One of the reasons people expect acknowledgement is for their egos.

There is no ego-tripping on the real Spiritual Path; on the contrary, the Path is about the slow *demolition* of the ego. When somebody tells you that you have been nominated to some great position because you are such an evolved soul, forget it; they're building up your ego. True Masters do not build up egos; they annihilate them. They make you humble and realize that you are only a speck of dust in the infinite Ocean of Reality.

And why does the real spiritual way of life begin with humility? Because of the magnitude of the task, the tremendous undertaking that has to be done, and because of the tremendous results when you get there.

There is absolute humility on the Way—at the start, middle and end of the journey. Praise and glory are insignificant on the Path; they neither add to nor subtract anything from the Ultimate Reality.

Shifting Consciousness from Outer to Inner

So how do we progress on the Spiritual Path? First, let us consider the natural progression of the materialistic human consciousness (which you could call the standard human consciousness nowadays). If you are an ordinary human being not on the Spiritual Path, the progression is horizontal; that is to say, you progress outwardly and physically because you are establishing yourself in physical consciousness in relationship to the physical world, trying to acquire more power over the physical world. And it doesn't go any further than that. If you become rich and famous, therefore, society rewards you. Look at sports stars: they achieve physical strength and skills, win a gold medal, and then everybody worships them. That is the way of the world.

Progression in the spiritual way of life is not horizontal but vertical. In spirituality you progress and expand inwardly, not outwardly. Now, what does it mean that in spiritual life you expand inwardly?

When you go on the Spiritual Path, the spiritual way of life, there is a gradual refinement of your consciousness. This is why worldly people cannot understand that way of life and why you cannot give spiritual techniques to worldly people: they *cannot* appreciate them, and in fact they might actually resist them, because their consciousness is purely physical and materialistic. (This is precisely why Jesus said that you should not give pearls to swine.)

When a person begins to live a spiritual life the first thing that happens to them is refinement. For example, those who listen to heavy metal music, or any aggressive, destructive or violent form of music, saturate their inner being with a rough, low-frequency vibration of the materialistic consciousness. But suppose one day they begin to listen to classical music. Then their inner vibration would start to be purified, their consciousness refined. That would be a sign of progress, and they would be on the Spiritual Path because they would be making a step from a lower vibration to a higher one.

It is the same when a person who is used to reading romance novels starts reading a spiritual book like the Bhagavad-Gītā. The romance novel represents the worldly level of awareness and nothing else. A spiritual book has a higher-frequency vibration, another dimensional level of awareness which, once you begin to tune into it, shifts your awareness from outward to inward, to a deeper inner region of understanding within yourself, a deeper level of Reality.

So any time your consciousness shifts or expands inwardly *you are making spiritual progress*. You do not need meditation to make spiritual progress; all you need is an inner shift of consciousness.

There was once a famous astronomer who was a hundred percent materialistic, who thought he knew all about planets and stars, the solar systems and galaxies. One night he was going for a walk and he looked up at the sky without his logical mind doing its usual calculations of celestial objects—and for the first time in his life he *saw* the stars! He suddenly realized the tremendous reality of those vast numbers and knew that it was not possible for non-aggregate matter to come together and form solar systems and galaxies—by what means? for what cause? So he suddenly realized that there must be an Intelligence, a God, or a directive force or something *absolute* behind it all. He had an illumination because he managed to shift his perception from the outside to the inside.

I'll give you another example, this time from the Warrior School. Most martial arts-type warrior schools are materialistic, focused on physical strength. In such a school you do a lot of strengthening exercises, working to make yourself strong and agile physically. But what if somebody told you that behind your physical body and all the space around you there is a subtle force, the *life-force*, and that rather than just using your muscles you should try to feel that life-force, because the body is just an instrument and does what the life-force wants it to do? That would change your whole understanding of the subject. It would move you from the outside to the inside, from the gross level to the subtle level.

Once you have made that shift, your whole reality changes, your view of life changes. You realize that within Life there are regions upon regions of inner realities, that Life itself is multidimensional. And whether you are following a Spiritual Warrior School system or a Yoga system or whatever, as you penetrate further and further inside, you become more spiritualized; you are making the Spiritual Journey. That *is* the Spiritual Journey.

Progress in spiritual life is a slow, steady integration of our internal reality with the external world, an inward movement in which you express the deep regions inside you but at the same time stay connected to the outside. Expressing the inner reality outside is important because *this* world is our field of service. If you go inside and remain in a transcendental state, who is going to help this Creation here? *We* are the agents of the Divine. The Warriors who ruled India in the ancient days of the Vedic civilization, four to six thousand years ago, understood this. They went inside, they acted outside; they went inside, they acted outside. They were in charge of armies, leading large organizations and kingdoms—not sādhus starving themselves to death in the forest. They went inside and served outside.

Spiritual progress is the total inward movement of your consciousness, and then coming out and expressing it in service in daily life. *That* is the key. Why? Because the Spirit of God is also in manifestation, active here in the physical world. If the Spirit of God were withdrawn, the physical dimension would collapse and disintegrate into the basic Universal Substance. God's attention must be here for Creation to be maintained, in the same way that your Soul's attention must be in your physical body for your body to be maintained, otherwise you would die.

So the further you progress spiritually and the more you become illumined inside, the more you must express it in service for the benefit of all, without discrimination. Because that is what God does. The Divine Consciousness has no favourites; it works for all.

The Male and Female Paths

This outer expression, that which is expressed *into* the world, is the Male side of the Way of the Spiritual Warrior; and the inner expression, that which is inside us, which we must connect with first, is the Female side, the subtle force, the life-force. This is why it is important when doing Spiritual Warrior techniques to feel the Female side, to feel the life-force, because that will guide you on the right path. The more we tune into the Inner Feminine, the more we can move outside us and do the right action, because the Inner Feminine has *another* sense, a different way of understanding things than the outer consciousness has.

You can see in the history of India that when the Kṣatriya, the Warrior Class, disappeared, the yogīs took over, that is, those who thought that the Path lies in going inside and staying inside and not dealing with the outside conditions. Then there was a gradual degeneration of India, where society collapsed because the holy men escaped into the jungle and did not care about society. Over the centuries the country became chaotic without the steady order of the Kṣatriya. The Warriors create *order* in society. First they create order and then they put the Spirit into it, making it holy, divine, in accordance with the Divine Plan. That is the Way of the Warrior; that is its function in planetary life: to create society's order and structure and to spiritualize it so that people can live normally, coherently and harmoniously.

Those who are always using physical strength and physical objects for physical attainment are doing the Male side, the outer side, and they *remain* on the outer level; they have no way of developing inner attunement, inner awareness and inner consciousness—precisely what the whole Spiritual Journey relies on. Whether you are a Yogī or a Warrior or a Zen adherent or a Taoist, it is always the inner attunement which is your basis: you start from within and work outwardly. That is the Way.

This means that spiritual progress has nothing to do with a single exercise or any one single technique. Some like chanting and do not like meditating; others like meditating and do not like chanting; others like physical exercises and do not like meditating. But the key is that none of these activities is *It*. That is because It is your *total inward attunement*. The Way is your total being moving inward and then your total being acting outward. It is your attitude to existence itself, your whole heart and soul and mind and body tuning in inwardly, accepting the Inner Reality, and tuning in outwardly and doing the outer work.

Once you understand the inner Female and the outer Male and apply that understanding in your life, you will accept people as they are, without condemning them, because you realize that that is what they are and that is how the life-force works or does not work inside them, and they can't do any better; if they could they would. So you do not react to them or let them affect the expanded vision you have of life, which embraces everything, the inner and the outer.

When you begin the Path of Discipleship you try to change other people, because you want to give them some guidance. But when you go further on the Path you realize that you cannot change other people— not only that, you should not even try. If you want to teach them, you yourself have to be a teacher. Your very existence is a sign for them, if they are able to perceive it or register it. If they are not, don't worry about it: it's not your problem. You stand solid, like a rock in the ocean. It makes no difference to you whether or not the ocean appreciates your solidity.

So stand in your own Light, in your own consciousness and realization. Move your Light all around the world. If somebody appreciates it, that's fine. If somebody does not appreciate it, that's fine too. It does not change you one iota—the rock that you are, the Light that you are, the *shining being* that you are. You are what you are and that's it. If they are able to tune into your Light, then they will be helped by it.

So the important thing is that *you* are the Way, the Life and the Truth. Stay centred in your own Beingness and radiate the Light just like the Sun does: to everyone in all directions. It does not say, "I don't like Pluto so I'm going around it." No, the Sun radiates its light equally to all. So your internal consciousness must radiate out equally, everywhere, *regardless* of the environment you are in. That is the key to spiritual progress, how you can really make progress in spiritual life. ✗

~ 18 ~

The Bridge
Between Worlds

The Way of the Spiritual Warrior is essentially the way of the Spiritual Path, but very few teachings are clear about how the Spiritual Path works. Many teachers may tell you about the Spiritual Path, that you have to meditate, chant or pray, but they do not really understand the *mechanism* of the Spiritual Path. As with anything, the Spiritual Path has a mechanism by which it works. For example, if you are an auto mechanic you have to know how cars work; otherwise you won't be good at repairing cars and nobody will come back to your garage. So with everything you need to know *how* it works.

Knowing how something works requires a deeper layer of understanding, and this is especially true of the Spiritual Path. A teacher can give you a meditation technique but it does not mean that he or she understands how meditation works. The religious traditions are like that, whether they are Christian, Buddhist, Jewish, Muslim, Hindu or Chinese: they give you the tradition but they do not understand how it works. It takes an Esoteric Teacher to know why and how a spiritual technique works, and to explain it scientifically. To simply meditate without understanding why you are doing it, or whether you are doing it correctly, is not sufficient.

So let's start with the fundamentals, for we need to build up an understanding of how the Spiritual Path works. First of all, you have to understand that you are multidimensional and the Universe is multidimensional. It is at this point that the regular teachers and orthodox teachings fail. They tell you that God exists, that you are a Soul, that you have to meditate or pray, and they give you some techniques and that's it. But they do not know the basis of the Spiritual Science—the multidimensional nature of the human being and the multidimensional nature of the Cosmos. Without this basic understanding, all they can offer are hit-and-miss teachings or techniques based on trial and error.

Many teachers of spiritual life also do not know of the multidimensional nature of Reality. They have an experience and they describe it to their students, who get a certain point of view of what spiritual life is or what Realization is. But then the students go to another teacher who has had a different experience from a different part of Reality, and then they get confused because one teacher says one thing and another says something else. The fact is that there are as many explanations as there are teachers, and the differences in their explanations are simply due to the fact that the teachers are experiencing Reality through different aspects of themselves, that is, they are experiencing different parts of Reality, so their descriptions are different.

The Buddhists, for example, have this idea that they have to look for SŪNYATĀ, the Emptiness, whereas the ancient Greek Mystery Schools looked for PLERŌMA, the total Fullness. And so it is with all the religions: through each realization they look at a *point* of Reality and emphasize that. They say that is *it* and you have to strive for *that*, not realizing that they have tuned into only a point of Reality.

So let's come back to the fundamentals once again: You are a multidimensional being, which means you have a physical body, a vital (etheric) body, an emotional (astral) body, a mental (mind) body, a causal (Soul) body, and beyond your Soul nature you are divine (the Spirit within you). And the World around you is also multidimensional: it contains the physical dimension, the etheric-physical dimension, the astral dimension, the mental dimension, the causal dimension, the Buddhic dimension, the Nirvāṇic dimension and the worlds beyond Nirvāṇa. This is something basic that you need to know because whatever you experience comes from one or other of these worlds, and then you know what layer of your Self, and what layer of the Universe, you are experiencing.

The key to this understanding is what I call *Building a Bridge between Worlds*. And according to the bridge you build will be the world that you are going to experience.

I will give you an example of a bridge between worlds. Since 1875 it has been fashionable for mediums to open their astral bodies and ask that some entity come to them. Nowadays they have refined the technique a little but they still go inside themselves, seeking and desiring for contact with some master or other entity, sometimes using an affirmation so that some spirit will enter and speak through them. In such a case, the bridge that has been built is a bridge to the Astral World.

Naturally, to build such a bridge you work through your astral body to get in touch with the Astral World, and you receive the experiences that are possible in the Astral World. The key thing is where the bridge you build is going to lead you, that is, which part of the Inner Universe. It is not the same for everybody. In this day and age we are told that we are all equal and we will all get the same results, that we are all already enlightened, we are all Buddhas. This idea is another New Age delusion. We are not all the same, the paths are not all the same, the end results are not all the same. How you build your bridge and where it takes you are what determine the results you get. It is very simple.

The Rules of the Inner Worlds

Each of the inner dimensions is vast and complete on its own, and you can have many kinds of experiences in the Astral World, the Mental World, the Buddhic World and the Nirvāṇic World. Buddha would describe Nirvāṇa in one way and the Christ would describe it in another way, and you would think that they were talking about two different things. So you have to expand yourself and understand the vastness of Creation, the vast possibilities of experience within the different realms of Creation, and then you will be able to interpret your *own* experience correctly. Otherwise, like the psychics, you will be deluded.

Every spiritual technique you practise is a bridge into one of the Inner Worlds, and you will get the corresponding results. Therefore you have to know what world you are entering and you also have to know the other worlds in case you do not make it and end up somewhere else. Nowadays people meditate and think they are in a mystical state of awareness whereas in fact they are only experiencing the Astral World. Remember, on the three upper dimensions of the Astral World there are some very beautiful realms, states and feelings—great joy, beauty, light and grace—so people experiencing that think they have reached the Heaven World.

When you are in a deeper state of meditation and reach the next level above the Astral World, what we call the Mental World or the Heaven World, you might meet a dazzling, shining angelic being—a real angel. An angel is not going to deceive you, but because the radiance of the Heaven Worlds is even stronger than that of the Astral World you may

---

One of the rules of the Inner Worlds is that each world is brighter and more radiant than the previous world, and that experiences in each world are stronger than in the one below. In the Astral World, therefore, your feelings, moods and desires are many times stronger than in the physical body. For instance, you may come across a radiant being that claims to be the Archangel Gabriel, and because that radiance is so much stronger than in the physical world, you will be inclined to believe that that being *is* Gabriel. People do not understand that just because the experience of the Astral World is intense does not mean that it is a *high* state of consciousness. It is an *intense* state. Those who are not initiated into the science of the Inner Worlds can easily be deceived.

think that it is the Christ Himself or the Buddha. That being never wanted to appear as Jesus or the Buddha, but because its presence is so overpowering and you are not familiar with that world you misinterpret the experience. You do not see that it is simply an entity that is brighter than you and lives in a brighter world that is natural to that entity.

Another rule of the Inner Worlds is that if a being appears to you, whether it is a discarnate human being, an angel or some other being, and that being enhances your ego—it tells you telepathically or verbally that you have attained a high level of consciousness, that you are the chosen one for the next generation or the like—that being is on the Negative side and you should not pay any attention to it. That is the power of glamour, the negative power that tries to entrap you, to take you away from the Spiritual Path.

Glamour is not limited to the Astral World; there is also glamour in the Mental World—glamour dependent on the power of the mind, which is another source of possible delusion. Mind power can be just as glamorous as emotional power. A lot of people develop their mind and think they understand everything and there is nothing more that can be known. That is glamour of the mind. In the nineteenth century the materialistic scientists decided that there was no God. But does that mean that there is no God? In their minds it was totally clear that there is no God, so they were deceived by the glamour of the mind.

So you need to be careful of both astral glamour and mental glamour. There is also spiritual glamour, which is even more subtle; in fact, it is the subtlest form of glamour of them all.

Spiritual glamour occurs when you have a mystical insight and believe that you are the Buddha or the greatest Master who has ever lived. This means that you have reached the Buddhic dimension and have experienced the sensation of Unity, the sensation that you are one with the world, with everybody and everything. This is the subtlest form of glamour because you feel at that moment that you have reached the end of the Path—beyond Oneness what else could be known? This is the glamour of the Buddhic dimension and many Mystics reached that stage and thought they had attained the ultimate possibility of being, so they didn't even try to go beyond it or think that there could be something beyond it.

This does not mean that the Buddhic World itself is glamorous; the glamour is in your *handling* of your experience, your *interpretation* of it. Remember, the worlds themselves are what they are. It is our judgment, our perception, our understanding and our explanation of them that is glamorous. Buddha reached Nirvāṇa but his attainment of Nirvāṇa did not make his ego grow any larger. No truly enlightened person would say, "I am it, beyond and above all else, and you must all listen to me." That is the glamour of Enlightenment and it has no place on the Spiritual Path. The Path is simple, direct and straight like an arrow. You either know or you do not know. If you know, you say; if you do not know, you do not say; but there is no glamour in it.

The Buddha is still learning about Nirvāṇa, the Christ is still learning about the Kingdom of God, and they will go on learning forever. You cannot say that you know the answer to everything. You have answers according to the bridge you have built and the world to which you have built it—and that is all. This keeps things in perspective and it keeps you humble. Whatever you experience in meditation is your experience at that time. You should not get stuck there because the next time you may experience something else, a newer revelation.

On the Spiritual Path there is always growth, there is always moving ahead, having deeper experiences, reaching deeper states of Enlightenment. Enlightenment is not something that happens to you once in a lifetime; it is ongoing. One of the great moments of Enlightenment is Buddhic Consciousness; after you stabilize yourself in that consciousness you enter Nirvāṇic Consciousness, a greater moment of Enlightenment; after you stabilize yourself on that level you enter Paranirvāṇa, an even greater moment of Enlightenment; and so on. Enlightenment is breaking through to a new level of Awareness, growing on that level until you reach the total possibility of that condition, and then making an effort to break through to the next level.

So your path is never finished and you have to put everything you experience in the right context. Then you will be safe on the Spiritual Path and be able to guard yourself from astral glamour, from mental glamour and even from the glamour of being spiritual. If you understand the true way of spiritual life then you will be able to walk steadily, with spiritual integrity. You walk in the Light of your Soul and the Light of your Soul is the only reality that guides you. You won't listen to astral entities that tell you how great and wonderful you are. The key is humility, humility, humility—at all times and in all situations. Then you can progress on the Spiritual Path.

~ 19 ~

THE WARRIOR IS
IN SERVICE TO THE KING

The Spiritual Warrior Path is based on the fact that there is a reality that your normal consciousness has but there is another reality
that your normal consciousness does not have, and somehow you have
to connect to that other reality and become part of it. In other words,
you are not complete as you are and you have to become something
else—the infinite possibility inside you.

Karma Yoga: Union through Action

If you follow the Way of Yoga you try to find that "infinite possibility"
through meditation, trying to reach beyond the normal self to realize
the Cosmic Self, the Universal Reality. This is a valid path that has been
practised for thousands of years. We call it the Path of Meditation or
the Path of Contemplation. Then there is the Path of Jñāna Yoga, or
Knowledge Yoga, where you are given esoteric knowledge, esoteric science, esoteric understanding, and through that knowledge you begin to
feel a larger reality pervading your being and you become transformed.

Then there is the practical way: the Way of the Spiritual Warrior.
Remember, I'm talking about the *Spiritual* Warrior, so you have to
switch your mind away from martial arts schools, where they are only
interested in fighting or physical development. I am saying that there

is a Way where physical action teaches you to become nonphysical and feel the Transcendent, where physical objects teach you to become aware of the Transcendental Reality shining inside substance. That is the Way of the Warrior.

When you follow an active path—what is normally called Karma Yoga in the East, KARMA meaning "action"—you try to discover the principle behind an action, what causes it, and the results of the action and how they relate to the Transcendent. Every action must have some relationship to the Supernatural within you, and the Way of the Warrior is about finding out how an action is related to the Supernatural, how an action relates to the Ultimate Reality.

The physical techniques practised in a true Warrior School are therefore not just physical exercises. You have to remember that they are spiritual exercises, forms of meditation and movement, or moving meditations. They are Karma Yoga, which means "union through action", that is, "union with the Divine through action". If you think they are keep-fit

---

Sword movements like the Cross, the Swastika, the Circle, the Wave and the Curl and magic symbols like the Runes and Sigils are representations of real forces and energies, patterns of how the Cosmos manifests itself, how it evolves and moves from one condition to another. Some of those patterns can be expressed in movement with your physical body, and through physical movements you can tune into their cosmic pattern, the archetypal forces that those movements represent.

When you are a Spiritual Warrior and you move your sword and the movement flows with your destiny and the destiny of the moment, the sword sings, making a crystal clear sound. If you are not one hundred percent tuned in, if your mind is wobbly or your emotions are not coordinated or your body is weak, the sword will not make that sound. The more off-key that sound is, the more you know that you are not tuned in.

Similarly, when you do a physical movement and you are totally tuned in, it seems to come from beyond you, as if it is not you who is doing it. That is because the Cosmos is working through you in that movement.

exercises, that's fine too because they will make you healthy, but you are not understanding the Principle of the Warrior Path; you are miles away from working as a Spiritual Warrior.

Even making a simple movement of your hand is actually a cosmic act; you can feel the energy of the Cosmos flowing through your hand. You are part of the Cosmos, part of the total Reality, part of Universal Space, part of Universal Intelligence, part of the All-Presence.

So the Way of the Warrior is about feeling that whatever takes place inside you is taking place in the Cosmos, and you are one with that Cosmic Reality. Anyone, no matter how unfit they are, can do a simple arm movement and try to feel where that movement comes from. What is that movement? What is causing it? If you are materialistic, of course, you will say that the nervous system is moving the muscles and this muscle is doing this and that muscle is doing that. But that has nothing to do with it at all. I mentioned before that the physical body, together with the physical world, is a reaction to Reality; it is not *Reality*.

What takes place in the physical dimension is the last stage of a certain sequence of cosmic events—the *last* stage, not the stage that starts something. So when you move your arm, it is not the beginning; it is the end result. First there is a mind in the action: you thought of moving your arm even if just for a split second. Then there is an emotional force behind it, a desire to do it. Finally, the life-force within you, the Prāṇa or Chi within you, executes the action and the body simply follows it. Even on the personality level, everything that happens starts from the mind and works down to the physical.

When you are enlightened, or when you are a real Spiritual Warrior, then you see the cause of every movement, you trace the causes from the inner dimensions and see how they work out in material Creation.

The Way of the Spiritual Warrior is therefore about tuning into cosmic forces and feeling how energy is working at a particular time and place in the history of the planet. Have you ever thought about the amazing power that must have been working in France during the French Revolution? In those days people were extremely dense in consciousness, and to make a whole nation alive and vibrant enough to change the structure of society took colossal internal energies.

Have you ever thought what forces could move a large country like Russia to rise up and change its system, as it did during the Russian Revolution? The First World War, the Second World War—these are more examples of tremendous forces generated to change the environment in certain countries and to change the world. They are all forces of *change*, but those forces have to be large enough to move millions of people.

So where do such colossal energies come from? History is movement, energy, change. To shake up society, to push people to rise up and try to become something other than what they are, takes tremendous forces— tremendous *internal* forces. And that was true for every major event in history right from day one, right from the times of Lemuria and Atlantis.

If human beings were left to their own devices they would just degenerate, going from very little action to the least possible action, spiralling down to the simplest common denominator. By nature, human beings are lazy and do not want to fulfil their evolutionary plan because it takes effort; they would rather take the easy way. But the easy way is not the way of evolution; it is the way of stagnation or even going backwards.

The Way of the Spiritual Warrior is the hard way. It is recognizing that you have to work hard, impose a strong discipline on yourself and achieve results. It is the way of evolution because you know you have to be more than what you started off as, and to do that you need a vision, a goal. And what is that vision or goal? It is Cosmic Consciousness, Divine Consciousness, Absolute Consciousness; it is control over the forces of Nature; it is understanding what motivates Life to be as it is.

This is when you understand the Law of Karma and the Law of Dharma (Destiny), when you understand that the Code of the Warrior is about discovering your true spiritual destiny, which is very different than working out your karma day by day. Once you find your true spiritual destiny, you can find the destiny of the group you are working with, the destiny of your nation and the destiny of the planet. And you can gear your actions to the best outcome for your group, your nation or the planet.

The Way of Service

So essentially warriors are servants, even on the physical level. The ancient warriors always had a master whom they served, maybe a warlord or an emperor or a king. Even the greatest of warriors were servants. And as a Spiritual Warrior you are also a servant: you serve the Spiritual King, the Lord Above All, who has been ruling the planet from the inner dimensions for millions of years and will do so until the end of time.

On that level you serve all Humanity and the whole planet under the direction of the Spiritual Hierarchy (the Spiritual Government of our planet), in the name of the Spiritual King and in accordance with the Divine Plan. This is what makes you a Spiritual Warrior, in contrast to an ordinary warrior. The Spiritual Warrior serves the King of Kings, the real King of the planet, the Shining Eternal Being that the Spiritual Hierarchy was established to serve.

The King knows the evolution of our planet, how the planet relates to the Solar System, how the Solar System relates to the Universe and how the Universe relates to the Divine Will that makes everything to be as it is—the First Cause. So the King is in service to the First Cause and the Warrior is in service to the King. This is why the Warrior Path is an esoteric path: you must have a deeper understanding of your own structure, the structure of the Cosmos and of the internal Hierarchies that rule the Cosmos, and what the real plan for the Cosmos is. That plan is in the mind of the King, and you have to be in tune with the King and serve the King consciously.

On the normal religious paths you look for God and do techniques and find God. You attain Transcendental Consciousness or Bliss Consciousness or Self-Realization or God-Realization. You enjoy tremendous internal Bliss and Joy and Light and Glory and you stay there; you have found your Kingdom of God, your Nirvāṇa. But that is not the Way of the Warrior. Finding the Kingdom of God is only a small part of it; the Way of the Warrior is *doing* the Kingdom of God. That is the big difference.

If you are a Yogī or a Mystic you cannot be in service to the King, because to be a servant, even in the normal understanding of the word, you have to be active. As a Warrior, therefore, you work for the benefit of all: first of all for your own group, the people you are training with on the Warrior Path, and then, by extension, for society and sometimes even for your country. On a more advanced level you impact the world consciousness itself, because it is your job to see the Divine Plan in the mind of the King and to know the next stage of evolution for our planet, and then to serve the King and bring that plan about, transforming your locality, society, culture or nation, or doing whatever the plan requires you to do.

Warriors work on different levels according to their internal level of understanding, to what degree they have absorbed the message of the King. The King works by Cosmic Intelligence—particles of Light that impinge on one's Soul-Consciousness and are then transcribed by the Soul into subtle messages that the personality consciousness can understand as a plan of action. Then you put yourself in service to the King and you learn the art of Service, because to serve the King is an art on its own, not something you work out mentally. If you try to do it intellectually you are not in touch with the King at all.

First of all, therefore, before you even start thinking about serving the King, you have to become at least a baby Spiritual Warrior, which means that you have to understand life itself, how things are. You have to understand people, what motivates them, what energies flow through them; you see where they come from, where they are going, what you can do for them, how they work, and so on. When you understand the forces of life around you and inside you and can work out your true destiny, you are a baby Spiritual Warrior, ready for your real Warrior training.

When you realize where your group is going—what the group destiny is—and begin to work for the group destiny consciously and intelligently, then you are a bit more than a baby Warrior: you are a child Warrior. You have a larger purpose and start to work beyond your own personal destiny to help your group fulfil its purpose, what it is supposed to do in the world according to its Dharma.

When you develop beyond that and become a teenage Warrior, then it is no longer just about your group. You work beyond the horizons of the group on a planetary scale, seeing how countries are changing, how the Earth is changing and working out what you have to do. Then when you finally grow up and become a mature Warrior, you work for the Cosmic Plan, you understand the vast sweep of Creation, the great tides of Evolution going through the Cosmos, the Great Breath of God. Your field of activity is the whole planet inside and outside, in different countries and in different dimensions, and you are fulfilling the wishes of the King, who always works according to great principles. Then you understand what it means to be in service of the King, to sacrifice your life to this great vision, the evolution of the planet itself.

Meditation and all the other spiritual techniques of the Warrior School, as well as the physical exercises, prepare you to become a baby Spiritual Warrior, but there is a danger that you think the Path is doing all those techniques and exercises, not realizing that they are part of something larger. That *something larger* is the vision you should hold in your consciousness, the goal you are working towards. It is like weaving a tapestry. In the olden days, a master weaver had a vision of the whole pattern of a tapestry, all the symbols and designs and how they all flowed together. He then started making the tapestry bit by bit, keeping that large vision intact, or else the pattern would not work out.

Accordingly, the physical exercises, breathing techniques and meditation techniques of the Warrior School are part of the large tapestry you are working on, the tapestry of making yourself a Spiritual Warrior—one who understands the *why* of things. In the beginning stages you know how things work but you do not know why. But as you become a Spiritual Warrior, it is the *why* that comes to you: the why of the Cosmos, why it is as it is, what it was in the past, what it is going to be in the future; and why Humanity is as it is, what it was in the past, what it will be in the future.

And as your understanding grows, you see more and more of the Divine Plan in your life. Understanding is part of the Warrior Way; without understanding there is no Warrior. You must understand *why* everything happens. This is where you become an enlightened Warrior: first you find the immediate cause and then go beyond that to the next cause and the next, until you come to the Ultimate Cause, that which is the cause of all Creation. That is what you must ultimately reach, and then you will stand in between "up there" and "down here", surveying the vast Reality and sensing what the Divine Will wants you to do in Creation. Then you will be a real Master Spiritual Warrior. ✗

~ 20 ~

THE QUESTION 'WHO AM I?'
DETERMINES YOUR LIFE

The question *Who am I?* determines your life. When you ask yourself *Who am I?* you can get not only the answer to the meaning of your life but also an understanding of why human beings are the way they are and why the planet is the way it is. In other words, what you identify with determines your life and what Humanity in total identifies with determines the destiny of the planet. It may seem like a simple question, but in fact it is quite profound.

If you are on the Spiritual Path, therefore, the question *Who am I?* is the number one question to ask in your life. It is really the basic starting point, and this has to do with the fact that human beings have three main possibilities for development, according to their different types of consciousness.

The physical types with their physical body consciousness dominate the planet. They are quite happy with materialistic life, simply eating, going to work, going to the pub and going to sleep. For them, life and consciousness are bounded by the physical world. Another type of human being is the emotional type. Artists have emotional consciousness because all art is based on expressing emotions, from the deepest depression to the highest ecstatic elation and everything in between. Another possibility for human beings is to work with the mind, and the intellectual types form a large proportion of Humanity, consisting of people in the sciences, technology, education, medicine and other fields where the mind is used. These types use their rational, logical, thinking ability—for everything.

On the personality level, therefore, when you ask yourself Who am I? you can say that you are the physical type, the emotional type or the mental type. And of course there are combinations of physical-mental, physical-emotional, mental-emotional in varying degrees.

These types are found across society and whichever type predominates will determine the destiny of that society. There are certain societies that are mostly physical, dealing with everything in terms of physical values, so their destiny will move along that line. Some are emotional and some are intellectual and therefore move along their respective lines. An individual or a society will develop along their dominant line, whether it is physical, emotional or mental, or a combination of lines. This explains why certain regions of the planet, certain societies and cultures, are the way they are: they are expressing certain qualities along their line or combination of lines.

On the personality level, therefore, every human being can be classified according to a type, and that includes the country they were born in, the race they were born in and the religion, group and family they were born in. There are artistic families and intellectual families, and all kinds of groups having their specialized lines, which show where their destiny lies.

The question Who am I? can tell you what your life expression is on the personality level, but what if we go deeper than that? What if we say that there is more to the human being than the personality? What if the idea of the Soul is not a mythology or a weird philosophical or theological idea but a fact, a reality? What if when you ask yourself Who am I? instead of saying you are a famous artist or a university dropout, you suddenly have the sensation that there is some other quality inside you that is timeless, eternal, boundless, not limited by any society, cultural structure, philosophy or religious belief?

When you ask yourself that question and that *other* appears, naturally your whole life will be different from that moment on, because all the things that were important to your personality are not going to be as important. When you reach that point of evolution, when you ask yourself Who am I? and you sense a vast, infinite potential existing within you, naturally it will override all the lower expressions inside you, everything of the personality nature, no matter what kind of family you were born into.

Suppose you were born into an artistic family of musicians, but when you ask yourself Who am I? you do not identify with what your family is doing; instead you identify with something beyond the emotions that needs to be expressed. Naturally, you will feel disconnected from your family. Or suppose you were born into an intellectual family, but because you feel that you are something beyond the mind, you feel out of tune with your family. In either case you cannot identify with the vision and goals of the rest of your family (or group, culture, religion or nation), because you know that something grander, something vaster—*something more important*—needs to emerge from you.

You then come to a crisis point, the crisis of the first step on the Path. This is when you begin to feel that you are an outsider in your own country, in your own race, religion or culture, in your own family, because you feel that the values people live by are not yours. You feel that their values are limited and limiting, based on a narrow understanding of life. You feel that there is a vast reality inside you that needs to be expressed. and you feel that expressing that vast reality is the meaning of your life. It is the answer to the question *Who am I?*

The Spiritual Path—a Group Journey

Then your whole life is turned upside down and the battle begins. You have to free yourself from your family and friends because they want you to keep you in their category, according to their way of being; naturally, they will not want to let you go. You have to break away from your limitations: the old patterns, the old culture, the old religion, the old society, the old ways of working and thinking. You feel that you cannot be a part of that because everything that is nationalistic, cultural or traditional is limited to the workings of the personality, to set forms that somebody invented in the past. You know that you are more than that and you have to free yourself so that you can go on the big Quest—the quest for the Holy Grail, the quest for the Ultimate Truth, the Ultimate Reality within you.

For some of you, whether to pursue that quest or conform to your environment may be a long struggle, until you break through and realize that you have to go on that quest no matter what, because life has no more beautiful meaning or higher purpose than the quest for Truth. Whether other people want to do it or not is their business, but they cannot limit you. Only you can limit yourself: by trying to fit in with what everybody does and wants you to be. If you do that, you cannot go on the Quest, not completely, not correctly, because something is holding you back. You cannot be free.

This is why the idea of ashrams, monasteries, warrior schools, and sacred places came about. People felt that they could seek the Truth with other pilgrims like themselves, so they banded together and went away from mainstream societies and formed monasteries, communities and groups so that they could pursue the *Inner Quest* in the company of others. Even the so-called solitary sādhus in the Himalayas are really not solitary because usually they form small groups of half a dozen or so. Even the Christian monks who went out into the desert, supposedly to meditate alone, tended to stay in the same area. People always felt the need to go out and work together in a spiritual community, even in small groups of two or three people, to seek the Truth, to find an answer to the fundamental question of life: Who am I?

This is the one and only question in life, and as soon as you move from the normal explanation of who you are to wanting to discover a deeper dimension of who you are, then you are moving out of the mainstream into the next category of human being, the category of the seeker, the disciple, the knight on a glorious quest for the Holy Grail. You are now at the stage that having realized that there is something deeper inside you, you have to do something about it, you have to do something practical in order to attain your vision or goal. Otherwise it is a philosophical idea that you can research and write books about; but you will not be on the Quest. Your quest starts when you begin to work *practically*: meditating, doing breathing techniques, sound work and physical movements. It is only through practice, through actual doing, that you will reach your goal.

This stage of the Path, the stage of practice, brings another life crisis. Crisis number one was to separate yourself from your family and the mass consciousness. Crisis number two is about how you are going to practise, when you are going to practise and who you are going to practise with. This is where group work is so vitally important, not because of companionship but because working by yourself is always harder.

Imagine trying to build a bridge by yourself! With a hundred people to help, the work would be much easier and more fun, and it would be done in no time. The spiritual life is like that, too. If you think you can do everything all by yourself, that you can fight the demons of existence single-handedly, you are in for a long, long journey. But if you travel with a group the journey is smoother and everything moves along faster, because the group itself is a higher reality, a higher being, than the individual.

A large organization has a power that an individual cannot have because a large organism is given more from the Cosmos, from Life itself. The ant needs to eat only a tiny amount of food; the elephant needs a lot more, so Life gives the elephant more because it is a larger organism. This means that a group is given more by Life than an individual working alone. This is the importance of the group, of coming together and working in the group environment of a true Warrior School.

You have to really *belong* to your group. Some people join a group but they do not really belong to it, that is, they want to pick up information and do some practices now and then, but their heart is not part of the Group Heart. A group is just a large entity with the same ups and downs as a human being: sometimes things go well, sometimes things do not go well. But if your heart is in the group, you will support the group through its crises. You will persevere to the end.

Remember, there has never been a spiritual or religious group in the history of Humanity, including esoteric groups, that did not have problems—schisms, interpersonal fights, breakaways, one disaster after another. Christ and his disciples and Buddha and his disciples had to face colossal crises like persecution—unbelievable problems! Just because you are on the quest for the Holy Grail does not mean that everything will be provided for you and you will always be blissed out. This is a dream that was never true and never *can* be true. When you are on a spiritual journey, you have endless battles to face. Look at the stories of the knights searching for the Holy Grail, who fought one battle after another, with giants, dragons and other bad knights; their whole life was one endless battle.

Group life is also like that: one endless battle. But you have to understand that that is not wrong, that it is a sign that the group is making progress. Many people join a spiritual group and then when something goes wrong they throw in the towel and leave. They do not understand that the challenge itself *is* the Path. If the group is not challenged, there is no Path. You have to understand the Cosmic Principle behind it, how the Light and the Dark work in the Cosmos, how the forces of evil attack the forces of good, how the Opposition tries to destroy a group. You have to understand that this is the way of *Life*. This is the Way of the Warrior.

The Law of the Light and the Dark

This is an occult law of spirituality: *If you are successful in the spiritual field, the worldly powers want to destroy you.* It is the Law of the Light and the Dark. It is the law for every spiritual group, and you have to understand it and not be afraid of it. Look at Jesus and His disciples: as soon as He was in trouble they all ran away. They did not understand that trouble comes when you are making progress in the spiritual field, that it is due to acknowledgement by the worldly powers that you are making progress, that the Way of Liberation is through struggle.

For example, in the Middle Ages there were contemplative orders of nuns who lived in little cells, with just a bed and a crucifix or a painting of the crucifixion, with blood dripping from the heart, hands and feet of Jesus. That is what they had to contemplate their whole life, and they weren't even allowed to talk. If you think they were living a simple life with no responsibility, that they had an easy time, forget it. They had a horrendously bad time—emotional disturbances, psychic breakdowns, and struggles with demons and all kinds of real and imaginary forces—because all they did every day was stay focused on a negative image: the Christ crucified.

So just because you are on the Spiritual Path, do not think that your life is going to be easy, that you will not have to suffer or fight for anything. Life on the Spiritual Path is an ongoing battle. But if your heart is in it, you do not give up; you go to your battle station and support your group; you ask: What can I do? What is my part in the fight? You must actually put this idea of the Warrior into practice, because it is easy to be a warrior in a cafeteria and drink coffee and think about what Warriors do. The life of the intellectual is easy because it only takes place in the mind. But in real life it's not like that at all.

In real life, when the battle comes you have to fight, because the battle is for the good of your whole group, for the liberation of the planet. There are no lone rangers in the Warrior School, but strong warriors fighting together for the Truth, no matter where the opposition comes from, whether from within or without, whether from society or from invisible forces or energies. The battle is on, and as a group of warriors you fight together and do not run away at the slightest problem.

The Way of the Warrior is not a bed of roses, but it is a glorious Path, and you can only follow it when you know who you are in the ultimate sense—a Divine Soul fighting for the forces of Light in this dark world. Only then can you be a Spiritual Warrior in shining armour with shining sword in hand, ready to do your part to turn this planet into a planet of Light. Only those who stand in the Light themselves can do that. Only those who understand what the Divine Will wants for us—for the whole of Humanity, not just one or two individuals—can do that.

There will always be problems, because they are part of the natural process of life on this planet and part of the Group Soul process. So you just go on. You take every problem and battle it until you conquer it, whether it is a physical problem, emotional problem or personality problem, or you think that you are not progressing fast enough, or you lack certain knowledge or understanding, or you have no time for practice. These are all problems but they are not signs that something is

---

There are all kinds of groups: bowling leagues, golf associations, knitting clubs. Every group can ask itself the question *Who am I?* But when a Warrior School group asks itself the question *Who am I?* the Group Soul says, "We are a group on the Quest, a group working for the Light, whose sole purpose is to increase the Light on the planet, to raise the Planetary Vibration."

Individual Group Souls can have group members in the Physical World, the Astral World, the Mental World or the Causal World, so those in incarnation work together with those in the Inner Worlds, and their total group function is to increase the Light of Knowledge, the Light of Wisdom, the Light of Understanding, the Light of Love, the Light of Action—all the ways Light expresses itself. For Understanding, Knowledge, Wisdom, Action, Compassion and Love are all vibrations of Light.

wrong; in fact they are signs that everything is going along gloriously. The bigger the problem, the bigger the glory, because as I mentioned, the Law of Life is that where the Light is increasing, the Darkness is increasing, and they must clash.

If you are a knight in shining armour, you will have a lot of opposition. If you are a knight in brighter shining armour, you will have even more opposition. And if you are a knight of all-blazing Light, you will have all the forces of the world aligned against you.

That is the Law of Life, and there is nothing wrong with that. You take opposition philosophically and positively, one day at a time. Instead of moaning, crying, blaming somebody else or running away, you see what the situation is and what you have to fight today. Tomorrow there will be another fight; the next day, another. Then you understand what the Warrior Life is about: fighting, yes, but fighting to let the Light shine more and more inside you; to let the Light shine more and more into your Warrior School; to let the Light shine more and more into the world itself. This is the Way of the Spiritual Warrior. ✗

~ 21 ~

ENLIGHTENMENT OF THE YOGĪ,
THE MYSTIC AND THE WARRIOR

When you begin the Spiritual Journey you think that Enlighten-ment is a simple thing: something happens to you and you're enlightened. Enlightenment is actually quite a big thing and it involves a multidimensional reality.

Part of that reality is listening to a Teacher. In that listening you receive Enlightenment in two ways: you receive Enlightenment in the form of knowledge, an understanding of things, but because the Enlightenment energy is multidimensional, in the actual listening an energy is transmit-ted to you on the inner levels that stimulates your inner consciousness, your inner being. So while you are listening you are receiving the energy of Enlightenment and something is shifting and moving inside you.

Otherwise you could do what the Hinayāna Buddhist monks do in Burma, Thailand and Cambodia. In that form of Buddhism the monks practise the Natural Breathing exercise day in and day out. That is a good exercise for dissolving the ego, but for them to get a moment of Enlight-enment could take many years because they rely on one technique, one process only, and because they do not have the energy transmission or a knowledge-field transmission from a Teacher.

The Enlightenment process is quicker with a Teacher because you approach it from different angles. First, you listen to a Teacher; that in itself sharpens your awareness and prepares you for Enlightenment. Then you receive different but complementary techniques and processes that also aid in the Enlightenment process. And then there is the subtle energy transmission. So rather than relying on only one process, this is a much more comprehensive way of working, one which expands the self and increases the possibility of Enlightenment a hundredfold.

To understand Enlightenment, you have to understand the idea of *continuum*, that everything is continuous with everything else, not only in the physical dimensions, the physical Cosmos, but also in the inner dimensions. This outer world is a continuum in itself and with the next inner world, which is a continuum with the next inner world, and so on. The continuum is endless, both horizontally (externally) and vertically (internally).

It is like the ocean. If you look at the ocean you can see thousands of waves on the surface of the ocean, all separate from each other. But at the same time you will also notice that each wave rises from the ocean and falls back in again—thousands of them, but *all* from the sameness, the oneness, the ocean. No matter how many waves come and go, there is a continuum beneath the waves: the ocean itself. It is always there, sustaining the waves as they come and go.

In the beginning stages of the Enlightenment process you only sense the continuum horizontally, that is, externally in physical space and time. You see the continuum underlying all things, between you and a tree and between the tree and the sky and between the sky and the farthest star. But that is not the whole story. You can see the continuum that joins everything together, but you sense that there is a deeper mystery behind it, a deeper, more fundamental reality; that is, you sense the continuum *internally*. Then you are aware that the internal continuum and the external continuum meet and form the Cross.

In the second stage of Enlightenment, which is Cosmic Consciousness, you are at the centre of the Cross; your consciousness has expanded inwardly, in Inner Space (the vertical arm of the Cross), and outwardly, in outer space (the horizontal arm of the Cross). And then the Cross gradually becomes larger and larger until it becomes the whole Cosmos, and you are "crucified" in the Cosmos—your consciousness permeates the All-Structure of Creation and you understand where in that All-Structure you fit in.

When you reach the third level of Enlightenment you see the whole picture—the Manifest Condition and the Unmanifest Condition. You see the realms of being and the intermediary dimensions, and you understand that God is still and God is active, that all is action and stillness at the same time.

At the fourth level of Enlightenment, where the sense of Unity inside you is so vast that it encompasses everything, you know that the most profound non-action and the most violent action are part of the great Ocean of Life, the great Ocean of Reality.

The Three Main Paths to Enlightenment

There are three main paths to Enlightenment: the Way of Yoga; the Way of Devotion (also called the Way of Mysticism or the Way of the Heart); and the Way of the Spiritual Warrior. Essentially they look at the Enlightenment process in different ways, and traditionally you followed one way or another; you were a Yogī or a Mystic or a Warrior. In our School we combine all three: Devotion (the Heart), Yoga (the Mind) and the Warrior (Action).

The Mystic—whether a Jewish Mystic or a Christian, Sūfī, Hindu, Buddhist or Chinese Mystic—approaches Reality through the Heart, through *devotion*. To open the Heart and sense the Divine Presence in everything with a tremendous Love for the Divine within themselves and outside themselves—that is the Way of the Mystic. For the Mystics, therefore, Enlightenment is a transcendental experience: they get disconnected from their physical body and from their mind, disconnected from their environment, disconnected from Creation, and they go into what they call a rapture or ecstasy, a kind of ecstatic trance. These devotee types would rather not go to work and do worldly things, which they find boring; they would rather stay in ecstatic trance and smile and be blissful.

In extreme cases they tend to be totally disjointed from the life process, and then they are called *God's fools*. You see them amongst the Sūfī and Hindu Mystics: men and women who are totally spaced out, always in a trance, who can't even feed themselves or move their bodies. They do not care whether they are clothed or not, whether they eat or not; they do not care about anything that happens around them. Their personality ego has disappeared but they cannot relate to *anything* at all in the world.

This is the result of an extreme longing for the Divine but without a corresponding desire to be in the world (because they do not have proper Teachers). Usually they are loners, with no awareness of group consciousness or social consciousness whatsoever. They are only concerned with their own inner experience. Their understanding of Enlightenment, therefore, is to be in a continual state of Bliss, ĀNANDA, dissolving increasingly more into that Blissful Consciousness within themselves.

The second path is the Way of the Yogī, which approaches Enlightenment through the mind. Those on this path are the Rāja Yoga types, such as Patañjali and Śaṅkarācārya, who use their mind as the focal point for entry into Liberation, or Enlightenment. Using the mind to attain Enlightenment can also lead to the problem of being disconnected from society. Many of these Yogīs withdraw from society and contemplate Reality, becoming disconnected from themselves and from the larger stream of life. They withdraw into the state of SAMĀDHI— they don't call it Ecstasy—and they experience and explore the inner dimensions of their consciousness. Like the Mystics, they have no sense for what they need to do for others or what they need to do for the outside world.

The third path, which is not well known because it has been long forgotten, is the Way of the Spiritual Warrior. It was practised in a previous age when Activity was the Way. That is to say, the Way was discovering who you were and how you related to the world outside of you: to a flower, to a tree, to the sky. It had to do with *relationship*. So the Way of the Warrior is a way of relationship: first how you relate to yourself, then how you relate to the Warrior group you belong to and then how that Warrior group relates to the larger world outside—what the destiny of the group is in the world and what your part in it is.

So the Warrior Path is the only one that is socially conscious; right from day one you are aware of your *relatedness* to things. Warriors are not concerned with enjoying God or Bliss or Inner Peace. What they enjoy or do not enjoy is not important; it is how they relate that counts. This is called Dharma, which means "right relationship or right action". The Sanskrit word DHARMA is difficult to translate because it means the rightness of all things: the dharma of a flower, is to be like it is; the dharma of a sheep is to be a sheep.

For the Warrior, right relationship—how you relate to others and what you need to do or not do about something—is always the highest level of attainment. For example, when people see some rubbish on the sidewalk they normally walk by and leave it there. But the Warrior says, "That rubbish shouldn't be there," establishing a right relationship, and then picks it up. As a Warrior you have to see how the little things you

---

Part of the Warrior training is to learn to see the larger picture. Most martial arts schools teach techniques and exercises and the pupils tend to get focused on a particular exercise or training and think that *that* is what it is to be a Warrior. They cannot see the totality of life because the proper Warrior Path was forgotten a long time ago. First of all the Warrior sees the larger picture, and then the Warrior sees how a particular technique or movement fits in with the larger picture. If you cannot do that you can never become a Spiritual Warrior.

do fit into the cosmic totality, and *then* you know whether it is your job to act or not, and in what manner you should act, in any situation. *Dharma.* That is the key word for the Warrior. *Right action.* And right action can only come from the right understanding of the total picture.

But remember, this does not mean that because you are a Warrior you always have to act, you have always to be busy trying to change everybody, trying to change the world and telling the government what to do. That does not make you a Warrior at all. Being a Warrior has to do with *skill in action*: you have to know when it is right for you to do something and when it is right for you *not* to do something. Most people think that all Warriors do is fight all the time, waging one battle after another, one conquest after another, one action after another. That is not a Warrior; that is an ignorant person.

A Warrior stands *still* when the Light is still inside him. And when the Light moves, then the Warrior knows it is time to act.

For example, when I first went to India I was greeted at the airport by hundreds of poor people. If I had given money to each of them I would have had to catch the next airplane home. I thought: Compassion is fine, but it has to have common sense behind it. If I give everything away now my trip is finished. So I asked myself: Is it my duty to help all these people? Is there not an Indian government that should be doing something about its citizens? So I gave up on the idea of giving away all my money.

Accordingly, in the early stages of Warriorship you think that you have to save the whole world, but as you grow into Warriorship you realize that some part of it is your duty, and you have to know what is your part and what is not your part. Obviously, the world is so large that other people have responsibilities, too, not only you. And this is where the fine-tuning of the Warrior inside you takes place. Just what is your part?

In other words, you have to discover what your dharma is—as a human being in a human society on *this* Warrior planet.

The devotee types say, "No, this is not a Warrior planet, this is a goody-goody planet." Well, yes and no. There is love on this planet, and there is also no love. As a Warrior you are realistic. You stay in your heart and express love and do everything the Mystic does, but unlike the Mystic, you also see the evil in the world. A Warrior says, "Yes, it's a goody-goody planet. But I keep my eyes open."

All Things to All Men

The Way of the Warrior is the most unique way because it combines the Way of the Mystic and the Way of the Yogī. When you are Warrior you are a full-fledged Mystic—you have all the wonderful Heart development of a Mystic—and you have all the Wisdom of the Yogī, the illumined Buddha Mind. But you are also something else: a *Warrior*. This means that all human potentialities shine inside you. An enlightened Warrior is everything—a Yogī, a Mystic, a human being, a divine being.

This is what Saint Paul was referring to when he said: "I am all things to all men" (1 Corinthians 9: 22). Saint Paul was a Warrior (and by the way, he was the real founder of Christianity, not Jesus). To be all things to all men means that you can help all men according to their need. If a person thinks he is a Buddhist you will help him in a Buddhist way, and if he thinks he is a Communist you will help him in a Communist way. So Saint Paul was a real Warrior: universal, broad, embracing all of Humanity *according to each person's need*. He did not say, "Come and follow the Christ because I am a Christian." No, he said, "I am all things to all men."

He could say this because the Divine Being is everywhere and we are all manifestations of the Divine Consciousness, without exception. Even the worst person in the worst place at the worst time is a projection of the Divine Being. This is what some people cannot understand: How can a terrible person be divine? It is a mystery, but it will be resolved when you reach the second stage of Enlightenment. In Cosmic Consciousness you see how everything is divine, even the most evil people.

You realize that they *are* divine, except the problem is that they do not know it. It is precisely because they do not *know* they are divine that they act in evil ways.

This is where the process of Enlightenment comes in: you have to make people realize that they are already divine, they are already enlightened, they are gods and goddesses walking on this Earth. Give them that knowledge and they will change, and all the negativity in their life will disappear.

The Way of the Warrior not only includes the Way of the Mystic and the Way of the Yogī, but it can also be practically applied in day-to-day living. It is not a philosophy and it is not something you do occasionally or when you meditate. You are a Warrior twenty-four hours a day, seven days a week, 365 days a year, all of your life and all of your lives beyond this life. When you die you are still a Warrior.

For the Yogī the Way is in stillness and not action. This is why Yoga literature is full of arguments about whether Yogīs should act or not act, whether they should just sit in meditation all the time. Even simple actions like eating were questioned. For a Warrior it is not a matter of discussion, because you know that one part of the Divine Being is always unmanifest and still, and one part is always in activity, and you know that you, the Warrior, stand between the absolute Stillness and the absolute Activity.

So the Warrior has a larger perspective, meaning that as a Warrior you see that there are times when it is your dharma to act (and the Cosmos not to act) and times when it is the dharma of the Cosmos to act (and you not to act). You see the total Divine Manifestation, the total interplay of Divinity, the complete Reality, and you know your place in it, what you have to do in that amazing picture. Whether you act or do not act comes from knowing the Dharma-field, the battlefield of life.

In the battle scene in the first chapter of the Bhagavad-Gītā, Arjuna started off by analysing the situation: Why do these great heroes and famous warriors on both sides have to kill each other? What am I supposed to be doing? This is the early stage of being a Spiritual Warrior. You wonder what you are supposed to be doing in life and if something is the right action or the wrong action. But as you get instruction and grow, and especially when the Inner Warrior awakens, then you *know*: this is the plan and this is what I have to do. And then you do it. The self is out of the way and you become an agent for the Divine. The Energy comes through you and it is no longer *you* who fights but the Christ within you, the Warrior within you, the Buddha within you, the Self within you. You are just an instrument for the expression of the Divine Manifestation.

The first thing Arjuna was worried about when the real Warrior awakened inside him was death, but not because he was afraid to die physically. No, he understood the inner dimensions and knew that when he died he would go to the Heaven World because of his past karma. That was not the problem. He was worried about death for another reason. Arjuna was mainly worried that many Master Warriors would fall, and he was questioning if it was right for them to die at that time. He knew that many would go to the Heaven World, or Devāchan, but wondered if they should live on and evolve themselves further so that they could enter the Buddhic World or even Nirvāṇa. That was the problem for Arjuna, not just the ordinary idea of death.

For the Warrior, death itself is not the issue; *where* you go after death is the issue. And the Warrior knows that this is also the problem for Humanity. If many people are dying in the wrong way they will go to the lower astral worlds, which is not part of the Divine Plan. So the Warrior is concerned about where people go, concerned about their destiny, and is always trying to lift them up so that they have a higher destiny, so that en masse they enter into one of the Higher Worlds, if possible; the first level of Enlightenment, if possible; Devāchan or beyond, if possible; the lower Worlds of Light, if possible.

So that is a brief explanation of the difference between a Mystic, who follows the Path of Devotion, a Yogī, who follows the Path of Yoga, and a Warrior who combines both paths plus another layer of understanding and purpose. As I mentioned, we practise all three Paths and combine them into one synthesis, which is why we practise many different kinds of techniques and exercises.

If you only do one thing, your consciousness gets locked into one thing and you are able to do one thing. In India there are many Yogīs who are only able to express Divinity through one practice or action. They express Divinity, yes, but they are limited; they are not the complete human being. The complete human being is vast: to be all things to all men, not just one thing to a few people who might like what you do. You have to be able to work for *all* of Humanity, for the planet itself—whatever is *required*. That is the Way of the Warrior. ⚔

~ 22 ~

ENLIGHTENMENT
IN AND OUT OF THE BODY

The Sanskrit word MUKTI means "Liberation, Enlightenment or Freedom", and there are two kinds of Liberation: DEHA-MUKTI, Liberation while in the physical body, and VIDEHĀ-MUKTI, Liberation outside of the physical body, or without the physical body. Essentially, Liberation, or Enlightenment (which means the same thing), is a transformation of the self, and that process can be completed in one's lifetime or in the after-death condition.

This is highly esoteric knowledge which ordinary religious teachers do not have. They tell you that if you are good you go to Heaven, but they do not tell you how to liberate yourself from Heaven (because there are better worlds than that). We will explain these two processes, and once you understand them you will be able to make rapid progress on the Spiritual Path and become enlightened in this lifetime or after you die.

We will start with the first part, Deha-Mukti, which is easy enough to understand. It means that you liberate yourself while you are in a physical body, while you are alive. This can happen when you have inner experiences through meditation, chanting, silent walks, sword exercises and other spiritual work that is part of the process of Deha-Mukti. But the question is: What is the Liberation process without the physical body? This is where you need an Esoteric Teacher.

Liberation where the physical body is not involved can happen in the after-death condition or in the dream condition, when you are out of your physical body at nighttime functioning in the Astral World. Videhā-Mukti means "Liberation *outside* of the body", so it does not matter whether you are in the Astral World in a meditative condition or as part of your dream life, or after you die and have left your body altogether and are in one of the Inner Worlds.

Videhā-Mukti is a complex process, but I will explain it to you so that if you have not completed the process of Enlightenment while you are still in your body, you will automatically be liberated when you step outside of the body, because you have been working with the other technique, Deha-Mukti.

The Law of Cause and Effect

I'll start with a simple observation. When the wind blows through a field of wheat, the wheat moves this way and that, but it remains wheat; that is, when something external affects the wheat it does not change its basic nature. But a human being is not like that. When something external happens to you, you change.

A human being has a basic centre, what we call the essential "you", what makes you to be you. In time and space, *you* are some sort of a self-existent reality. When something happens to that self-existent reality from outside and you experience sadness, joy, pain, pleasure or whatever, that experience affects the self within; so, unlike the wheat, you react. And this is why being a human is a huge problem: everything that happens to us from the outside is processed on the inside, and the inside state, rather than being immovable, changes.

The state of Enlightenment is not like that: enlightened people remain calm, centred, unmoved whatever happens to them in the outer world—on the physical level, or even on the astral or mental level. All the outer things are happening in their mind, body and emotions but the essential self is unmoved. For the average human being, however, the essential self is pushed this way and that, according to what kind of experience is coming through from the outside world, creating causal factors that force them to come back into incarnation.

If you have been a good person and have built up a lot of good qualities, you are still not liberated because those very qualities will bring you back into incarnation; you have to express them again in the next lifetime. And if you have been a bad person the same thing happens: those bad qualities will have to be expressed again in the next lifetime. This happens life after life after life; most people have incarnated thousands of times.

This was the great dilemma for all the Sages, Saints and Masters and all the great religious figures of history—how to break the Law of Cause and Effect, the chain of bondage in which human beings are imprisoned. They receive outer impressions, take them in and react, creating equal after-effects in the Inner Worlds which force them to return again into incarnation, where they do the same thing—over and over and over again. Humankind is trapped in this physical world, in this physical condition. In the esoteric language we call them *Prisoners of the Planet*; the planet is just one big prison for human beings.

Is there any way to break this cycle? Is there any way we can be free and only come into incarnation when we want to, rather than being forced into incarnation by the Law of Karma? There is a way: the process of Videhā-Mukti, Liberation outside the physical body.

So, how does it work? Everything that comes to you from the outside is filtered through what in the West we call the ego, the sense of "I am". In Sanskrit there is a beautiful word for ego: AHAṀKĀRA, which means "I am the doer". Everybody has an ego, of course, and it is precisely the ego that makes sure that everyone stays locked inside the prison of the self.

When you were a baby, for about the first year of your life, you did things without an ego. You just responded to outer stimuli. When you saw mummy's face, you cried. When you saw your daddy's face, you cried even more. You reacted to outer stimuli spontaneously, without an ego sense, without the "I am the doer" sense. But by the toddler stage you started to develop your ego, and when you threw your first tantrum, your ego was completely developed. From then on you functioned as an ego for the rest of your life. The problem is:

> As soon as there is a switch in your consciousness from doing something without any sense of "I am doing it" to doing something with the sense of "I am doing it", then that "I" attracts everything you do to yourself—good, bad and indifferent—and registers it.

The "I" not only attracts it but also keeps it in a registry. In the esoteric language the registry is called the Akashic Record, but it is really a subtle inner consciousness. In Buddhism it is called ALAYA-VIJÑĀNA, which means the "hidden mind or storehouse mind (the mind that stores things)". In modern psychology it is called the *subconscious mind*—and that is exactly what the subconscious mind does: it registers and stores impressions.

So all the impressions you have received since you developed the sense of "I am" are stored in your subconscious mind. As you go through life, therefore, the store of impressions in your subconscious mind gets bigger and bigger, especially if you go through bad times or suffer many hardships; then the impressions in your subconscious mind become very strong.

The stronger your subconscious impressions, the more karma you have. Karma is simply the result of all the stored-up memories, whether you are aware of them or not. Those stored-up memories cannot keep accumulating forever so they have to be released by the Law of Nature— as karmas, the things that happen to you as a result of what you have put into your subconscious mind.

Imagine that every life you put stuff into the Alaya-Vijñāna, the storehouse mind. If you have lived, say, a thousand lifetimes the karma from each lifetime is stored in your causal body, your Soul body, so you as a Soul have to release it, otherwise your causal body would be enormous. So when you come back in your next lifetime those forces pour into your "I" consciousness in a massive wave, and all kinds of things happen to you again—sickness, unhappiness, good luck, bad luck.

While you are working out some of your past karma, however, at the same time you are creating new karma because you are storing other impressions you are receiving. And that goes on life after life after life, in an endless cycle. You come in, work out karma but at the same time create new karma. It is a process that leads nowhere.

So, when does it all end? It doesn't, if you just follow that pattern.

Is there a way to free yourself from that pattern? First of all, you have to understand that in *this* lifetime you can make a decision, what in the esoteric language is called "entering the stream of Enlightenment". In this lifetime you can decide not to go around this wheel of death and birth (SAMSĀRA in Sanskrit). You are born, go back to the Astral World, go back to the Mental World, go back to the Heaven World, and then come down again, ever, ever on that wheel. And all because of Ahaṁkāra, "I am the doer", the entrapment in your own self.

So, how are you going to break away from the ever-turning wheel of death and birth? That is what Liberation is about. Remember, being liberated does not mean that you are not going to do anything for the rest of eternity. It means that you are free internally. You incarnated this time because you had to; if you are a liberated person you have a choice to incarnate or not; you are free. Freedom means internal freedom.

The Secret Knowledge: Selfless Action

Breaking away from this wheel of birth and death is what Liberation is about. As I said, the key is to understand that since your ego developed at around the age of one, you have been claiming actions for yourself and they go back into your subconscious mind. So when you meditate, do not think, "I am meditating now" or "I want Enlightenment now."

Do not use the word *I* at all because if you do, you are working from the ego and it becomes another stored-up impression. Even the best of all actions becomes an impression that goes into your subconscious mind and has to be worked out in the future, *if you do it with the sense of "I am the doer."* It's as simple as that.

The basic lesson, therefore, is to become self*less*. This is a tricky point where the yogīs got confused. If you read ancient Yoga literature you know the yogīs argued about whether they should do anything at all—whether they should eat or not, whether they should ever get up from their meditation seat or not—because they thought that if they did nothing they would not create karma and therefore would become liberated. The whole idea behind their way of life was that you did not get involved so that you might become free, but that is a false idea because non-involvement does not help anyone. What is more, if the non-involvement is done through the ego, then you are still bound by the Law of Karma.

They thought that action itself was the problem, and there are still yogīs in India who do not want to act, or do not dare to act, because they think they will get trapped into reincarnation. This is because they have yogic knowledge but not esoteric knowledge, the Secret Knowledge.

According to the Secret Knowledge you do not have to stop *acting*, but you have to act *self-less-ly*. That is, you act normally but without the ego behind it. If *you* are doing the action, you are storing up impressions in your subconscious mind. But if you do the action as Nature moves, as the great Cosmic Life-Force moves through you, then you have not stored anything; the effects of the action are stored in the Cosmic Mind, the Infinite Mind.

An enlightened Sage, Master, Warrior—an enlightened person—is active in the world, but he or she does not store up a single moment of karma. All actions go back to the Infinite Mind, the Omnipresent Consciousness, the essence and substance of the Universe, *not* to the person who is doing the action. This is the great secret of the liberated

Sages like the Buddha. Whatever they do does not come back to them and therefore they always remain free inside. They are free, they are not bound by the Law of Karma and they can move in any dimension of Space wherever they want to. This is the Secret Knowledge.

It is nice to know that you can be free, but how do you apply this knowledge? When you meditate, just meditate, with no ego in it. When you do anything, just do it, with no ego in it. You do not have to withdraw from anything; you will be doing the same things but without the sense of "*I* am doing it". Your actions will still be effective—in fact, they will be more effective—and internally you will be free.

But even if you start acting selflessly from now on, even if you have entered the "stream of Enlightenment" and are practising selfless action, you still have past karma stored up in your causal body that you have to work out.

I've been teaching for a long time and I've learned that people think that if they are doing the correct practice and are becoming selfless, then they should be totally blissed out and free from all problems for the rest of their lives. Unfortunately, it doesn't work that way because the past karma—what we call *residual karma*—will still be coming at them. They will still get sick, die of cancer, or whatever, *but* they will be working out their karmas, day by day, moment by moment—and not creating new ones.

So whatever happens to you, just accept it. I find it interesting that the orthodox religions have a kind of understanding of this. In the Jewish, Christian and Muslim religions they talk about accepting the Will of God, that whatever happens to you, God wanted it, so you just accept it. It is not actually God who wants those things to happen to you; it is you, your past, but they do not know that. If something is happening to you now, there was a past cause for it, something you did, so just accept it; it needed to be worked out. But, again, *accept it without the ego*. If you apply your ego to the situation you are back at square one.

This is a problem for people who are on the way to Enlightenment. They can fall back and re-apply their ego. Buddha was tempted and had to fight against MĀRA, the Great Tempter, the Opposition, and Jesus Christ was tempted and had to fight against Satan. These events are symbolic. What they mean is that Jesus and Buddha had past residual karmas to deal with. Of course, they dealt with them correctly—they did not use their egos—so they stayed liberated.

The best thing is to do what the Warrior does: live your normal life and within that life act in a way that does not bind your ego, that is, without self-interest. A real Warrior is a person of service, who lives only to do things for others, and the idea of getting something out of it does not enter into the Warrior's consciousness.

So if you want to follow the way of out-of-the-body Liberation, then from now on you have to do everything as a service. If you work in a restaurant, it's a service. If you teach at a university, it's a service. If you switch your way of thinking so that everything you do is a service towards others, then you are becoming a true Spiritual Warrior, and what is more, you are in the process of liberating yourself in the afterlife because you are not leaving any impressions in this life.

There is a good example of selfless action in a story about the Desert Fathers. Much has been written about the Desert Fathers, preserved in Latin in the Vitae Patrum, the "Lives of the Fathers", and in Greek in the

---

The two processes of Liberation, or Enlightenment, are: doing spiritual work, especially in a group like the Spiritual Warrior School, and at the same time changing the way you do things in your life, acting without ego, acting without leaving a trace. If you watch a bird flying across the sky, you see it for a while and it disappears. There is nothing again, just space. Your actions should be like that: you do something because it has to be done and in that moment there is an imprint. But because you did it without ego, once it is over it disappears and leaves no trace.

Philokalia. (Both are sources of amazing Christian teaching that most modern Christians do not seem to know about.) The Desert Fathers were Christian monks who lived a simple life and had virtually nothing. One day, robbers attacked a group of these monks. They took the only thing they could find from one old monk who was in his eighties—a bowl. But the monk also had a crucifix which they hadn't seen. As the robbers were leaving, the monk ran after the leader, yelling, "Hey, you forgot the crucifix. Here, take the crucifix, too." Then something snapped in the leader of the robbers and he gave up his life of crime and became a monk.

This shows the importance of acting selflessly: it frees you from accumulating more karma, elevates you to a completely different level of reality and even changes the lives of others because it communicates *something* to them, an intangible reality, a higher reality.

Thus, in the process of liberating yourself you are also liberating other human beings. You give them another reality, not with philosophical ideas, but through your beingness. That is because the energy of Liberation is a real energy, a subtle vibration that is communicated to animals, people, plants, to everything. So while you are liberating yourself or maintaining your state of Liberation, you are exuding an energy that other people can pick up. You are helping the greater work of liberating the whole planet, helping the whole of human society turn around and become truly human, not inhuman as it is now. You are part of the great process of Planetary Transformation. ✷

23

THE ENERGY OF
ENLIGHTENMENT

The first twenty-five years of the twenty-first century is one of the
most dramatic historical periods in the life of the planet, and it will
determine largely what happens to Humanity during the rest of the century. You could say that it is the planet's crunch time, when the planetary
destiny is going to be changed either for the better or for the worse.[9]

First of all, for the past sixty million years of evolution of our planet,
our Sun has been exposed to all kinds of energies and vibrations as it
moves through different locations of space within the galactic system, but
now our Sun has come to a region of space where it is being bombarded by
very high-frequency vibrations, vibrations that it has never encountered
before. The Sun is trying to absorb this extra energy so that it does not hit
the planetary structures within the Solar System and disturb them too
much, but there may come a point when it will not be able to handle the
extra energy. If that happens the Solar System will be flooded with such
high-frequency energies that life on Earth will radically, fundamentally
change, either in a destructive direction (toward materiality) or in a posi-

9. The cosmic energies affecting the Solar System, and their effects on the planet, are de-
scribed in detail in the authors trilogy of works: *Planetary Transformation: A Personal Guide to
Embracing Planetary Change* (Sounding-Light Publishing, 2010); *The New Planetary Reality: The
Coming Avatāra and the Nine Paths to Enlightenment* (Sounding-Light Publishing, 2012); and *The
New Heaven and the New Earth* (Sounding-Light Publishing, 2014).

tive direction (toward a speeding up of human evolution)—depending on whether we respond to it negatively or positively.

This negative or positive reaction is what the Bible refers to as "the separation of the sheep and the goats" (Matthew 25: 32). Remember, the New Testament is not written in philosophical language; it talks about ordinary things, so it says that when the big changes come, Humanity will be separated like the sheep and the goats—those who go with the new and those who do not.

This means that we can expect, along with huge upheavals in society, a certain amount of unsteadiness in the planetary structure, which could mean increasingly bad weather and unusual weather patterns—no summer in some places, no winter in others. The weather is just one way our Mother Earth reacts to external influences, but there will also be other reactions—eruptions of volcanoes, earthquakes, strange phenomena in the sky, and so on. These are external reactions but there will also be internal reactions because all the extra solar systemic energies are also impacting on our Astral World. This means we will see more people channelling and having psychic visions, more people with psychic powers, and whereas nowadays intellectualism is the normal thing, at that time psychism will be normal too, another side effect of the whole planetary mess-up.

Another problem is that the Energy of Matter—BRAHMĀ, "God-into matter", the Third Aspect of the Holy Trinity (BRAHMĀ-VIṢṆU-ŚIVA)— is increasing, and the materialists respond to it very well. So the materialists will respond to the materialistic energy and develop the power of materialism … Then who is going to do the work of Enlightenment?

The Light of Nirvāṇa

The Energy of Enlightenment has nothing to do with all those other energies. The Energy of Enlightenment, or BODHICITTA in Sanskrit, is the steady Light coming from the Nirvāṇic World, which is the steady centre of the Cosmos. From there the Light comes down to the Buddhic dimensions, then to the Mental World (the Heaven World), the Astral World (called the Astral Light in the Esoteric Language) and right down to the Physical World. It is a universal Light that shines through all of Space all the time, and always will.

It is important to understand that world picture and how you are going to fit into it, and whether you will be able to sustain yourself when those great transformations come. And the only way to do that is: attach yourself to the Energy of Light, the Energy of Enlightenment, the Light-Consciousness, because it is always stable and will remain stable under all conditions. Even if the whole Solar System disappears, that Light—the Interior Spiritual Sun, the Light of Nirvāṇa, the Light of the Kingdom of God—remains ever unchanging no matter what transformations happen in the lower dimensions (the Physical, Astral, and Mental Worlds).

Because of all these massive happenings on Earth, and also because most people do not know their own inner direction, many people will be distracted and will feel restless inside, and there could be a major shift in people's attitudes towards either the positive or the negative side.

Remember, this option has always been there for Humanity, but unfortunately in the past people did not respond correctly. There was a great energy of renewal that precipitated the French Revolution, but Humanity responded to it with violence. There was a great energy of renewal that started the Russian Revolution, but Humanity responded to it with violence. There was a great energy of renewal that precipitated the First World War and the Second World War, but the people responded to that energy negatively.

Now there is a massive energy again, an even bigger one, so the question is: How are we going to respond to it?

Many people nowadays want instant Enlightenment, but there is no such thing. Some people have psychic visions and experiences like astral travel and think they are enlightened; some have Kuṇḍalinī experiences and think they are enlightened; and some experience a religious frenzy at a fundamentalist meeting and think they are enlightened. So first of all: What is Enlightenment?

Enlightenment is really Light, Light-Consciousness. You can have all kinds of experiences but they are not the Enlightenment that Buddha spoke of: Illumination, the complete liberation from human and planetary conditions, which means nothing can touch you because you are always centred in your own Being, always centred in the Light. Those other experiences are just transitory stages—still part of the Enlightenment process but not *the final, complete Enlightenment.* The Bright Light of Nirvāṇa—that is the final, complete Enlightenment. Nothing less.

That Light is within you already but first you have to locate it. You may find it in the Third-Eye Chakra or in the Heart or Crown Chakra, but after you locate it, you have to hold yourself steady in that Light, which is perpetually shining, unmoving, immovable. Your house can collapse around you, the world can blow up, but you remain steady because no cosmic phenomena, no planetary phenomena—*nothing*—can touch that Light. Why? Because the Light is beyond the worlds of Creation; it is part of the uncreated Universe, the uncreated Reality, which is not touched by whatever happens in Time and Space whatsoever.

If you cannot hold yourself steady in the Light you will feel a sense of restlessness, a physical, emotional and mental restlessness, feeling that you are missing something or you are not getting anywhere, that you should be doing something else. It was prophesied even in the New Testament that the "elect", those who had already stepped on the Spiritual Path and were destined for Enlightenment, would be lead astray and distracted by psychic phenomena and all the chaos in the world (Matthew 24: 24).

And you who are on the Spiritual Path will be unstable, too, because you will get pressure from the outside world, from the Astral World and from all kinds of sources, and you will want to go along with that pressure, like the people who were swept along, like leaves in the wind, by the French Revolution, the Russian Revolution and the two World Wars.

So it is important to first of all understand the esoteric side of things and secondly find the source of Light within you and abide by it no matter what other people do or don't do, no matter what the world condition is. What is more, you also have a responsibility in this, because the Energy of the Light is trying to penetrate into Humanity. The Light of Nirvāṇa is not like an electric bulb; it is an *intelligent* Light, it is the Light of God, the Mind of God, *Cosmic Intelligence*. It is a supercosmic, intelligent Mind made of Light.

That supernatural Light is descending into Creation, into the Solar System, and at the same time there are all these cosmic vibrations influencing the Solar System, forming what we call the Cosmic Cross—the descending Light as the vertical arm and the waves of electromagnetic forces and high-frequency vibrations as the horizontal arm. The story of the Crucifixion in the New Testament was really about the Cosmic Christ crucified in the temporary Jesus. Jesus was a human being and the Cosmic Christ was the descending Light, the Light of Nirvāṇa, and His crucifixion was a symbol of what is happening now with Humanity.

Human beings will be "crucified" between the Light-Energy coming down and all the natural energies and manifestations impacting on Humanity. There will be so-called supernatural manifestations (*so-called* because they will actually be psychic energies or events). People will have visions, perform miracles, foretell the future and heal, and they will think they have attained the Kingdom of God. Remember, there is nothing wrong with healing and performing miracles, but it is an intermediary stage, not on the level of Nirvāṇa, the realm of Light.

The materialists will be swept away with the material energies, the material stimulation of the planet, and the psychics will be swept away with the psychic stream, with the astral energies that will be bombarding the planet from the Astral World. But the true spiritual disciples will hold themselves steady in the Light, and only they will understand what is behind the cataclysmic events.

Working for the Forces of Light

Ideally, the Forces of Light—the Saints, Sages and Spiritual Warriors who work for the Light and go by many names: the Spiritual Hierarchy, the Forces of the Christ, the Planetary Light Forces, the Kingdom of the Light—should win. They should be able to establish the Kingdom of God on Earth. But they have the same problem today that they had two thousand years ago: Humanity is spiritually ignorant. The Buddha came and explained all about the Spiritual Path and Humanity did not go along with it. Christ came and explained all about the Spiritual Path and Humanity did not go along with it. (In fact, He could not even get one village, Jerusalem, to go along with it!)

Now we have run out of choices; people will have to respond whether they like it or not. In those days they could say, "Come back next time, Buddha, and I will listen to you" or "Come back next time, Christ, and I will I listen to you." Now there is no next time: you are either in or out. If you really want to help, you have to switch over to the side of the Spiritual Hierarchy and work with those beings who are consciously trying to enable the pure Light of Divinity to manifest on this planet—because if you do not work for them, then you are against them.

The Christ said that if you are not with Him, you are against Him (Luke 11: 23). This is not because you are consciously against Him (or the Forces of Light). It just means that if you are not helping you will be part of the mass of Humanity that gets swept away. And this time it will be even more urgent. In the past, our Solar Logos did not have the same problems and the planet was hit with cosmic energies but not on the scale that is about to happen now. So now it is even more important that you maintain your focus on wanting to be enlightened and wanting the planet to be enlightened, because only the Universal Light, the Light of Nirvāṇa, can stabilize those conditions.

As I said, the times are changing fast and the situation is becoming more and more critical. If we do not do the right thing, history tells us that we will have an age of misery and suffering. On the other hand, we could have a Golden Age, the most amazing age that ever existed on this planet, better than Atlantis at its peak, better then anything any philosopher has ever dreamed of. But it will not happen until we have Light-Workers, *real* Light-Workers—which is another problem. There are many people in North America who call themselves light-workers. They are mediums and psychics who work with psychic and astral energies and forces, not with Light, but they call themselves light-workers.

So you have to distinguish between what is psychism and what is the true Light within you (and within Creation). It is only when you have reached that Light and can work with it that you are a real Light-Worker. The planet needs Light, not psychic phenomena; it needs Light-Warriors who have the same ideal as the Christ and the Buddha, the ideal of the Kingdom of God within you. That is the vision and you have to work towards that and nothing less.

What is your idea of Enlightenment? Is it some sort of a physical, psychic or Kuṇḍalinī experience, or a miraculous power? If you hold that view, you will be stuck on the intermediary stages and you will easily get distracted. If anybody with magical powers comes along, you will

---

The Light is an invisible force, and as that invisible energy works inside you it will radiate out to other people. When the Christ gave this Light to the disciples He said, "Now go out and teach the world" (Matthew 28: 19). When they started panicking and asked Him what they were going to say to people, He told them not to worry, that the Holy Spirit would guide them.

By surrendering and allowing the Light power (symbolized by the Holy Spirit) to work through you, you will say exactly the right thing to the right person, spontaneously. Then you can be working for the Forces of Light twenty-four hours a day, all your life. All you have to do is make the big switch—to the Light. Be aware that you are a Light-Worker in the true sense, and do not worry about what to do: you will be guided to do the right thing.

immediately rush after them because they can do something you can't do and therefore you will think they are enlightened.

If you do that, you are not holding the idea of Enlightenment correctly in your mind. Nothing below Nirvāṇa should be your goal or vision. Otherwise you will get swept away in those currents of energies, which is okay, but you are not going to help our Planetary Hierarchy establish the Kingdom of Light on Earth. There is only one Kingdom of Light and if you want to work for the Kingdom of Light you have to dedicate yourself to it.

The Forces of Light, from which all the great Teachers have come, have been keeping this planet going for thousands and thousands of years. They are the ones who have kept the life of the planet at a stable level, but now they need you more than at any other time because of these colossal cosmic happenings.

So you have to decide: Do you want psychic powers or other intermediate-stage experiences? Or do you want the steady Light of Nirvāṇa, the bright, eternal Reality? Can you say, "Yes, I am a Spiritual Warrior, I am part of the Forces of Light. All that matters is Light, Light, Light—being in the Light, releasing the Light, giving Light to the world"?

If you hold that as your vision, then you can move towards it and work towards that vision, knowing that you will get there because you will get help. If your vision is unstable, however, the Light Forces cannot help you, for the simple reason that you are under the sway of the forces of Super-Nature—the astral forces, the mental forces and the forces of the causal dimensions. That is because you are working through your solar plexus, so the Light-Current cannot work with you. It is just not possible. But if your vision is stable, if you know that your ultimate goal is the bright Light of Nirvāṇa and that is where you are going—no ifs, no buts, no maybes—then you are seeking the proper Enlightenment and you will get there. It is important to understand that you need to be steady internally before the Light can work with you.

So your task is to understand what you are looking for. In the early days people only wanted Enlightenment for themselves, and there are still many people in the world who think that way. But we are all part of a living, breathing Humanity that needs to be liberated, that needs to be brought face to face with the Light. In this cosmic scheme the group is more important than the individual.

As a Spiritual Warrior you are part of a team working for Planetary Liberation, working to create understanding in the minds of people so that they can be with the Light and release the Light into the world. And when these momentous problems come, you will be on the right track and be able to hold yourself steady in the Light because you know that that is your job. In a real battle situation the commander might give your team an order to hold the fortress while another team has another task. If you are a good warrior you will hold the fortress until you die. In the meantime the other warriors can do what they have to do for the larger plan of the war.

There is a war going on now on this planet, a war between the forces of ignorance, materialism and delusion and the Forces of Light. It has been going on for thousands of years but now it is more pressing, and the real Spiritual Warriors have to come forward and say, "This is our purpose: we will hold our planet no matter what, even if we all perish."

So you have to make a commitment to be an agent for the Light, a Spiritual Warrior helping the Forces of Light. If along the way you become psychic or develop miraculous powers, that is fine. If you can use them for the good, use them; if not, then do not use them. It is not an issue. The issue is to channel the Light, to hold the Light inside you and be a Light-Warrior. There is no power greater than the Light, no wisdom greater than the Light. The central pillar of Life is Light—it always has been and always will be.

If you can understand this you will join and do it willingly, not because you will get something out of it, not because Buddha or Christ will give you a medal, but because you know that this is your duty as a human being to your planet. If you are an intelligent human being you will see the plan, its purpose and *your* destiny in it, and then nothing will matter except that you fulfil your destiny. Otherwise you will be just another human being running around wanting this and that for yourself, and you will be swept along with the great tidal waves sweeping the planet, because you were not aligned to the Real, the eternal values that the Christ, the Buddha and all the great Masters have been trying to teach:

Hold steady to the Light, enter the Kingdom of God, be in Light-Consciousness! ⚔

24

THE ART OF THE
SPIRITUAL WARRIOR

The Art of the Spiritual Warrior is difficult to explain because most people associate Warriorship with fighting. In the movies, what do warriors do? Fight. What do soldiers do? Fight. What does everybody do? Fight. So society has a false impression that to be a warrior means that you have to kill people for social, religious or political reasons, or any reason whatsoever. Unfortunately, this is a completely wrong idea because the Spiritual Warrior is actually a sacred person, a spiritual person.

A Spiritual Warrior becomes an outpost for the Light-Energy. You cannot become a Warrior unless you work with Light. This is important, because all the forces of the Cosmos are made out of Light. Any energy, even the most materialistic energy like electricity, magnetism or any gross physical energy, is just a lower degree or frequency of Light. The Spiritual Warrior works with the higher frequencies of Light, with the Divine Light itself.

The Art of the Spiritual Warrior means that as a Spiritual Warrior your life flows spontaneously from the Infinite, that energies from a spiritual dimension are flowing through you. So the energies move your sword, or you move the energies with your sword (or whatever weapon or movement you use). You and the Cosmos are inseparably connected: whatever the Cosmos is, you are; whatever you are, the Cosmos is.

There are two ways of making any movement: one is to learn it by heart so that you can do it subconsciously and the other is to do it with full awareness of the Divine, with full awareness that every action is a divine action that emerges from Infinity, from Higher Consciousness, from your Higher Self. This means that you are training not to win a championship but to transform your inner being, to become a particle of Light through whatever movement you are making, because whatever movement you are making is only part of the movement of Life itself. So the Art of the Spiritual Warrior is something you do twenty-four hours a day.

Training with a sword or other weapon is only secondary; it teaches you to focus your mind on a principle, say, the principle of living in the moment continually. But once you have mastered that principle it starts functioning inside you all the time, which means that you can apply it anytime, when you are talking to somebody, when you are at work, when you are in crisis. This is what distinguishes you from normal martial artists who train very hard and master a certain skill. Naturally, that skill is reflected in their lives, but not one hundred percent of their lives, because they only understand a principle through actually doing their martial art.

A Spiritual Warrior, on the other hand, understands a principle under all conditions, no matter what he or she is doing, because Warrior skills are an extension of martial arts skills into every part of the Warrior's being. *That* is what makes a Spiritual Warrior.

Many people spend a lot of their time developing themselves through the martial arts, and that is good, of course; it is an excellent development for the person. But they do not understand what that involves: they should become martial *artists*. Notice that the word is martial *art*; it is not martial *fighting to death* or martial *killing*. An art is a creative activity, so the very term tells you what warriors should be—artists who create through self-discipline and by awakening the inner powers within themselves. Warriorship is an art, a creative activity, not a matter of simply killing people.

Clear Mind, Spontaneous Action

The Warrior principles are few. The first principle is: *There is neither success nor failure; no action is successful and no action is a failure.* Normally, if you succeed in life you are very happy, but if you fail you feel down that you have not achieved your purpose in life. But once you understand this principle and apply it in your life, you can relax. Gone is the idea of competition, gone is the idea of winning a prize, gone is the idea that you may fail.

For the Spiritual Warriors there is no success or failure. There is only action. And the result of the action, whatever it is, does not belong to them but to the Cosmos; therefore they have an even mind and nothing disturbs their tranquillity. If you can apply even this one Warrior Principle in every part of your life, it will change you one hundred percent; you will become a new person. When you do something it won't matter whether you succeed or fail; you just do the action in the moment, spontaneously, as it flows out of you, and whatever happens, happens—and you are quite happy with that.

This is why the ancient Master Warriors, when asked by their disciples, "When did you truly master the sword?" would reply, "When I hung up my sword." In other words, the sword was truly mastered when it was not being used anymore. This means that you do not need the sword because everything that the sword taught you, you do *automatically.* You are applying the *principles* you learned through your weapon all the time; you do not need to think about it, to look at a situation and figure out which principle you are going to apply. There is no thinking. The mind is clear, the action spontaneous.

But even if you learn a principle you can still miss the point; that is how subtle this art is. The art is not a marital art, yet it is; and it is not about learning principles, yet it is. The Art of the Warrior is just doing … just doing … just doing. That is why it is so difficult to put into words.

The Art of the Warrior is absolute and utter *simplicity*, though you train and learn complicated movements because they teach you something. But even if you spend hours and hours every day developing those qualities and you master them, that's still not *it*. It is still not the Art of the Spiritual Warrior.

The Art of the Spiritual Warrior begins after that, but you have to go through all the training and develop yourself. Why? Because if you want to go to university you have to go through preliminary training—elementary school and high school—otherwise you cannot handle the high-level knowledge of the university. It is the same in the Warrior School: you have to practise certain movements and techniques as part of your preliminary training for the real understanding, which you could miss unless you did the preliminary training. All the physical training, therefore, is only to prepare you for the *higher* learning, the *higher* training, which is *all inside you*; it has nothing to do with anything outside of you.

To understand this you have to understand this principle of *only doing*, without thinking about success or failure. If you make a movement and you are striving too hard, trying to be a perfectionist, you will fail even if the movement is perfect. You fail internally because you have strayed from the principle of no success and no failure—the evenness and harmony of the Cosmos. Many people who try to be successful have to be internally disharmonious to achieve it. They are tense, agitated.

In the olden days Warriors learned all kinds of sword techniques for discipline, for understanding principles, but they very seldom applied them in real battle situations because they were too cumbersome and complicated. In a real battle you just did one movement, and you either lived or you died. In the movies Bruce Lee does all kinds of flying leaps and somersaults, but if you did that in a real battle situation you would be cut down before you finished the first move. In a real fight you would be absolutely simple, with minimal action, minimal movement, minimal force. You would just do whatever the situation required, immediately, spontaneously. Now!

They want badly to succeed, so they put a lot of effort into it, but they are out of harmony with the Cosmos, out of harmony with themselves and out of harmony with Life as it is in the moment.

This is why it is so difficult to explain in words what a Master Warrior is. The Master Warrior is somebody who lives life just as it is. I will give you an example: Some of the best Master Warriors were Zen monks. There is a story of a young disciple who asked a Zen Master Warrior, "What happens after you are enlightened?" The Master replied, "Well, before enlightenment I used to chop wood. After enlightenment I am still chopping wood." And that is all there is to it. There is no failure, no success, and nothing has seemingly changed.

But *everything* has changed, although it is impossible to describe in words. The Master Warrior *knows* how things are. The student is still seeking, questing, inquiring, wanting to know, wanting to achieve something, wanting to be successful, afraid of failure, afraid of not having enough knowledge. For the Master Warrior, if it's snowing, it's snowing; if it's raining, it's raining; if he's sick, he's sick; if he's well, he's well. *Just as it is.*

In the Stream of Enlightenment

So the Art of the Spiritual Warrior is about inner harmony, at all times and under all conditions. *And that you cannot produce wilfully.* It is not a mental structure, not something you can produce by simply saying, "I am now peaceful" or " I am now in harmony." Those are good thoughts—but that is all they are. The Warrior really *is* in harmony, without thinking about it.

This happens through a subtle process: you realize that the things you are doing have already been done even before you do them; the things you are thinking have already been thought before you think them; and the things you are feeling have already been felt before you feel them. And everything that happens to you has already happened and you are just going through the motions. *It has all been done for you already.*

Then you settle down and your life is in harmony; you no longer have to worry whether you succeed or fail, whether you pass the exam or not, whether you get this job or not—everything has already been done. If you're meant to live in the gutter, you live in the gutter. If you're meant to be the head of a company, you are the head of a company. And if you're fired, who cares? But it is not that you don't care; it is not a kind of an unintelligent indifference. You are settled *inside*, settled in the bosom of the Father, or if you like, in the great current of Life itself, and having settled in you do not struggle anymore.

Whatever you do not expect happens. You do not expect miracles to happen, so they do. You want to be simple and non-intellectual, so you get knowledge. You want to be meek and inoffensive, so you get strength. You get whatever you need. A fish just flaps its tail and moves through the water, automatically. It doesn't have to work out how to do it. The problem with human beings is that they are always trying to work out *how*. How am I going to deal with my family? How am I going to deal with my angry boss? How am I going to pass the examination? How am I going to earn a living? Their minds are always working things out and they always want to be something other than what they are. If they are poor, they want to be rich. If they are rich, they want to be super rich. If they are super rich, they want to be mega rich. There is no limit to wanting to be something else.

When you want to be something else it disturbs the equilibrium inside you. Once that balance is disturbed you go up and down, swinging from happy to unhappy, from misery to ecstasy, because you are not in harmony with yourself, not in harmony with the Cosmos. Once you understand this you will realize what an amazing journey life is, and then your destiny will open up and you will realize that you always had that destiny but just were not in it. The train had always been moving except you were not on it. Now you are on the train, you are in the movement of things, what the Easterners call *being in the Stream*.

This is the Art of the Spiritual Warrior: you have to enter the Stream in order to cross it and become a Spiritual Warrior. You cannot do it unless you enter the Stream. That is what we try to do in the Warrior School, because it is only by wading into the Stream that you can get to the other side. On the other side is where you become a Spiritual Warrior, with the full potential of being what you really are.

When you are a Spiritual Warrior you realize that all the activity and training you went through is actually counterproductive, but you also understand that as a student you had to go through that to get to this stage of understanding. You had to go through all the fights, trials, struggles and tribulations until you suddenly realized, "Hey, I'm already there. I don't need the sword anymore; I'll hang it up in the cupboard." This is when Warriorship is not a science anymore but an art, the art of living itself, and you begin to *live* life full on, without any fear, worries or doubts about yourself.

In the olden days the real Spiritual Warriors went into battle not caring whether they were going to live or die. They said, "If destiny requires that I die, I die; if destiny requires that I live, I live." Either way it did not disturb their inner tranquillity. Why? Because they were no longer in the Stream; they were on the other side.

On the other side of the Stream there is only harmony and equilibrium, only one continuum of existence. You die, you are still in the continuum; you are born, you are in the continuum. You are in this world, you are in the continuum; you are in the Heaven World, you are in the continuum. Wherever you are, you are still in the continuum. Therefore your mind is tranquil; there is no need to worry about anything, no need to struggle for anything.

You can understand these principles at any moment: you are sleeping and you suddenly wake up. It is like Enlightenment: when it comes, it comes spontaneously; it is not pre-planned. You cannot say, "I'm going to be enlightened by tomorrow afternoon at three o'clock." It doesn't work that way. You struggle in the Stream, do your best at what you think you need to do, and then suddenly it comes. When it comes to you it is very simple and you realize that you have been enlightened for a long time. The only difference is, you did not know it and now you know it. Enlightenment is a style of living; it is as simple as being where you are and not wanting to be somewhere else.

That is what it means to be in a state of Enlightenment and that is what it means to be an enlightened Spiritual Warrior. If you need to fight, you fight. If it's time for peace, then it's peace. Whatever you need to do in whatever occasion that arises, you do it spontaneously, without pre-planning or thinking it out.

The Art of the Spiritual Warrior is just to be what you already are—nothing more, nothing less. It does not mean that you will never encounter negativity, that everybody will be nice to you and send you good wishes all the time. During the time of the Christ, the time of Buddha, the time of the Zen Masters, the time of all the great Teachers in all parts of the world, there were wars, people were killing each other and there was disease and poverty—just like now. But those conditions did not alter the inner reality of the Masters.

So the Way of the Spiritual Warrior is about being in the moment and being what you are. And it involves your *whole life*, not just your training. Training is fine but that is not what the Art of the Spiritual Warrior is about, not until you transfer what you learn from your training into your life, your day-to-day living. *Then* you are there; you have crossed the Stream. Then you have mastered the Art of the Spiritual Warrior. ✣

PART THREE

~

THE SPIRITUAL WARRIOR SCHOOL

THE INNER TEACHING

~ 25 ~

THE SPIRITUAL WARRIOR
SEES GOD INSIDE HIMSELF

Everybody on this planet is meant to be a Spiritual Warrior. But eighty percent of the population have no understanding of the Spiritual Path, and within the remaining twenty percent who are tuned in, the majority are tuned in wrongly, mainly due to lack of proper teaching. So I will try to explain to you what it really means to be a Spiritual Warrior.

First of all, you can only become a Spiritual Warrior when you have released the power of the Warrior inside you, and to release that power inside you, you have to go inside yourself. In ancient times there were three types of schools—warrior schools, devotee schools, and wisdom schools—but they had only one objective, common to all of them, and that was: entering inside yourself. If your consciousness is always turned outward, then the Divine Power *inside* you cannot manifest.

I'm talking about a real power and how it is expressed. Whether it is expressed in the art of war or in music, scientific research, medicine, politics or any field of life, it is all the same Divine Power. But you need access to it in the first place, before you can start manifesting it physically to change the world condition.

So the first requirement is that you have to enter inside yourself, and then bit by bit you have to go through the stages of finding the Divine Power inside you and then expressing it. One possibility is the Way of Yoga, which is practised in India. There, they specialize in meditation techniques for acquiring siddhis, or magical powers. That was the original purpose of the HAṬHA YOGA system, for example. In Sanskrit, the word HAṬHA means "very hard, very difficult, requiring tremendous power", and the system was devised to completely master the physical body, in every aspect from breathing to the heartbeat, and through that mastery attain psychic powers. It was the same in China, at the Shaolin Temple, where the monks developed and awakened psychic, or occult, powers through hard physical training.

The Way of the Warrior, therefore, is just another form of Yoga. The only difference is that the yogīs of India used passive methods, suspending bodily activity by holding body postures and their breath for long periods of time, while the Warriors did exactly the opposite, engaging in strenuous activity for hours and hours every day.

So there are two systems—one passive, one active—but for the same end: to feel the Divine Energy and Power within and express it either in terms of miraculous powers (siddhis) or the powers of the Warrior.

Connecting to God in the Heart

To awaken the power within us, we first have to move our attention from outside to inside. Whether you belong to a martial arts school, a warrior school or a yoga school, it is the same principle: before the Deity within you can become part of your external life, you have to contact

---

Yoga postures are only a means of developing power inside you; they are not an end in themselves. In the West the idea of Haṭha Yoga has degenerated to keeping fit and healthy and reducing stress, which is fine but nothing like its original vision and ideals, which are still practised in India today. The real Haṭha Yoga Schools aim to develop internal powers. It is the same with martial arts: nowadays people practise only for physical fitness and maybe to gain self-confidence, but they have no idea of the immense possibilities behind what they are doing.

the Deity within you. So the basic requirement is simply to turn your attention inside. And this may take years, depending on which system you follow, how you follow it, whether you have a good or bad teacher. A real Spiritual Teacher will tell you that it is not the outer action—the technique or process you are doing—that counts; it is your internal connection through that technique, how you connect to the internal reality of the Divinity within you. It is a process of *connection*.

So for many years the training is about learning to connect. The first big shift is taking your attention from outside concerns to inside concerns. Having established that, you have to persevere with your meditation until you begin to actually feel the presence of Divinity, which is like an all-pervading Energy.

The easiest point of reference, that is, the first centre through which you can feel the Divine Presence is your Heart Chakra. In other words, your first experience that the Deity dwells within you, and within everybody else and the whole Cosmos, comes through the Heart. The first step, therefore, is to move your attention to your Heart and try to feel the presence of the Deity inside you. This step in itself is amazing because it will readjust the way you think about everything in life. It will readjust your conception of religion, your philosophy of life, your conception of who you are—everything will be thrown out and you will be radically changed.

For example, if you were brought up in one of the orthodox religious traditions, such as Christianity, Judaism, Islam, Hinduism or Buddhism, you were told that there is a God somewhere *out there*, that there is a heaven somewhere *out there*, and that you will go to that heavenly place and there you will meet God. But it's all *out there*. When you enter the Heart, however, you realize that God is not out there but actually right inside you. And what is more, you do not have to wait until you die to see God; you can see the Deity right now, in this very moment. When you enter the Heart, your whole understanding of religion will be shattered and you will have to revise it to a completely new level.

With this comes another change: how you look at life. Previously, if you were a good Muslim or Roman Catholic or Jew, you were told by the authorities that you have to be good, and they told you why: if you are bad you will go to hell; if you are good you will go to heaven. Since this was a rational reason, you tried to be good so that you could earn the right to go to heaven. Once the Heart Chakra is penetrated, however, and you begin to feel the presence of the Divine inside you as a natural fact, you will not be concentrating so much on *trying* to be good; you will actually *be* good, because you will realize that any time you are not doing something good it causes some kind of tension or maladjustment inside you. You will find that the state of goodness is your natural, normal state, and any time you have even the slightest feeling of anger or discord, it will upset something inside you—an internal harmony or an internal reality.

So it is not merely a philosophical idea: you try to be good because the Pope or the Dalai Lama told you to. You are good because when you do something wrong you feel it inside; it actually hurts. It is not necessarily a physical hurt but an internal discomfort that tells you that you have moved away from your centre, which is the inner connection with Divinity. And this applies whether you do something wrong physically, emotionally or mentally. An angry thought towards somebody registers in the Heart just as powerfully as if you had actually done something in anger. It makes no difference to the Heart whether it is a bad thought, emotion or physical action; the result of discomfort inside you will manifest in the same way.

At this stage you can become supersensitive. You have connected to the Heart and can begin to sense Cosmic Harmony, which is the first manifestation of the Divine Presence, but the start of this process can be difficult as your Heart becomes increasingly more sensitive to your own disharmony—and the disharmony of others and also the world itself. This happens to spiritual people in all the religions: they become depressed when they enter this stage because they see the agony of the world. They see that there is so much suffering everywhere, so much violence and disharmony, and they get swamped and lose hope for the world and Mankind. This is how existentialist philosophy arose in the West. Originally, the first existentialist philosophers were people who had sensitivity to life, but then they realized that life was a total mess and they lost their hope for Mankind. So they got into a negative stream of philosophy.

But there is a positive stream inside everybody. On the innermost layer of a person, beyond what even the person can touch or understand, the Divine Presence is shining all the time, no matter what wrong the person has done. Beyond the physical self, the emotional self and the mental self there is the same positive, dynamic point of Light in everyone. The presence of the Divinity is within every human Heart—I'm not talking about the physical heart but the Spiritual Heart of every human being—without exception. Even the worst dictator who ever existed had the same Divine Presence shining inside him.

Forgiveness of Sins

Entering the Heart will revolutionize your whole way of thinking about people, and you will realize that the fundamental problem of Humanity is that people are not tuned in to the Divine Presence within them. On the Soul level, as Souls, we are all in harmony with the Divine Life itself, but on the personality level people are out of tune with that harmony and because of that they manage to do all kinds of negative things—think negative thoughts, feel negative feelings and perform negative actions. This is at the root of the Roman Catholic idea of confession and the forgiveness of sin.

The original idea of confession was that you went to the priest because you had a sense that the wrong you did must be rectified in terms of your awareness of the Divine Reality inside you, of your relationship to God.

You knew that you had to do something to re-establish the connection you had lost by doing something wrong. The priest would then tell you to say ten Our Fathers and fifteen Hail Marys and go to mass—that is, to put your life back onto a spiritual track so that you would regain your internal harmony and re-establish your connection with God. That was the original idea behind confession and the forgiveness of sin, returning to the state that you had lost, but nowadays this is not understood.

If you understand this, however, you know that you do not need to go to a priest. Let's say you had a wrong thought or got upset about something. All you have to do is sit down and meditate and re-enter the Heart. The Heart knows that what you did was wrong, so the wrong is dissolved and you move from disharmony to harmony. You do not need to go to church. You rectify your relation with the Deity by yourself for the simple reason that the Deity is within *you*, not in the Church.

This is where the Church went wrong and strayed from the original idea of releasing people from inner disharmony. People began to think that only the Church and the priests had the power to forgive sins. What they did not know, and still do not know, is that the power of forgiveness is inside you. The Divinity *is* inside you and that Divinity is the power that forgives you, provided you establish the right connection again.

I am sure that when you were a child there were times when you got annoyed at your parents and screamed at them. When you thought it over and apologized, however, they forgave you. At that moment you were harmonized internally because you felt that yes, you had sent out a wrong message, but then you took it back. Now, when you take back your anger you re-establish the right connection with your own Heart, the centre of positivity inside you, and everything is well. You no longer have to feel guilty.

This is another problem nowadays: you are taught to feel guilty for your whole life. This comes from another wrong teaching of the Church, that you are born a sinner and cannot help it. Well, we may be sinners, but we *can* help it, because we can *return to the Source*—the Heart, the Divine Presence within—and that source is always positive, always good, always harmonious and always loving.

Jesus taught this life principle as forgiveness, forgiving yourself and forgiving others. If somebody has done you a wrong, well, you forgive that person. If you have done someone a wrong, then forgive yourself. Forgiveness simply means: releasing the negative thought, feeling, or action from your system. Look at the Middle East. There are two sides and neither forgives the other and they have been fighting for two or three thousand years. They do not live the law of the Christ: forgiveness. And when you do not live by forgiveness, the negativity and violence keep coming back and coming back and coming back.

The process of forgiveness starts with the understanding that the initial violent act was an outer act; it had nothing to do with your internal life nor with the internal life of the other person. As I said, within the innermost Heart of everybody is the Divine Self, the shining presence of the Deity. Once you realize that, you will not engage in negativity against the other because you know that they are acting through ignorance. They are like demons obsessed by outer reality, ignorant of the

---

As a Warrior you first seek the Divine Presence inside. That is step number one. And the easiest way to do that is to enter into the Heart. When you first enter the Heart you will discover that the Divine Reality just appears to be there, like a kind of stillness and peace. But later on, the next revelation is that the Deity within is not like a still life painting but is *dynamically active*, continually moving, continually maintaining Creation.

This is the start of the next stage, when you learn what this activity is, what it means for you and what your part in that activity is. *Then* you become the Spiritual Warrior. Because once you have sussed out your part in the great cosmic drama you can start using the same power of the Divinity to start acting. You act through the Divine Power *as it expresses itself through you in your particular situation*.

internal Reality. So do not engage, do not fight back. Forget the idea of an eye for an eye because that keeps negativity going. Just disengage.

You realize that there are trillions of situations for trillions of beings—angels, humans, animals—and that the one same Power acts through all of them. You also realize that if all humans would only tune into the Divine Presence within and start acting from that Divine Principle, this planet would turn into a planet of Light, with immense fields of Light coming from within and blazing out into the Solar System.

When you reach this level of inner development of the Heart you will understand that your part in the Divine Action is to teach, to heal, to inspire others—or whatever. Every human being has a pattern of the Divine Law inside them that they are supposed to be acting out in their lifetime. There are general patterns of activities for human beings—obviously, all healing people are engaged in healing and politicians are engaged in politicking—but within those patterns there are individual variations, individual themes. You have to discover what your variation is. If you are a healer, then what is *your* speciality in healing? What does your internal Heart tell you that you can do? How does your life-force need to express itself?

This is the stage of Service, when you have realized the Divine within and you allow the Divinity to shine through you, in whatever field you choose or whatever abilities you may have. But it is important to discover how to use that internal connection to express the special skills you have in life *correctly*. The dark warrior uses his skills for purely selfish ambition, for his or her own advantage and progress, and the Warrior of Light uses them for the benefit of all. So the lesson here is: first enter into the Heart and then begin to express your communion with the Heart in action, for the benefit of Humanity and the planet. ✑

THE MYSTERY OF
THE HOLY GRAIL

The mystery of the Holy Grail will help you understand that the Warrior Path is a Spiritual Path of the most profound nature, symbolized in the West as the quest for the Holy Grail by the Knights of the Round Table and in the East as the quest for Immortality by the Chinese Spiritual Warriors.

Originally, the real Knights of the Round Table—the initiated knights of France, Germany, Britain and other countries in Europe—and also the great Chinese Warriors, such as those from the Wudang Mountains, had spiritually enlightened Masters without whom the Warrior Schools could not have existed. The Teachers unveiled the mystery of the quest, what a Warrior should be seeking, but when the Teachers died, of course, the knowledge died with them.

In all the great traditions, therefore, the later generations did not understand what the quest was about, and it is that misunderstanding which is normally portrayed in books about the Knights of the Round Table and the Chinese Warriors. So their stories read like far-off memories of knights on a real quest mixed with materialistic ambition and ideas of worldly conquest, along with glimmers of truth. That, of course, is how it is in this world: everything spiritual after a while becomes degenerated into a material concept.

A good example today is Yoga. The original meaning of the word YOGA is "conscious union with God". Now, how many Yoga students today really think that what they are doing is consciously uniting with God? In fact, in America there are advertisements for Yoga classes actually claiming that Yoga is not a religion, that it is not about spirituality, meaning to say it is only about physical exercises. That is how degenerated things have become! After a while, even the most spiritual knowledge becomes swallowed up and absorbed in materialistic consciousness, and then the materialistic consciousness denies that there ever was any spiritual connection in the first place.

That is what happened over the centuries to the great Spiritual Warrior Schools, including the Christian Knights of the Round Table, who originally had a spiritual vision or ideal that slowly degenerated and became a worldly quest. This is why the Warrior Path is not portrayed correctly. Even modern movies like *Crouching Tiger, Hidden Dragon* or *Hero* or *The House of Flying Daggers* have about a seventy-percent correct representation of the Warrior Path, but they do not portray the real Path because the real Path is highly esoteric and you have to be a Warrior yourself to understand what it is about.

So what is this quest for the Holy Grail and what is this quest for Tao, or Conscious Immortality?

I am using these two major systems as examples: the Chinese system of Tao and the Christian system of the Holy Grail. In the stories about the Knights of the Round Table, whether in English, French, German,

---

In the West there is the story of St. George, who slew a dragon, and there is a place, Draguignan, in Southern France, named after another dragon slayer. The dragon, of course, is a Chinese symbol of the Kuṇḍalinī Force, the Feminine Force inside us and inside Nature, which is a clue to what the quest for the Holy Grail is really about.

Spanish, Hungarian, etc., the main idea is that the knights had to look for the Holy Grail. So they went to their local bishop or priest and got their blessing and then rode off in search of the Holy Grail. The problem was that nobody knew where the Holy Grail was or even what it was, so they went from one country to another and fought battles against each other and their enemies and even against monsters, demons and dragons, thinking that was part of their quest for this mysterious Holy Grail.

Unfortunately, the writers of these stories had a fertile imagination but no real Esoteric Knowledge, because the Holy Grail is not a physical thing at all. Nor is the Tao, although the Chinese warriors went out looking for a fountain that would make them immortal when they drank its water. So by that time the knowledge had already degenerated, but the basic idea that the knights and warriors had to look for something, that there was something sacred they had to sacrifice their life for, was correct. But those who had not been initiated into the Esoteric Knowledge never found what they were looking for, and many of them died in misery because of their lifelong quest.

Of course, the normal understanding of the Holy Grail is that it is the cup that Jesus drank wine out of at the Last Supper, or the cup that Joseph of Arimathea used to collect Jesus' blood when He was speared while hanging on the cross. So the knights' stories were based on looking for a cup or a spear, and when they found it they would become immortal, that is to say, they would have omnipotent powers. Even the Germans during the Second World War were looking for this cup and spear, as did many people over the centuries. Of course, nobody has found them yet because, as I said, they are not physical things. Christ did have a cup, of course, and there was a real spear that He was killed with, but they are not objects of a quest for immortality, nor do they have anything to do with it.

The Way of the Spiritual Warrior is the quest for truth, but the truth lies somewhere within things. It is a spiritual quest and the Cup and the Spear and the Fountain of Immortality are only symbols of a deeper mystery that I'm going to tell you about.

What we are really questing for as Spiritual Knights, or Spiritual Warriors, is an invisible reality. The Physical World, the Astral World and the Mental World are part of what we call the *Lower Creation*, which is perishable. The Buddhic World, the Nirvāṇic World and the worlds above are part of the *Higher Creation*, and relative to the Lower Creation they are eternal.

Of course, the most unstable reality is the Physical World, as you know, because in the Physical World everything is changing all the time; everything is being demolished and transformed into something else. The astral dimension is also unstable. After death, you will exist for a while in your astral, or psychic, body. The intellectual types will only stay there a short time because they do not have much resonance with the astral dimensions, which are based on emotions; the more emotional types will stay there longer.

Similarly, those of you who are intellectual will go to the Heaven World (if you manage to get there), and the more intellectual you were, the longer you will stay in those dimensions, because the Heaven World is a world of pure thought-structures, where your mind can explore all the possibilities of physics, science, mathematics, philosophy, theology, metaphysics or whatever. You can spend thousands of years in the heavenly dimensions, but afterward you have to move on and come back into incarnation again.

No matter how long you stay in any one of these worlds, you eventually have to move on because in these regions of Creation you cannot stay forever in a particular condition—which is why you cannot find the Fountain of Immortality on Earth because immortality, of course, is a condition in which you never die. In the Physical World, Astral World and Mental World, there is no condition in which you never die, so none of these dimensions contains the Fountain of Immortality or the Holy Grail.

So if you want to become a Spiritual Warrior, this is one thing you have to understand from day one:

Your quest will never be fulfilled here, in this reality. It has to be fulfilled in another reality.

What we have to establish about the Way of the Spiritual Warrior is that it is *spiritual*. You have to understand that there is a tremendous spiritual dimension within us that can only be approached by spiritual means. You cannot approach it by developing physical powers or psychic powers or mental powers. *That is why this quest is so difficult.* If you were told that there is a holy cup or a fountain of youth that will give you immortality, you would immediately want to figure out how to get it. But you—the personality—cannot go on this quest; you have to employ another part of you, a part you that you are normally not aware of.

You can call it the Self within you or the Fundamental Reality within you or the God within you or the Living Soul within you—whatever you like to call it, there is something in every human being, within the deeper regions of the Heart Centre, that is *not part of this Creation*.

You have a physical heart and an etheric heart, which maintain your physical body and are part of this Creation; an astral heart, which maintains the functions of your astral body and is part of this Creation; a mental heart, which maintains your mental body and is part of this Creation; and you have a causal heart, which is a half-material, half-Light reality but is also part of this Creation. But then beyond that, in the Buddhic dimensions, you have the lowest stage of the Spiritual Heart, which is *definitely* not of this Creation. And within that is the real Spiritual Heart, which is like a dynamic Light whose every scintillating, oscillating "atom" is a moment of eternity.

In the East they call it the Jewel within the Lotus, because the lotus flower represents the Heart Centre: Ōṁ Maṇi Padme Hūṁ. Ōṁ Maṇi: the "jewel"; Padme: "within the lotus"; Hūṁ: "we dissolve in it".

In the West they call it the Rose in the Heart. Whether it is symbolically called a lotus flower or a rose, it is a deeper reality within us, which is our essential immortality. We are connected through the Heart to that great Jewel within us—or if you like, the Holy Grail or the Fountain of Immortality—the Conscious Immortality within us.

To summarize: firstly, the Quest is not physical, emotional or mental; and secondly, there is another reality in a spiritual dimension where the real Quest takes place. The question is: How do we approach that other reality? How do we link this world with that world?

This brings us to the hidden meaning behind what we call the Holy Grail. The Holy Grail is a symbol of the Feminine Principle. You have to go through the Feminine Principle in order to approach the Spirit within you, the Principle of Immortality within you. That is what the quest for the Holy Grail is really about.

If you read about the Knights of the Round Table and the great Warriors of China, you will notice that there is always a female in the story. Before a knight went forth on his quest, he always had to present himself to a lady and get her blessing. She would give the knight her scarf or handkerchief and thereby became his subconscious mentor throughout the quest. He would be thinking of the lady and would have to conquer enemies and find the cup or whatever he was looking for and then take it back to the lady. Only then would his mission be completed.

The writers of these stories, although they had forgotten the truth, still knew, without knowing why, that somehow a female had to be involved in the quest. In the East, too, there was always a lady who was a protector or represented a divine reality, and the quest was done in her name or by her power. In these stories the physical female stands for something profound—the Spiritual Female—because to go from *this* reality to *that* reality there is only one bridge, and that is the Divine Feminine Consciousness, or the Feminine Principle.

This is why in the West there is Our Lady, the Virgin Mary, who acts on our behalf with the Christ, and why in the East there is Quan Yin, who acts between the warrior and the Absolute Reality, Tao.

Accordingly, we have to understand that there is a Divine Feminine Consciousness in Creation and She plays an important role in the quest for Immortality. In the modern age Our Lady's function is totally misunderstood because it has been materialized. Nowadays people pray to Our Lady to find them a parking spot or to win the lottery, which is a warped understanding of who She is. She is not just a cardboard figure you pray to for things, but the *Feminine Consciousness of the Deity Itself*, the Feminine Mind of God. She is all-powerful, a real cosmic irresistible *Power*.

So the idea that the knights had a lady who blessed them before they went off on a quest is really the materialization of a spiritual idea. And the spiritual idea is that there is a Divine Lady within Creation and She will appear to you and guide you and help you through your trials and tribulations, if and only if you invoke Her presence. At least the Christians know enough to pray to Our Lady, which means they invoke Her presence, but then they tell her what to do. (It's like praying

---

Most people know the story of how Buddha sat under a bodhi tree and stayed there until he attained Enlightenment, but what they do not know is that before that time Buddha endured twenty years of severely hard discipline, doing all kinds of painful Haṭha Yoga exercises that reduced Him to skin and bones.

In fact, Buddha was rescued by whom? A female. (Females always come to the rescue!) A village girl found Him when He was on the verge of dying, and she sensed that unless something was done for this poor holy man he would die very soon. The village girl then offered Him something to eat.

At first, the Buddha would have nothing to do with the woman, for He had become used to the harsh disciplines, the masculine, punishing way of life. But after a while He began to feel another energy coming from the young woman, who was gentle, loving, kind and compassionate. That gentle force stirred His consciousness and He accepted the food, and the village girl fed Him until His health was restored.

to God and then telling God what to do!) All you have to do is make yourself available to Our Lady and She will know exactly what to do on your behalf for your Salvation—how to take you from this world to the other world, how to make your spiritual quest successful. Whether you call Her Our Lady or Quan Yin or whatever, the *Feminine Consciousness* is the key to it all.

What does this mean? The Worlds of the Higher Creation (the Worlds of Light) are the Worlds of Conscious Immortality, where you are conscious and you know that it is forever impossible for you to die. You perceive Conscious Immortality in Nirvāṇic Consciousness, when you know that you are immortal not as an idea but from a deep internal experience—although the word *experience* is of course meaningless in this case because an experience in Nirvāṇa is not like an experience here. In *that* experience you are conscious that you are immortal, that God and the Universe are immortal, that there is a Reality that is imperishable. Even if this world here were blown apart by atomic bombs, it would not make the slightest impact on that other reality—nothing. It would not even be noticed in that other dimension, not even registering as a vibration in the Worlds of Light.

The secret behind the quest for the Holy Grail is that first of all the Grail is inside you and secondly that the quest is your life. That is why every aspect of the Warrior's life is meaningful.

There is not just one standard type of Spiritual Warrior. Some had great worldly responsibilities—they were kings or emperors; others had family responsibilities—they were married and had children; and some had no worldly responsibilities—they were monks. As a Spiritual Warrior you have your own unique task, or dharma, to fulfil according to what you are. If you are a king, then your dharma is to guide a nation or fight against enemies; if you are a monk, your dharma is to contemplate and preserve the Sacred Knowledge and hand it down to the next generation. Every Warrior has a dharma to fulfil.

The function of Our Lady is to help you fulfil your own dharma, the destiny of your individual life, and this is why the Christians still have a far-off memory that if you pray to Our Lady She will help you. But the problem is that most people do not understand that She is a spiritual help, that She is meant to help take you to the Kingdom of God, to mould and change you and help you along your *destiny line*.

Your destiny line is different from your karma. You have to understand that Our Lady's function is to help you through your *destiny*, not through your karma. You have to work out your karma yourself, without invoking Our Lady or the Divine Presence. If you are a student and fail your exam because you have not studied, don't invoke Our Lady; it has nothing to do with Her. You have to distinguish between your personal karma, which you created (and continue to create), and the function of the Divine Presence, what the Divine Being is supposed to do for you. Having made that distinction, you will find that Our Lady will help you fulfil your dharma, or your true destiny.

Our Lady is the servant of God, if you like, acting between the vast spiritual dimensions and the dimensions of this world. If you invoke Her correctly, She will help you through the problems and struggles you encounter in life because that is Her job. You do not have to tell Her what to do, just be respectful and reverential towards Her and *allow Her to do Her job*. Being a Spiritual Warrior has much to do with awakening the Feminine Consciousness in the Heart, and with surrendering to that

---

Our Lady, the Feminine Principle, is concerned more for your overall development than the trivial things that you should be dealing with yourself. She is concerned for your Soul, for your Heart, and building the Shield of Light that every true Warrior has—which is the knight's "shining armour". The shining armour is the Body of Light, the inner body of radiant Light that you create and build through the Art of the Warrior.

Feminine Consciousness so that She will take you to the state of Conscious Immortality. It is about shifting your awareness from the created dimensions to the uncreated dimensions, the boundless fields of Light where Conscious Immortality is to be found. And Our Lady's function is to help you do just that. ✗

~ 27 ~

THE WARRIOR AND THE
FEMININE POWER

The so-called feminist movement has nothing to do with what we call the Feminine Power, the Feminine Energy, the Feminine Consciousness, the Feminine Principle, and so on. Feminist ideas are masculine, intellectual and aggressive and have nothing to do with the Feminine Principle, which has three aspects that must be mastered in order to become a Spiritual Warrior. There is the Passive Principle (which is the gentle side of the Feminine), the Uniting Principle (which unites the male and female energies) and the Dynamic Principle (which is the all-consuming power of the Feminine).

Today we do not understand the Feminine Principle because the world is all masculine, that is, the consciousness with which we function in the physical body at this particular time of our evolution is masculine. It's what we call *objective consciousness*, meaning that it relates to objects all the time, and it is an activity of the Masculine Mind. It is the awareness of objects separate from each other.

Another aspect of masculine consciousness is the intellectual workings of the mind. The mind functions by thought and each thought is separate from the other: you think about the train, then you think about God and then you think about your girlfriend or boyfriend and then you think about what you're going to have for breakfast. Each thought is a separate "object" in your mind, except that it's not on the physical level but on the mental level, on the Mental Plane.

So you engage in two separative actions: on the Physical Plane your physical consciousness cuts things into separate objects and on the Mental Plane your mental consciousness—the lower mind, the rational, reasoning, logical mind—cuts things into separate thoughts. Both activities are masculine and have nothing to do with the Feminine Principle.

Unfortunately, in today's so-called scientific age, everybody is forced to follow the masculine line. The modern education system tries to make everybody intellectual right from day one, at the kindergarten level. Not one iota of education involves the Feminine Consciousness—which is a real disaster that no one is aware of. Even if you are the most logical thinker in the Universe, you are still functioning on the masculine consciousness level (and not even at the highest part) and you are not in touch with or have any sense of the Feminine Principle. Intellectual development, even if pursued for a thousand years, can never put one in touch with the Feminine Consciousness.

During the last thousand years, as you know, the male has been dominant in all cultures. Now we have to go beyond that history because it is not relevant today. Today we have to move forward into the twenty-first century, not backwards. And what does this century require? Harmony, the balancing of the Male and Female. Why? Because men and women are both living Souls!

On the level of the Soul there is no male Soul and female Soul. The Soul is simply the Soul, a bright, radiating spark of Light, and we are all bright, radiating sparks of Light. Divisions occur only in the outer personality expression. If we want to be Spiritual Warriors, therefore, we have to go beyond those divisions to the natural, real state, which is the Soul Nature within us, the Bright Light within us.

The Feminine Power and Atlantis

In the early days of the Atlantean civilization we used our feminine consciousness. This means that our basic awareness was on the level of the Astral World, that is, we had *astral consciousness*, which is one hundred percent feminine. We had only a vague awareness of the objective world, this physical dimension. We were mainly aware of the *inside* of objects and only vaguely aware of the *outside* of objects, which to us had the same reality as thoughts have nowadays. We functioned from our internal nature and that was our feminine consciousness.

Today Nature is an outside thing. When you go to school and learn about seashells, for example, you look at photographs of seashells in schoolbooks and then you learn all about their sizes, colours and what they do—all outside, just physical dimensions and characteristics. And it is the same with every topic in school: you learn only the outside and absolutely nothing of the inside. In Atlantean times, however, you knew what a seashell was from the inside—how the life-force functioned through it, what creative stresses created it, why it was created in such-and-such a way, what intelligence shaped it and what its inner purpose was. You knew these things spontaneously, automatically.

China was the only country where female warriors were trained equally with male warriors. Other tribes, races and countries thought that only males should be warriors, that the male was supposed to be the archetype of the warrior, and they trained only males. But China was unique in having both female and male warriors, without the slightest distinction between them. The interesting thing was that although the males used the Feminine Power (with tremendous and miraculous possibilities), it was the female warriors who expressed the Feminine Power fully, who completely embodied the three aspects of the Feminine Power: the receptive, or passive, aspect, the uniting aspect and the awesome power aspect. That is why the Chinese female Master Warriors were impossible to beat on any level.

In the time of Atlantis the Master Warriors were one hundred percent in touch with the Feminine Consciousness and had complete control of the Astral World, which is like a colossal sea of Light, Colour and Sound, a resounding sea of primordial, intelligent Energy. Within that sea are the Elemental Kingdoms of Earth, Fire, Water and Air (which have nothing to do with the elements of earth, fire, water and air on Earth). The Warriors could control all the inhabitants of those kingdoms and could manipulate astral forces *at will* for their purposes. They had Nature at their command.

But that was in the early days of the Atlantean civilization, when it was on the rise. Later, during its decline, people began to misuse their knowledge and astral powers until half the population became black magicians. The misuse of the great primary forces of Nature spread like such a disease that there was only one course of action: the Spiritual Hierarchy had to destroy the whole continent. Otherwise, the planet would have become a planet of black magic, an irreversibly negative force in our Solar System, and it would now be at a worse stage of evolution than it is.

After Atlantis was destroyed, the new generations, those who had been saved and put into places like Egypt, South America and the Gobi Desert (which was an island in those days), were not taught the secrets of Atlantis; they were not taught how to master the forces of Nature. That knowledge was purposefully withheld, so many generations of Humanity grew up not knowing how to live in tune with the forces of Nature because the Spiritual Hierarchy was worried that they would recover the Ancient Wisdom and fall back into a cycle of destruction. But over those hundreds of thousands of years there were a few people here and there who were initiated into the techniques of moving their consciousness into the Astral World and controlling the forces of Nature, so that knowledge was preserved.

In terms of evolution, the loss of astral consciousness was not too bad because people became more focused on their physical bodies and on conquering the physical world. People withdrew from the psychic power, the tremendous power of the Feminine, and since the beginning of the Āryan dispensation, around eight thousand years ago, they have been developing their minds, which at first were rudimentary. They devised techniques for developing the brain, so civilization today is all about body and mind—*all masculine.*

But with that we lost a dimension inside us and we are getting further and further away from reality, because being in your mind is not reality. You can think of an apple for one million years and it's still only a thought; you won't know anything about an apple. The delusion of modern civilization is thinking that you can know about something by thinking about it. But you can't. Thinking is just an activity of your mind; it is not knowledge. You see a diagram of an atom in a book and you think you know about it. But do you? You only know the atom when you are right inside it, feel the stress of its life-force, feel its creative energy. Then you know it.

You know a human being when your aura penetrates the aura of another person and you see how energies move inside the person, the basic forces behind the apparent bodily form. If you want to be a Warrior you have to be able to work from the inside, because in the midst of battle you have to know your enemy from the inside, know exactly what your enemy is thinking and feeling, otherwise you will be defeated straight away.

The Feminine Power and Mediumship

Nowadays the Feminine Principle is mysterious and not understood due to the evolutionary changes that have occurred on the planet, but the understanding of the Feminine needs to be recovered. To do that, first of all, you must understand that your normal mind as it normally functions is not feminine. Your thinking processes are not feminine. The objective awareness through your five senses is not feminine. Therefore you know that thinking is not the way to approach the Feminine; in fact, the more you think, the less feminine you become. But there must be ways to recover the powerful Feminine Kingdom that has been lost—and there are.

Unfortunately, mediumship is not one of them. There have always been mediums, of course, and mediumship has been especially popular since 1875, when it became a craze in the United States. Today it is still considered a cool thing to be a medium by many new agers. But mediumship is the wrong way to try to recover that lost reality, because as a medium you open yourself up and say, "Anybody, please come in." You do not say it mentally but internally, in the attitude of your astral body and auric field.

This is what I call unprotected psychic development and it is very dangerous because anything *will* just come in, mostly deceptive spirits or delusions of one's own mind. This explains why a lot of mediums and channellers have warped vibrations, by which I mean they do not have the right energy source; their energy does not conform to reality. So mediumship is not the right technique.

In the West mediums try to recover the Feminine Power but with the wrong process and understanding, and in the East the process of recovering the Feminine is also wrong but in a different way. The West has the wrong way of trying to get in touch with the passive side of the Feminine—mediumship is essentially passive—but the East has the wrong way of trying to get in touch with the dynamic side of the Feminine—awakening the KUṆḌALINĪ force, which is the dynamic aspect of the Feminine Consciousness.

This idea of awakening the Kuṇḍalinī is becoming popular in the West (like channelling used to be). There are hundreds of authors writing about how to awaken Kuṇḍalinī, but—my goodness!—they do not know how dangerous their teaching is. Most people are far from ready to awaken Kuṇḍalinī. If they awaken Kuṇḍalinī while their consciousness is still objective and intellectual and the vibration of their bodies is still dense, they will end up in the nearest psychiatric institution or as suicides or with some other serious problem.

You don't just *awaken* Kuṇḍalinī. The dynamic side of the Feminine Power can be incredibly destructive. The Hindus knew that; they call it KĀLĪ—an awesome power that can create, or annihilate. When the dynamic power of the Feminine is released it can do miracles. That is why the Kuṇḍalinī Yogīs wanted its miraculous powers; and of course the great Kung Fu and other Chinese Warriors also used the miraculous powers of the awakened Kuṇḍalinī.

So it is important to be careful when considering New Age authors and ask yourself: Do they have real knowledge? Do they really know what they are talking about? Have they been initiated into this science or are they just exercising their intellect and trying to be cool? You have to have discrimination in these things.

The Feminine Consciousness is still inside us, but because of the way society works we no longer take any notice of it. Even today some girls are born along the feminine line because Nature has not changed in spite of Humanity's efforts to destroy it. Some young girls are feminine until they start going to school, and by the time they are fourteen or fifteen they are just as masculine as the boys because the whole education system has turned them away from feminine energy and toward masculinity. The tragedy now is that every female is expected to be masculine. In the early days males were males, females were females, and the balance of Nature was maintained.

The Three Levels of the Feminine Power

A leftover of the Atlantean feminine consciousness that we still have nowadays is called *instinct*. Instinct is part of your feminine consciousness. You could say it is the most basic part of your feminine consciousness because it warns you of danger, that is, it's about self-preservation. Often you hear about teenage girls who go to one party after another and meet unfortunate circumstances on a deserted street. What was not operating in their lives? Instinct.

People do stupid things because even the most basic part of Feminine Consciousness is not functioning inside them. If it were, at least their life would be preserved because the Feminine Consciousness is a motherly consciousness, the instinct of a mother to preserve her child. (It's sad to say but many mothers nowadays have no motherly instinct and do not care about their children, again, because they are out of tune with the Feminine within themselves.) The point is that even the most basic part of the Feminine—instinct—no longer functions in a large number of people.

In the Warrior, instinctual response is a must. A good warrior walking along a field will know there is danger ahead or behind a hundred meters away, two hundred meters away, five hundred meters away, because he or she has the feminine power of self-preservation. When you are a Warrior in battle, it is precisely this power that you use. Your sword moves instinctually and the enemy behind you falls dead, without you even seeing or hearing them. Instinct saves a Warrior's life many times. Young warriors think that all that matters in battle is that they have big muscles and a macho attitude. In a battle that does very little for you; instinct will do much more. One small part of the Feminine Power is more powerful for saving your life than having big strong muscles.

Instinct is one of the passive powers of the Feminine. Her other passive powers are what we call psychic powers—telepathy, clairvoyance, clairaudience, clairsentience, reading other people's thoughts. These are not siddhis, the miraculous powers, but psychic powers, that is, they are functions of the astral body and the Astral World. As I said, in the time of Atlantis psychic powers were as normal for humans as logical thinking is nowadays, because our astral bodies were functioning freely in the Astral World and we were astrally conscious. Of course, some people still have remnants of the Atlantean consciousness and are therefore born with psychic abilities.

The next level of the passive side of the Feminine Consciousness within you is *knowing*. There is a part of the Feminine that simply knows, not based on any rational reason or physical senses. I will give you an example: Is there a God? If you are a rational and materialistic person you will research and find all the arguments for and against the existence of God, and in the end you will conclude that the question is open and needs further research. That is the approach of the male intellectual mind.

On the other hand, a person who can use his or her feminine consciousness will simply say, "Yes, God exists." No thinking, no analysis, no dissection, no consideration, no theorizing about it; just knowing. This is why it is difficult for the materialist to understand the spiritual disciple, who simply knows that he or she is a Soul, that there is a God, that there is a Divine Plan. This knowledge is inborn and there is no need to rationalize or argue about it for years and years. Anyone with the slightest bit of feminine consciousness would not deny the existence of Intelligence in the Universe—God or whatever you like to call it.

What the Feminine Consciousness *knows* is always correct. The Feminine in us reveals knowledge from the inside, and we become all-knowing because of the all-Wisdom, all-Knowledge power of the Feminine Principle. ✗

~ 28 ~

THE WARRIOR SURRENDERS
HIS HEART TO THE INNERMOST

The state of your Heart shows the stage of evolution you have reached in all your lifetimes, in your total reality.

There is a correspondence between the Heart and every part of your being: your physical heart corresponds to your physical body and your etheric heart to your etheric body; in your astral body you have your astral heart and in your mental body your mental heart; in your causal body you have your Causal Heart; in the Buddhic World, the first plane of unities, you have your Buddhic Heart; and in Nirvāṇa you have your Nirvāṇic Heart. The Heart is always the central part of you, whatever plane of existence you are on, and it gives you life and a sense of reality on each plane.

The Heart is the controlling factor, the hub of the Wheel of Life, the source from which every action takes place on each level of your being. On the physical level, if your heart decides not to function, as you know, you will not win the Olympics. And it is the same on all the levels. When your etheric heart is malfunctioning there is no Prāṇa coming into your etheric vital body, and then you die because there is no life-energy to maintain you in the physical world.

So the Heart is the centre of your being, but that is only one aspect of it. In its totality, the Heart is where you are in Creation. If you look at the Heart of a person, spiritually, you can tell exactly what level of evolution they have reached in the total scheme of things. And if you are a spiritual disciple, the Heart is the measure of how far you have progressed on the Spiritual Path.

The first stage of the Spiritual Path, therefore, is the discovery of the Heart, and as you carry on with the various Warrior meditations and spiritual exercises you will begin to experience aspects of the Heart that can be summarized by the following key phrases.

Full of Gold

One experience you may have in the early stages of practice is that the Heart is *full of gold*, like liquid gold or golden light. This experience connects to the Buddhic region of the Heart, which is quite common when you are doing a devotional practice. Devotees may experience the gold part of the Heart in the early stages of the Heart practice because they work through the physical heart directly into the astral heart, which is the emotional seat of the Heart. Because of a unique correspondence in the internal structure of the Cosmos there is a direct link from the astral to the Buddhic dimensions, which bypasses the mental and causal dimensions.

So if you are chanting devotional mantras to God or feeling intensely devotional you can enter the higher region of the Astral World and from there, by reflection, you can flick up to the Buddhic World, the World of Unity, where you will experience the pure Golden Light of Wisdom of the Buddhic Heart. Incidentally, this is why Buddhist monks wear saffron or golden orange robes: the colours represent the colour of the Heart in the Buddhic World.

When you begin to experience the Golden Luminous Light inside you, you know that your Heart Chakra is open to the Buddhic World, and then the World of Unity becomes accessible to you. That is why devotional schools say that the Path of Devotion is the quickest way to God, which is true—if you are truly and purely devotional and are doing the right practice.

Lotus Flower

Another way the Heart is often experienced is like a *flower*. In the East the Heart is symbolized by the *lotus* and in the West it is symbolized by the *rose* in Christianity and by the *lily of the valley* in Judaism. The Heart appears like a flower with petals, which you can see when you enter into the etheric, astral, mental or Causal Heart. It is not a flower, of course, but an energy vortex that, to the Mystics who experienced the Heart, looked like a beautiful flower—not static like a picture but with energy currents streaming from it like petals.

Space/Cave of the Heart

Another thing you will discover when you enter the Heart is *space*. A materialistic person thinks that space is out there, between the trees or between our planet and the Sun or between our Solar System and the other Solar Systems or between one galaxy and another. As far as the worldly consciousness is concerned, space is some kind of emptiness between objects—there's a star, then an emptiness, another star, more emptiness, and so on. But when you enter the Space of the Heart, or what is also called the Cave of the Heart, you discover that Space is nothing like that; Space is actually not empty but, on the contrary, completely full. And what is more, the "objects" that you see are actually the emptiness, like temporary *bubbles* in Manifestation.

Expressed in a different way, Space, which stretches to infinity outwardly and inwardly, is a total fullness, and within that fullness objects—universes, galaxies, worlds—appear like the bubbles that form when water starts boiling. Beneath the bubbles there is the vast Water, the whole Omni-Space, an infinite, boundless Sea of Substance. And the Universe is just a bubble inside that, an alteration of the homogeneity of Space. And *that* is the *unreal* part of Space: that which is forever stable and real is Space itself.

It's like a big joke: you see physical objects and think they are real and the "space" between them is unreal, and it's actually the other way around. This is a great mystery that you will discover when you enter the Space (the Cave) of the Heart, a discovery that will make you rethink your whole idea of reality.

Consciousness

You will also discover that this so-called emptiness is Consciousness, Pure Consciousness. It is the source of the intelligence and consciousness of all beings in the Universe; it is your consciousness and the consciousness of an animal and a plant; it is the consciousness of an angel and the consciousness of a Buddha, a Christ, a Solar Logos, a Galactic Lord. No matter how small or vast the consciousness, it comes from the one Consciousness you discover in the Heart, which is infinite, boundless and pervades everything in Space.

So you discover two things: first you discover that Space is not empty and then you discover that Space is absolute, boundless Consciousness, and that everything that lives in the Universe has its consciousness from that source. And this leads to another discovery: *you* are part of that infinite, absolute, boundless state of Consciousness; you as a living conscious entity in the Universe are Pure Consciousness, without objects, without limitations of any kind. This is simply the discovery of your true

---

Most people do not know the difference between their consciousness and their mind. Do you remember the great cry of Western civilization during the so-called Age of Enlightenment: "I think, therefore I am"? Well, it is completely wrong; you are, and *therefore* you can think. *Consciousness* comes first, *being* comes first, *life* comes first. It is materialistic stupidity to believe that your ability to think gives you reality. It does not; you must have the reality first before you can think. No, in real life Consciousness comes first and the rest of you—your Soul, your mind faculty, your feeling faculty, your vital force and your physical body—comes out of Consciousness.

nature, what you really are when you have recovered the Kingdom of God inside you.

And then you realize that your mind, and all its thought-producing faculties, is below you, and that the real you can function without your mind, without your feelings and without your physical body. This is of course shocking for materialistic people because they normally identify their consciousness with those things. They have the illusion that they are conscious because those *things* exist, not realizing that their consciousness is *before* everything.

Full of Bliss

So one of the mysteries of the Heart you can experience is that you can transcend all the structures you normally use and identify with, and still be alive! And not only alive, but blissfully alive! In fact, it is only on that level of awareness that you begin to understand the limitless joy of Bliss Consciousness—because the Heart is full of Bliss. By *Bliss* we mean a joy which cannot be altered or changed for all eternity, because in the state of joy that is Absolute Consciousness or Absolute Intelligence there is no degeneration. It is above the level of Creation, in a realm of existence that Creation does not touch.

In Creation, which includes the Causal World, the Mental World, the Astral World, and the Physical World, everything changes—things are born, grow, decay and die—so there is suffering. But above the Causal World, starting from the Buddhic World to the Nirvāṇic World and the worlds beyond, the idea of being born and dying does not exist. Everything is eternally shining brightly, always centred in its Absolute Reality; therefore the idea of degeneration does not exist and therefore the idea of suffering does not exist.

So the Heart is *full of Bliss*, from one eternity to the next, and this is another great gift you will receive when you fully complete the Journey of the Heart.

City of God

The experience of the Heart as being Pure Consciousness and full of Bliss is on the Buddhic level, but below that, in the Causal World, which is the highest region of the Mental World—still within the Creation level but in the uppermost regions of Creation—the Heart appears as the *City of God*, BRAHMA-PUTRA or INDRA-PUTRA in Sanskrit. This expression came about because when you experience the Heart in the causal dimension you will see the most beautiful geometrical shapes and patterns, multidimensional structures so perfect that you know no human mind could have created them. And once you get over the shock of the perfect beauty and harmony of the Causal Heart, you will discover that within that perfect city there is the sense of a divine presence, as if there is a king or ruler in the city, a power that has ruled since the beginning of Creation—which is why it is called the City of God.

So within your Heart you find the City of God and its Perfect Ruler, who is also the ruler of planet Earth and the ruler of you as a living being in Creation. When you experience this in your meditation you will begin to be sensitive to the fact that you *must* live by that rule, and this is what drives the Mystic, the Yogī, the Warrior towards perfection. You see this unimaginably beautiful city, you realize that within it there is a Ruling

---

When I first experienced the City of God in the Causal World, many years ago, the experience reminded me of the "heavenly Jerusalem" mentioned in the Bible (Hebrews 12: 22). Obviously, there were some Mystics amongst the Jews in the olden days who saw a city made of gold and sparkling jewels. When I saw it, it was like that: a city shining brightly with luminous translucent light and colours, with perfect shapes and forms. I was in my causal body and the experience was so overwhelmingly beautiful that I did not want to come back into my other bodies. But I knew that I had to come back, to fulfil my mission, but after I returned I cried and cried for days afterwards. It was like being in a state of perfection and then being thrown into a dungeon. It took me weeks to recover.

Intelligence that maintains that perfection and then you sense that it is the ideal perfection toward which all things will evolve until the end of time. Then you realize that there has always been a plan for the whole downward Involution, which is why the lower regions had to develop, and you know that the final goal of Evolution is that perfection that exists in the City of God, the Absolute Perfection in the Mind of God.

Then you will discover that not only is the whole Cosmos striving for perfection but also *you* are striving for perfection. And you will discover that this striving for perfection, which has been driving you through all your previous incarnations, is a remembrance of the City of God, and of the Divine King who rules that ideal perfection; and there is no way you can escape the *need* for that Perfection, which is your inward drive.

In the popular imagination the City of God became the lost city of Shang-Ri-Lah, but the real city is not at all lost; all you have to do is enter into your Heart Centre, move to the causal dimension of the Heart and then through the Causal Heart you will enter the City of God. This is a reflection of the larger City of the Planetary Heart, the Heart of the Planetary Logos, which is a reflection of the still larger City of the Heart of the Solar Logos, which is itself a reflection of the Cosmic Heart. Each connects you to the other: from the City of God within you, you can enter the tremendous City where the King rules the planet, and then if you can go beyond that in your meditation, you can sense the awesome Throne of Power of the Solar Logos, the inconceivable power that rules the Solar System.

That power has to be contained and it *is* contained within the City of God, which at the same time protects you, if you are not evolved enough to be able to experience it. This is why Evolution has to unfold *slowly*, so that we develop gradually and become able to take increasingly greater power, increasingly greater possession of the Divine Kingdom. It is only when you have reached a certain point of evolution that the total Kingdom can be manifested to you.

Light

Another Heart experience you will encounter is Light, which is a common experience for Mystics who enter the Heart. The Light has many sources. You can experience the Light of your own Soul, the Light of our Planetary Logos, the Light of the Solar Logos or the Light of the Universe, the boundless, absolute Universal Light. These are stages of development. First the Light seems to be only relevant to you, then you realize that it is actually planetary, directly relating to the planet, then it is Solar Systemic and then it is related to the Cosmos.

Divine Self

Along with the experience of Light in the Heart you may also experience the Divine Self. The Divine Self in the Heart is your own Soul, and you experience yourself as a living, breathing spiritual entity—the Living Soul—as against your personality. When you think, when you feel, when you act, you are in your personality manifestation, the personality self. But when you experience the Divine Self within you, you move out of your personality self into that which you really are, the Living Soul. And that Living Soul is radically different from you as a personality; you cannot imagine that they are the same person, but they are.

Before you incarnate there is a moment when you are in your causal body in the City of God as your Divine Self, that is, the divine, immortal being we call the Soul or the Living Soul. Then you begin to descend into incarnation, forming a series of shields around you: first a mental body, which blocks out the vision of the City of God inside you; then an astral body, which blocks out the remnants of the Light of the City of God; and then an etheric-physical body, which completely wipes out the City of God from your awareness; and finally a physical body, which is the end of the story: you do not see, hear or do anything whatsoever in the inner dimensions. The physical body is only meant for you to be active in the physical world, so you lose your divine nature—or rather, the *awareness* of your divine nature. And this is why we need to have meditation techniques to rewind the process and make everybody realize that we are divine Souls.

God-Realization

So the Heart itself becomes a means of Self-Realization (the realization that you are a Living Soul) and God-Realization (the realization that God is part of you and you are a part of God). This is not a philosophy but something you can experience. Once you enter the deeper layers of the Heart you will sense that there is a divine part of you, which is you, and then you begin to realize that apart from your divine nature there is a greater *Divine Principle* inside you, which is God. And then at an even later stage of unfoldment you realize that you and that Divine Principle are not two different identities, not separate realities, but are actually one. This is God-Realization, Union with God.

So you can see that the Path Within is a huge path, and a hugely rewarding path, according to the degree of your evolutionary attainment. When you reach God-Realization you have completed your task as a human being on this planet; there is no more that you need to do for yourself; your evolutionary path is completed. The rest of your life is spent in service, either moving on to a higher evolutionary stage in the inner dimensions or coming back into incarnation here and teaching Humanity. You have completed your schooling—technically you have attained the state of Freedom, Realization or Liberation (MUKTI or MOKṢA in Sanskrit). Your life has no other meaning than to see the Divine Plan and do what you can to unveil that plan to Humanity, to help people tune into and manifest the Plan.

This is the story of the Heart. It is not a philosophy, because you can experience all these things. All the great Mystics, Yogīs, Sūfis and Saints tell the same story in their own language, according to their own culture and background, but the Interior Realization, the Path, is always the same. Female Mystics like Saint Theresa, for example, describe their experience as being in a garden with birds singing and beautiful, sweet-smelling flowers, and being embraced lovingly by their Beloved. What they are trying to say is they are in the City of God and see the beautiful bright structures and colours and then feel the presence of the King. It does not matter whether you are a Buddhist, Christian, Muslim, Jew, Chinese or Japanese; a real Esoteric Teacher will know exactly where you are at, what level of inner experience you are having, by the words you choose and the feeling behind what you say.

I want to inspire you that this Journey is much more amazing than you think, and if you work hard the rewards are more than you could possibly imagine, more than what science-fiction writers could dream up. Because of their materialistic thinking, their idea of immortality is to hook up your brain to a computer, which will keep your brain alive so you will become immortal. They make all these attempts to become immortal because they do not know that *they already are immortal*. You do not have to attach your brain to a computer, which is part of this perishable world anyway, as you know. All you have to do is practise meditation and you will *know* that you are immortal.

Obviously, you have to spend a few years in meditation, yes, but in any discipline you have to spend a few years to master it. So if you practise meditation you will have results, and the results have already been described by others who went before you. There is nothing mysterious about it; it's very scientific: do this practice, get this result. If you want to attain immortality, just enter the Heart and you are immortal; the shadow of death will not touch you. Yes, your physical body will die but that is not You; it is just your temporary manifestation which you put on because you had to do certain things. But the real You lives in a continuum of eternity beyond Time and Space that nothing can disturb.

The Warrior of the Heart

This is a process of awakening the Heart and it involves three different stages, each using a different syllable of the ancient Primordial Sound Language. You start with the sound of ŌM; with that you *penetrate* the Heart Chakra. The ŌM sound is a directed, inward sound, so it takes your consciousness away from the world, away from your environment, and directs your energies inside you. When you have gained some measure of success in this stage and you can enter the Heart Chakra and feel its activity, then you start using the sound of RĀM, which *expands* the Heart Chakra. Once you have penetrated into the Heart Chakra and expanded it, in the third stage you start working with the vibration of KLĪM, which is a *uniting* sound, the power of Love.

The reason we start with the ŌM sound is because that sound is sharp and directed, like an arrow. It cuts through things, so when you turn it inside towards the Heart Centre, it cuts through the veils of the Heart. This is to do with the science of the Heart Chakra. First of all, within you there is a shining Spiritual Heart. It is luminous; it is total Intelligence, total Knowing, total Love, total Compassion and total Oneness with all things, but it is covered over with layers. First it is covered with all your emotional stuff, your feelings, moods and desires. On the next layer there are all your subconscious impressions from the past, by which we mean not only your life up to now but also your many past lives. Then of course the last layer is your physical consciousness.

Because the ŌM sound is like an arrow, it penetrates through these layers. When you do the meditation practice you will feel that you are penetrating through them. First you will become aware of subconscious impressions, maybe something that happened to you recently or impressions that happened to you sometime during this lifetime. As you penetrate further you come to the region of feelings and you discover many kinds of feelings, moods and emotions.

The arrow keeps penetrating further and further until you suddenly come to a luminous state of being inside you, a state of Absolute Intelligence, Absolute Consciousness and Absolute Bliss. Then you have penetrated all the coverings and have entered the real Heart.

This is what Jesus was referring to when He said, "The Kingdom of God is taken by force"(Matthew 11: 12). He was explaining one of the Warrior Principles, using words that people could understand because normally a king takes another kingdom by force. Applied to spiritual life, this means you have to force yourself to do what is needed; you have to *discipline* yourself. Remember, Jesus spoke in ancient Aramaic and many words had different meanings than what they have today. So when He used the words *by force*, He meant "with willpower, direction and purpose", what in Sanskrit is called TAPAS, which means "fiery zeal". Tapas is an essential quality of the Warrior: the zeal, the power, the will, the drive to *do*. With this zeal and the directed energy of the ŌṀ sound you will be able to enter the Kingdom of God within you by force.

The other sounds have different qualities than the ŌṀ sound. RĀM is expanding and it expands and develops whatever action you take. That is not the right way of entering the Heart, but once you have entered the Heart with the ŌṀ sound, you use the RĀM sound because it will

---

With this exercise you penetrate the Heart Chakra (ŌṀ), expand it (RĀM), and unite the two actions with the power of Love (KLĪM). Then you have a Heart that is like a blazing sun or fire that continually regenerates itself from the inside.

That is how the Sun, our Solar Logos, functions: it works from the inside out. It penetrates into its own inner being and gets the substance material from its inner higher being and radiates it out into the physical dimension. It is an inward penetration and outward radiation, all in a single act of Love, Self-Surrender and Self-Sacrifice. The Solar Logos is doing nothing else but sacrificing himself until the end of this period of time. There is no gain for him. It is an act of self-sacrifice; the Solar Logoi are the greatest Self-Sacrificers.

expand your Heart, as well as your experience of bliss and joy in the Heart. Then you add the third quality, KLĪM, which is the vibration of Love. Then you understand that you, the planet, the Solar System, the whole Cosmos is made out of Love and is maintained by Love—Divine Love.

In the New Testament, Saint John, who was the most advanced initiate among the early Christians, defines God as having two qualities: "God is Light in whom there is no darkness at all" and "God is Love" (John 1: 5; John 4: 8, 16). Another quality that Saint John did not mention is *Bliss*. God is Light, Love and Bliss. For some reason the Christian writers never mention it. KLĪM is that loving power of exultant bliss and ecstatic joy.

Expressed in terms of the Primordial Sound Language, therefore, this is the Divine Trinity: ŌM is the luminous, imperishable Self inside you; RĀM is the all-pervading presence of the Deity; and KLĪM is the Divine Compassion or the Divine Love that embraces and unites all things in the Cosmos. The Self is everywhere. The Divine Presence is everywhere. And the Divine Love is also everywhere. You can therefore experience these qualities of the Divine when you practise this exercise.

If you are a devotee you can awaken the Heart and there is no doubt that you will be filled with Love, but it is just that: an overwhelming sensation of Love. But when you awaken your Heart as a Warrior, when you become a Warrior of the Heart, the quality of Love (KLĪM) blends with infinite Intelligence (RĀM) and infinite Power (ŌM). You are connected to the threefold power of Divinity and become the Ideal Warrior. ✗

Practice

~

ŌṀ-RĀM-KLĪM Heart Meditation

Stage One: ŌṀ …

Intone the ŌṀ sound aloud a few times, with a prolonged Ō sound. Then focus in the Heart, putting your attention in the middle of your chest, and intone the ŌṀ sound mentally with the Ō sound less prolonged. Do not repeat the mantra over and over, but pause between each intonation and abide in silence.

Stage Two: ŌṀ-RĀM …

When you can enter the Heart and feel to some degree the activity of the Divine Presence within, you can add the RĀM sound. First intone aloud just the ŌṀ sound three times and then the RĀM sound three times. Then intone ŌṀ-RĀM many times, first aloud and then mentally, with your attention focused in the Heart.

Stage Three: ŌṀ-RĀM-KLĪM …

When you can penetrate into the Heart and expand it, you can add the KLĪM sound to complete the mantra. First intone aloud just the ŌṀ sound three times, then the RĀM sound three times and then the KLĪM sound three times. Then intone the full mantra ŌṀ-RĀM-KLĪM many times, first aloud and then mentally, with your attention focused in the Heart.

(Note: Normally, each stage could take a few months, but this can vary depending on various factors—your dedication and ability, how often you meditate, and so on.)

THE KNOWLEDGE
OF THE WARRIOR

First of all, there are four kinds, or levels, of knowledge. There is the knowledge that you get at school, which relates to material things in the physical world: you learn about trees, bumble bees and God knows what else. Then there is the knowledge of the priestcraft. In every religion there has always been a priestcraft that maintains the knowledge relating to non-material things—the idea of a soul, the idea of a Divine Being, the idea of angels, the idea of invisible worlds. This knowledge was valid and inspired the masses to understand that life is not merely what they see, but much more. In this way, the priestcraft performed an important function for people (and will continue to do so in the future).

Then, there is a deeper knowledge than that of the priestcraft: the knowledge of the magicians. In the ancient cultures, the magicians were special people who learned, for example, how to tune into the psychic dimensions or how to develop healing or magic powers. Magic can be white, black or neutral, so depending on the leanings of the magicians, they could do white magic, which is healing and helpful to people; black magic, which is destructive; or neutral, which can go either way. This level of knowledge is more esoteric and deeper than the knowledge of the priest. The magicians had a deeper understanding of how energies work in the Cosmos and how they could use their mental and psychic powers.

But there is another kind of knowledge, deeper than the knowledge of the magician and the priestcraft: the knowledge of the Warrior. I will try to describe what this knowledge is, which is quite difficult to do, because if you want to be a Spiritual Warrior you will have to focus on this field of knowledge.

The knowledge of the Warrior is nonverbal, a direct, inspired knowledge that comes from within, an invisible field of knowledge and awareness that keeps pouring in twenty-four hours a day, seven days a week; it is not something you can learn from a book. And if you are a Warrior, that direct knowledge comes out of you every moment. When you meet a person, the Intelligence inside you knows that person directly, from within, and it is the same with every situation in your life, with *anything*. From the time you wake up in the morning until you go to sleep, that awareness of all things is there inside you.

As I mentioned previously, the Chinese Kung Fu Master I knew did not believe in studying books but learning through practice. By *practice* he meant that you should learn to know yourself, because if you do a martial arts movement right, the energy flows right; if you do it wrong, it flows wrong. And that cannot be learned from books, and it is not something somebody else can teach you. You can only learn it yourself, through practice.

So the martial arts are an excellent training ground to know yourself, but in ancient times they did it the other way around. In the traditional Warrior Schools in China, Mongolia, Tibet or Japan, and even in Europe in the Middle Ages, most of the Warriors-to-be became monks first before they became Warriors. This meant that they had to spend years in seclusion, in meditation, learning breathing techniques, learning to commune with the Divine Principle within, and so on. They first became monks and attained certain inner realizations, inner states of consciousness, and then they were trained in the martial arts, in the physical warrior techniques.

This does not mean that it has to be done that way. I just want to point out that historically pupils in the Warrior Schools had spiritual training before they had physical training. Of course, one can receive spiritual training simultaneously with warrior training, which is the system we are using. It is the modern way, or the way it should have been done in the first place, because the two—the spiritual training and the physical training—work together very conveniently.

The Warrior Consciousness

The state of the Spiritual Warrior is Cosmic Consciousness, a universal field of Awareness. It is an unconditioned state (which is why it is so difficult to describe). In this consciousness you see your exact position in a situation and that of the other person, and you know whether it is right for you to respond because it is what the situation requires, or whether you do not need to respond in any way whatsoever. As I said, this is not a book-learned knowledge. A book cannot teach you when to respond or not respond, when to do this or that. You have to be in that higher consciousness where you see the whole situation and know whether you need to do anything about it or not.

Until you begin to have glimpses of that Warrior Consciousness you will try to become a Warrior in your mind. But you can never become a Warrior in your mind. You can do your practices and meditations and mentally work out why and how to do things in various situations, but you will not be a Warrior because the Warrior is *spontaneous*, in the moment, acting according to the situation, according to the environment.

Essentially, a Warrior is boundless and free and because of that he or she can make the right choices. That is the important thing. You have to be free to be able to make the right choice, and from the right choice springs the right action. If you are emotionally or psychically tied to a relationship or to a situation, you cannot make the right choice. You respond, the other person responds, and you argue. If you are internally free, that situation is just part of an infinite ocean of reality around you, and you see your existence as part of an infinite series of existences. So you can stay calm and choose to either stay and try to work things out or go your separate way. Because you are not tied to any event, any particular space and time condition in your life, you are free and you can act *out of love*.

Note that your action is not a mentally calculated action; it is a loving action, because that sea of reality around you is an ocean of Love that includes everybody and everything. In that sea, *you* feel right; it's the situation that is off-key. You can remedy it or disengage from it so that it disintegrates. As a Spiritual Warrior, you see in that infinite ocean of Intelligence that everything and everybody has a destiny, from an atom to a planet to a galaxy. You sense that destiny, the life-force working through an object or a person; you sense what is behind it, what is motivating it. And then, because you are free internally, you can respond to it correctly, knowing how much it is in harmony with the Cosmic Reality around you.

This is why it was difficult for ordinary people to understand the actions of the ancient Warriors, which were apparently illogical, not what people would expect. That is because the Warriors lived according to a different field of knowledge, the Warrior Knowledge, the fourth degree of Knowledge.

In the ancient systems, all the great Warriors were trained by Spiritual Masters, who gave them the initial inspiration for self-exploration. From a Spiritual Teacher you get inspiration and the motivation to do the work required for your own perfection, your own liberation, your own growth and progress. The Teacher gives you a push, not just verbally but internally; a psychic or spiritual energy that wakes you up to the need to meditate and do other spiritual work; an inner push that helps you discover your true Self.

That is because the environment where you are born conditions you into a set culture. If you are born in China, you become Chinese. If you are born in Germany, you become German. Your parents and the whole environment create a certain structure you fit into. Then you think that is what you are. But where is your freedom? You've lost it. Once you identify with your environment, with whatever culture you were born into, you have lost your inner freedom. A Warrior is different. A Warrior is beyond culture, beyond any identification, a cosmic being.

That is why the Warriors were so good at breaking traditions—not because they did not like a tradition or thought it was bad, but because they were free from tradition. They simply had no need for it. There is nothing wrong with tradition, but as you evolve, as you become a true Warrior, you realize that tradition is just there, and you are beyond it.

Ordinary people are bound by tradition, doing things because they think they have to, or because it gives them a sense of identity, a purpose in life. But when you are a Master Warrior you are a universal person. If the tradition fits and is useful, you do it. If it does not fit, you don't do it. You do what the moment requires, what the energy inside you requires, what the Spirit within you requires.

In the early days of the Shaolin Kung Fu School the pupils were monks first, spending many years meditating and discovering themselves, and then became Warriors. But centuries later when the Shaolin School degenerated and lost its spiritual connection, the pupils who came into the school did only the physical training. They did amazing things with their physical training and developed tremendous powers by focusing on one ability. Some could smash stone blocks with their head, for example, and some specialized in pulling trees out of the ground.

But there was nothing behind these feats; there was no longer any spiritual connection; they had lost the Art of the Warrior. They developed physical skills but were no longer connected *within*. So what if you can pull a tree out of the ground? Physical strength is not a sign of intelligence.

The true Warrior is *intelligent*—in fact, the greater the Warrior, the greater the intelligence. If you want to be a Warrior, therefore, that is what you have to aim for. And that is why spiritual training is all-important, apart from the fact that it liberates you, that it gives you a meaning to life and an understanding of the process of life itself.

When you are a Warrior you stand in the Light and see the Dark, and you see the play of Light and Dark, holding the vision of both inside you. And then there comes a moment of *Illumination*, which is the sure, direct knowledge. In that moment, it is not your mind telling you what to do. No. There is something else inside you that tells you to go this way or that way, or stand still and do nothing at all. The guidance is within you in that moment—and it comes in moment by moment—so you know what to do. ⚔

~ 30 ~

THE POWER
OF INSIGHT

I want to tell you about how to have insight in your life. I will start with materialistic consciousness and give you an analogy of how it works. Suppose you want to find out how a car goes. In terms of materialism, you look at the wheels of the car and first argue whether the wheels are moving on the road or the road is moving under the wheels. You can spend years analysing and discussing that until you finally establish that the wheels go round on the road. Later, somebody questions that explanation and claims that the wheels are not moving, that it's only an apparent motion. So then the materialistic minds decide to do more experimentation and analyse the tires, and then measure the friction between tires and the road, and on and on.

That is the materialistic view of life, which only looks at the wheels and the road and does not take into consideration that the car has other parts, namely, an engine that actually moves the wheels. This does not figure into their consciousness because the engine is of another quality, so they refuse to have anything to do with it. Even if, theoretically, they considered the engine and tried to figure out what was making the car go, they would not get the right answer because ultimately the engine is just an intermediate reality: behind the engine there is a driver, which is a different order of intelligence, one the materialists will certainly not consider at all.

This is a rough physical example, but the worldview of the materialist is that what we see is reality; there is nothing else and therefore all the laws of life must be explainable just from what we can observe physically. Materialists do not consider that physical things might only be effects, that is, that everything that happens to you in life is only an effect, not a cause; that everything that happens in Creation and all the laws known to science are only effects, not the causes of things—they are just the wheels moving on the road.

Behind those effects there are the intermediary causes—the inner worlds, the inner energies, the inner stresses within Creation that produce and work out into manifestation. And behind those causes is the Primary Cause: the Spirit, which is an even higher reality. That is to say:

Spirit motivates energy and energy motivates matter.

This is important because when you apply it to yourself it will give you insight into your life.

Most people think according to my car analogy; they look at the effects. They do not try to figure out causes—not on the intermediate level and certainly not on the absolute level. While human beings maintain a materialistic state of mind, life is just one dislocated event after another, just a series of mishaps and chances, like the theory of how the Universe came into being, how it just happened that matter suddenly decided to form itself into solar systems and galaxies, just a haphazard happening in empty space with no intelligence or order or plan behind it.

When you look at your life do things just happen to you? If you've had a car accident or a disease or your wife or husband left you, do you think it just happened, that's just how it is? But is it just how it is?

To understand the mystery of your life you have to start off with the fact that everything that happens to you has an immediate cause, a secondary cause and, beyond that, on a much higher level, a primary cause. In other words, what happens to you physically is on the material level. Behind that there is an energy level, a different order of reality, a series of invisible energies and forces that make things happen in your life. And behind that is an Intelligence, which is your Soul, a completely different order of reality again, which it has its own motives that bring about events that manifest in physical life.

To practise Insight Meditation you take an event in your life and try to find out why it happened, rather than blaming somebody for it. You look at a situation and go back in your mind until you see something you did or did not do that caused that situation. Then you will have an insight into how your life has evolved and how you are actually creating situations. But that is not where you stop; that is still only the intermediary level of causes.

Then, try to reach your Soul level. Sense yourself as a Living Soul and sense the reasons why the Soul allowed it to happen, because the Soul allows things to happen for definite reasons. It is a much higher order of intelligence because it understands the cause behind the cause.

This is not an intellectual exercise; you have to use another sense. Take an event that happened to you and then, without thinking or intellectualizing, try to flick back through the events that led up to it, tracing the causes back to the beginning of this lifetime. If you feel that the

---

Your Soul had a plan for each of your past lives, it has a plan for this lifetime and, if you fail, it will have a plan for the next life. The Soul plans out a successful life, but if you fail, it will make another plan so that you can be successful the next time. The Soul is eternally optimistic. It makes plan after plan after plan, no matter what disasters you create, because it lives in a different reality, beyond time and space.

The Soul learns from the events of your life, except that it learns through subtle Light-vibrations. Every event, as far as the Soul is concerned, is a Light-vibration, an imprint of Light, and the Soul learns by the alternation of Light patterns. Your Soul arranges a pattern of Light, you go through the event and if it does not work out you do it again. That is how the Soul learns. It is a subtle kind of learning.

cause is something beyond that, then try to sense what happened in a previous lifetime. Remember that things that happen to you in *this* lifetime may have been caused by something you did in this lifetime or in a previous lifetime, or it could have been ten or a hundred lifetimes ago because in the eternal continuum the energy stream is eternal. Energy cannot be destroyed; it can only be changed or transmuted.

The important thing is to try to figure out what is happening to you now. In the beginning you might think this technique is inaccurate or that it is not easy to do properly or to find the right answer. It is an internal sensory exercise of going back, back, back, and sometimes you will see clearly why something is happening to you. It is about understanding the Law of Karma, how action and reaction work in your life.

I'm trying to say that Insight Meditation is actually one of the most powerful tools for making progress on the Spiritual Warrior Path, progress in meditation and in Soul Awareness. If you do this meditation regularly until it develops into a habit, then you can begin to live intelligently, seeing the causes behind the results, the energies and forces that moved you in a particular direction. Then, if you go to the deeper layer of the meditation process, you might perceive what the Soul had to do with it, why the Soul allowed it.

But remember this is not guesswork and it's not a mental exercise. It is a process of self-illumination, and if you master it you will be able to master your destiny. You will control the life forces and how they move and manifest in your life. You will have exactly the life you want.

Practice

~

Insight Meditation

The word *insight* means the ability to perceive clearly and deeply a problem or a situation with a sudden understanding; to understand profoundly your mental processes and the mental processes of others; an immediate understanding of what is transpiring.

In Insight Meditation you sit in your favourite sitting posture. It is best to use the heels posture or cross-legged posture, but you can use any other posture, including sitting in a chair with your back straight. In this meditation you *observe* what is going on inside you—your thoughts, feelings and experiences. You observe, and this is the key: you become the Silent Witness, the Silent Observer. Then try to get a sense of how the observer is different from that which is observed; how thoughts are different from the thinker; and what is the consciousness that perceives all of this.

This is a subtle meditation, for you are not looking for anything nor is there a seeker who expects to find anything. You simply and innocently *observe* all that is going on inside you.

Take one particular event and silently observe what happened without condemnation, judgement or self-criticism, and extend that observation back and back to a general pattern of forces or energies inside you. The insight is:

That which is ever moving, ever changing, ever passing away—your thoughts, feelings, moods, desires and sensations and all the world events—is the Unreal, or the not-Self. And that which is unchanging, that which is luminous and brightly shining, whose nature is Being, Consciousness and Bliss—your Soul—is the Self, that which is the Real.

As you go through this cycle of events in your mind, first you come to see what is not real—all the shifting energies and results—and then what stands behind it all: the shining Being, the Soul, which is the Real, the focal point of your life in manifestation.

Notes

This is an advanced technique. It puts you on the road to understanding how your life works and how you can control it. On a higher level, when you are on the verge of becoming a Master Warrior, you will rely on insight to suss out where things are coming from (what level of Reality) and what your correct response to the situation should be.

When you are a Master Warrior you deal with Cosmic Life. Your life-wave is large and goes back thousands of years into the past and forward thousands of years into the future. You consider the total effect that all your lives have had on you and how you are creating effects for your future lives, not only for yourself but also for future generations. You are dealing with what I call Cosmic Destiny. You work out what your right action is at a particular time and create the best situation so that the best outcome will be manifested in the future.

~

Life moves like a wave. The top part of the wave is the internal dimensions, the after-death states, and the bottom part of the wave is the physical manifestation. So the wave moves down into the Physical World and then goes back into the invisible inner dimensions, gathers energy and comes down again. If you can grasp your life-wave and understand what produced this life and its events, then you can go back and see where the life-wave is taking you in this life and the next.

This is when your Cosmic Life begins, because when you are on a high level of consciousness, what is called Cosmic Consciousness, you know your place in the Cosmos. You know why you are as you are, what your purpose is in the total scheme of things and the best way to bring about that purpose. You will still make mistakes, but because of your ability to tune in, you will know if you have made a mistake and how to improve your action to get better results in the future. It is a learning that goes beyond the personality, feeling what the Soul is and how it acts in the whole picture until you are able to work through the Soul itself.

~

Insight Meditation develops *Cosmic Insight*. You can actually read the mind of God and understand the original plan of things and why things are not working, why things are off the plan. You can see why certain religious groups are the way they are, and what the Soul plan was that did not get fulfilled. Every religion had a divine impulse and your inner consciousness can sweep back to the origin of that religion and see how it is out of touch with that divine impulse. You can look at the whole history of a race or nation and see why it has gone wrong, how it is not following the plan it was originally intended to follow.

~

Here is another way to practise Insight Meditation, a way of developing Soul connection and bringing Insight into your life:

Sit still and listen inside. You can listen either in your right ear or in your heart, and see if you can sense the movement of your Soul. Try to sense where your Soul is at this moment, not in terms of location but in terms of consciousness. Listen patiently and see if you get an instruction, message or impression of something you are supposed to be doing now. This is not an intellectual exercise. The Soul does not tell you to get off your backside and go to work. That is your mind. The Soul imparts an extremely fine, subtle impression, and then you *know* instantaneously. So it is a matter of tuning into your Heart or right ear and seeing if you can touch the Soul and feel its subtle reality and what its message is for you for now. ✗

~ 31 ~

THE CODE
OF THE WARRIOR

Movies like *The Last Samurai*, *Troy* and *Crouching Tiger, Hidden Dragon* give us some perspective on the warrior system, but you might have noticed that their perspective is a bit confused. In *Troy*, the warriors have no principles. In *The Last Samurai*, they have principles but they are mixed with local superstitions, as they are in the beautiful movie *Crouching Tiger, Hidden Dragon*. So the question arises: is there a code for the Spiritual Warrior?

In other words, if we want to bring about a Spiritual Warrior School, is there a code that we have to live by? Are there principles we have to live by? It is not enough just to have fighting skills. Anybody can have fighting skills. And in fact, most people in the warrior system have fighting skills but no principles; or if they have principles, they are identified with political aims, money or name and fame. *Troy* is all about name and fame and the Knights of the Round Table in Europe were involved with politics. The Chinese warrior system was also mixed with politics, with warlords fighting each other, using their skills to destroy each other for political reasons or personal glory. None of it was about spiritual principles.

On the other hand, the Ancients had a Warrior Code, a spiritual code to live by. In ancient India, for example, in the times of the Vedas, eight thousand years ago, the warriors had a strict code in accordance with Natural Law. Of course, it was lost over time and today's generations do not have that code at all. If you train to be a warrior without principles, you become a fighter, not a Warrior. The ancient Warriors were full of virtue, power, magnetism, because they had something else besides fighting skills: they had the Warrior Code inside them.

The Warrior Archetype

You have to understand that the Warrior type is a spiritual type. It is only because Warriorship has been debased over the centuries that it became just about skill in war. A warrior became just a machine to kill another warrior. That is not the original but the *debased* Art of the Warrior. The further you go back in time, the more you realize that the ancient Warriors were majestic beings. They had a noble manner and dignity. A force emanated from them that was not based on their ability to kill but on internal virtue, internal realities.

This brings us to another question: Is there an archetype of the Warrior? Because if there is no archetype where did Warrior Schools come from? How could there have been great Warriors even in the days of Atlantis? Where did the *idea* of the Spiritual Warrior come from? If there is a system there must be a source, even if it is long forgotten.

In a state of Higher Consciousness, I asked the Infinite Mind, the Cosmic Intelligence permeating Creation, what the source of the Warrior

---

Principles are an important part of the Warrior School system because without principles it is just a school of martial arts. If you watch the Kung Fu movies of China, you notice one thing: They just kill each other all the time—because they have *no principles!* Fighting is not a principle. When you are established in the true Warrior art, fighting is the last thing you do, if you ever fight at all. The purpose of martial arts training is to give you strength, focus, energy, skill; it has very little to do with killing. To be able to act in life skilfully, you have to have the Warrior Code inside you.

was. The answer I got is that there is an archetype of the Warrior, a spiritual archetype, a being of Infinite Light, a tremendous Spiritual Warrior who has existed for millions of years on this planet, in the invisible dimensions. It is the true Warrior, standing eternally in the Light, a being who has all the absolute dignity, majesty and virtue that any warrior has ever had or can have in the future.

When you tune into that archetypal figure, then you understand what it means to be a Warrior, and you understand why there are warriors among the human species. Most of the ancient races were warrior types, basing their whole social structure on warriorship, *because this planet is a school for warriors*. Other planets have other qualities but on this planet the humanoid type is a warrior type, and the planet, in its evolutionary unfoldment, is a school for warriors.

If the planet is a school for warriors, then there must be a prototype, an archetype to work to. As I said, there is. The archetype is a great Being and every warrior meets that Being when he or she has reached a certain level of development and is admitted into its presence. This does not happen in the Physical World: you are not led into a mysterious cave somewhere in India and introduced to a physical person. This is a spiritual being made of Light, a being whose consciousness is Light—the Warrior of Light who represents the strength, power, dignity, wisdom and majesty of the true Warrior, who is the very embodiment of Spiritual Warriorship.

The Warrior School is the Earth's planetary school because not every planetary life is as violent as ours. Ours is based on violence because we do not understand the Warrior Path. Originally the Warrior Path was a struggle between the Soul and the Personality, between Spirit and Matter, the temporary life-stream versus the Eternal Life-Stream. There is a maladjustment between them and the Warrior has to adjust things until the Cosmic and the Human merge into one.

The Warrior of Light is a *real* being, a dynamic, pulsating living entity existing in the inner dimensions, a perfected Warrior that we all can evolve towards. By the end of Humanity's life cycle on this planet we will become that perfected Warrior *in physical incarnation*, and that Being will exist until we reach perfection.

Only when you have reached a high point of evolution in your own existence are you *allowed* to see that Being even for a moment. If you met now you would be annihilated. There is such a powerful Light coming from that Being that you would not be able to stand it at this stage, unless you yourself become a Warrior of the Light. When you do, you will not only understand who you are and what you ought to become but also what the planet ought to become, because the Eternal Warrior stands for planetary evolution, for the perfection of Humanity, for what the human species will become when God's Divine Plan is accomplished.

In my book *The Warrior Code* there are 365 aphorisms, 365 principles or rules of Warriorship.[10] They came about as a direct response to the question: What should a human being do to approximate the ideal image of that archetype and become a Spiritual Warrior? Obviously, becoming a Warrior changes your life; it is about something other than what you are. To do that, you have to have some rules and principles. And that is what is in that book: the principles that will make you a Warrior, instructions that came from the invisible realms and were put into writing so that you would know what to do to become a Warrior.

In the Warrior School, besides things like meditation and martial arts training, you also have to work with principles, because if you are the most skilled fighter but have no principles you will not be a Warrior. There is a big difference between a fighter and a Warrior standing in the Light. It is a completely different reality. And to get to the point where

---

10. Imre Vallyon, *The Warrior Code: 365 Aphorisms of the Spiritual Warrior* (Sounding-Light Publishing, 2011).

you are standing in the Light, you have to start applying principles, not because somebody has told you to be good but because you understand *why* you need to be good; principles that you recognize and apply automatically, because you recognize that they are in harmony with your own being, with others and with Creation, and because you know that they will change your life radically and immediately.

Even one of the principles in *The Warrior Code* will change your life if you apply it, for it will open up Infinite Intelligence inside you. How that book works is magical because the principles have issued forth from the mind of the Warrior of Light and are impregnated with the quality of the Light. As soon as you begin to use those principles you will be zapped with the Light-Energy. The words of the Warrior are ancient, eternal and indestructible because they stand for Truth, which has always existed, exists now and will exist forever, until the end of the cosmic cycle of Evolution.

In the Inner Worlds there is perfect harmony. The Warrior of Light stands in that perfect harmony, and the rules and regulations of the Warrior come from that perfected condition. So when we apply them in our daily lives we begin to move towards that perfected condition. Even if you just learn five or six of the Warrior rules, they will radically change your life; in fact, any one of them will transform you straight away.

I'm sure that most of you have had problems in life, right? It's the rule of life. But when you have a problem, the essential question is: What are you going to do to solve it? Will you solve it according to a true Warrior Principle? Or according to what some worldly authority or religious figure tells you to do? Will you stand in your own Light, in the image of the Warrior who blazes out the Truth inside your consciousness, and act according to that?

A Warrior Aphorism

Let us take one of the Warrior aphorisms in *The Warrior Code* as an example:

> Order in the midst of chaos. Love in the midst of hate. Light in the midst of darkness.

As I said, this is not just a clever thought or idea. So what does this aphorism actually mean and how do you apply it? Suppose you have a problem—a family problem, a problem at work, a problem with your situation, a problem with some other person. You can deal with that problem in different ways according to your knowledge and understanding, but what if you say, speaking like the Spiritual Warrior, "Order in the midst of chaos. Love in the midst of hate. Light in the midst of darkness"?

The Spiritual Warrior says that there is order even when there is apparent chaos, there is love even when there is apparent hate and there is light even when there is apparent darkness. Accordingly, when you say this aphorism you are re-establishing an ancient Truth Principle. The Warrior within you knows that there is Order in the Cosmos even when this world seems to be chaotic; there is Love in the Cosmos even when everybody seems to be full of hate; there is Light in the Cosmos even when the world appears to be dark. They are invisible, hidden, subtle, but they are there, and the Warrior tells you to get in touch with that Order, that Love and that Light within you.

This is a true Warrior Principle, eternal and indestructible. This is the Ancient Warrior speaking inside you. At that moment, you rededicate yourself to the Spiritual Warrior within and the Warrior can get in touch with you. You will hear his voice bright and clear: "Create Order. Create Love. Create Light."

At that moment your life changes. First you become transformed by the Light itself because you allowed yourself to become a Spiritual Warrior in action, in a real life situation. These principles tell you how to live life. It's one thing to learn martial arts, to learn fighting skills, but it's a very different thing to live life itself, out there, in the workplace, at home—in the world. That is the test of the Warrior.

This aphorism tells you that you must be in the state of Order because the perfect harmony of the Cosmos is Order; you must be in the state of Love because the eternal rule of life is Love; and you must be filled with Light because the only real thing in the Universe is Light.

Then you begin to live like that, to respond to situations in such a way. You will realize that in the world people act disorderly, they act hatefully, they act in a state of darkness. But you know that they do this because they are not in the Warrior School, they are not in the Light of the Warrior, they do not stand in Divinity. So it does not matter what the other person does or says, or what the situation is, you focus and become that Order, Love and Light. Then you begin to radiate a colossal energy stream out of you that will change the situation and the people around you. It is quite magical.

I will give you a practical example. Suppose you have had a fight with your boyfriend or girlfriend or with a relative or your boss. Your first reaction is to respond in kind, to get angry, feel sorry for yourself, and so on. What if you say, "Order. Love. Light"? What if you say, "I stand in the eternal Order, in the field of Love, in the field of Light"? And that is all you do. You remain compassionate and loving, standing in your own Light, believing in the perfect order of things, being a Spiritual Warrior.

The duty of the Warrior is to establish himself or herself in the Warrior Code, the rules that a Warrior embraces. That is what gives the Warrior dignity and majesty, what makes the Warrior noble. You can be very strong physically but that does not give you manner and bearing. What gives you real strength and real manner is the spiritual quality inside you. And what gives you the spiritual quality is working with the Warrior Principles, moving bit by bit closer to the perfect image of the Warrior of Light inside you.

After a while the situation will change and you will be free of the negative impulses coming towards you. It is like self-defence. In Aikido and other forms of martial arts, for instance, you learn to defend yourself but not to attack because there comes a point where you are so strong that you do not want to kill, because life is sacred for you. You know that all life is one, that even your worst enemy is full of Divinity. When you are a Spiritual Warrior you do not destroy the other person, you just protect yourself.

Being a Warrior means being a Warrior twenty-four hours a day, 365 days a year, for your whole life. It is not something you do only today. You meet every situation and every person in your life with the Warrior Principles. Whatever circumstances come to you, you exude those principles from inside and act as the Spiritual Warrior. ⚔

~ 32 ~

THE WAY OF THE WARRIOR
IS ACTION

Action and Intelligence

In a sense, the Way of the Warrior symbolizes the way of life of a Western person, by which I mean a person who lives in the world, in contrast to a monk, nun or sādhu; that is, the type of person who is active *in* the world.

In Buddhism and Hinduism, the Principle of Action and the results of action have been taught for several thousand years, but for some reason in the West, people just act and hope for the best, without understanding the Way of Action. We need to understand action and how to utilize it so that our lives become more as they should be.

First of all, everybody acts all the time. It is impossible to go through life in the world not doing anything. So you have to act one way or another all the time, from the time you are born until the time you die. But what most people do not know is that every action has a consequence, whether they are aware of it or not.

By *action* I do not mean only physical actions but all your thoughts and emotions, your whole personality complex, whether the action is through a thinking process or a feeling process or a physical process—every action in the personality sphere below the Soul level, which includes this world and the subtle worlds up to the Causal World. Everything you do in that sphere has a result. Once you have had a thought or feeling or performed an action, therefore, the result is there, whether you perceive it at that moment or not. In a way, that is the tragedy of the Western World: we do not understand the Principle of Action. If you want to be a Spiritual Warrior, it is imperative to understand the Principle of Action.

So everybody in the world acts. Some just go about acting haphazardly, going through life in an aimless way, getting knocked or pushed this way and that. They have no internal structure to act intelligently and just act according to the circumstances presented to them or the situation they find themselves in. (Whether you act intelligently or unintelligently, however, you are still producing results. It makes no difference to the Law.)

There are millions of people like that, people who are driven left and right by all kinds of circumstances and act unintelligently in all the three spheres of action. And there are people who are a bit more with it, more developed, more intelligent; they have a plan, a purpose, a goal or vision in life. They want to make a good living and have lots of money, which requires a certain amount of intelligence, and they purposefully work towards their goal. Such a person is what I call a *relatively* intelligent person, not a really intelligent person.

Real Intelligence is what makes a Spiritual Warrior different from the average so-called intelligent person. There is an incredibly big difference between the intelligence of a Spiritual Warrior and that of the average person, a heaven-and-earth difference.

To live your life as a Spiritual Warrior your intelligence has to be much greater than the average intelligence because of the profound consequences of a Warrior's actions. As I mentioned, the Warriors were the heroes of ancient days. They had an impact on societies and nations, benefiting many generations and transforming human consciousness on a large scale. To have such an impact, you cannot be just an ordinary person, the type of person who gets up in the morning and does not know what to do until somebody tells them; you can't have a purpose-less, meaningless existence.

That is the bottom rung of the ladder of Intelligence. Now let's go to the top. First of all, there is a Universal Intelligence. We may call it the Cosmic Mind, the Infinite Mind of Light or the Mind of God or the Mind of the Absolute. There is an infinite field of Knowledge, Understanding and Wisdom throughout all of Creation, an infinite field of Intelligence that is responsible for the whole manifestation of the Universe as well as its evolution and its final perfection and annihila-tion at the end of time. And then there is human intelligence—human beings struggling through life, some with some intelligence, others with no intelligence at all.

So there is a big gap between the standard human being and that mighty, infinite Cosmic Mind. The great Heroes of old stand some-where in between the Infinite Intelligence and the intelligence of the masses. This means that there have been human beings who evolved out of the ordinary and towards that super-ordinary state of Intelligence. Nobody can reach the Intelligence of Deity; that is obvious. There can be only one Deity, only one Absolute Intelligence, and that is the Abso-lute Intelligence Itself. But there are, as I said, people who have attained in-between stages where they could perceive and act from a superior intelligence—you may call it Superconsciousness, Higher Conscious-ness, Cosmic Consciousness or Supernatural Intelligence.

The task of the Spiritual Warrior is to develop that Supernatural Intel-ligence, a level of intelligence that *has to be developed*. It is not something you can pick up at the supermarket when you go shopping. You may remain at the ordinary level of intelligence for thousands of lifetimes, and many people do. Remember, by *intelligence* I do not mean the function of your mind, your thinking process. That has nothing to do with Intel-ligence, that's just your thought processes, and everybody thinks all the time. Just because you can think does not mean that you are intelligent.

Intelligence has to be developed and perfected through conscious effort. The great Heroes did not suddenly emerge out of the masses and become Buddhas or Christs. They developed those levels of intelligence, or rather, they developed their *connection* with the Superior Intelligence, with the Mind of God. And through that connection they could understand, they could see destiny, they could act in ways that had an impact not only on their immediate environment but also their whole community, their whole nation and ultimately the world itself.

Developing Real Intelligence

The question is: How do you develop Intelligence? Well, strange as it may seem, it is not through the process of thinking at all.

To understand what life is about you have to develop your interior faculty, and the interior faculty is not developed by thinking but by *not* thinking. Modern education develops your thinking to the ultimate degree of activity. The more you think, the more educated you are, according to the modern standard. But the ancient standard was: no thinking *what-so-ever*. And the more "no-thinking", the better educated you were. This is what actually leads you to Higher Intelligence. You cannot attain Higher Intelligence by thinking. You can think until the end of time but you will never get there. You will not even get off the ground.

The Spiritual Warriors *know* that this Superior Intelligence exists and consciously train themselves to develop it. They don't sit back and say, "Oh, these are nice philosophies and ideas; now let's go to the beach." The Warriors say, *"How do we get there, what do we have to do to get there?"* And then they do it. It is important to understand that this high Intelligence exists but it does not come to you without action. You can read many beautiful philosophies—and people churn out philosophies day in and day out both in the East and in the West—but that in itself will not develop your level of intelligence. That just activates the thinking mind; it does not lead to Intelligence.

This is why in all spiritual training systems you first learned to stop your thoughts before you even began the journey of education, and this is why the ancient Spiritual Warriors—the Chinese, Japanese, Hindu, Buddhist, Greek and Roman Warriors—concentrated on stopping the thinking mechanism. It was so basic, like the first letter of the Spiritual Warrior alphabet: stop thinking; just be. *Be*—and thereby be able to receive the universal energies that move in and out of the planet and all around you.

Even before you could *step* on the Spiritual Path you had to be able to stop your mind, stop your emotions and be receptive to the universal vibrations around you—what life is actually about! There is another dimension to life, which is how life really is. Everything we describe in Nature exists only in the human mind, not in Nature itself. Do you think that a horse thinks it is a horse? You would be shocked if you entered the consciousness of a plant or an animal and realized what it really is, which is nothing like how science describes it. The thought of being a horse does not exist in the horse consciousness whatsoever. It only exists *in the human mind.*

That is why in ancient times people said that human intelligence is Māyā, or unreal. It is like a delusion because it does not correspond with Nature. In the Dark Ages of Europe they thought the Earth was flat. Notice: they *thought* the Earth was flat. They argued about it and the Church killed many people because they didn't believe the Earth was flat. But was the Earth actually flat? Of course, it wasn't flat; it was still round. It made absolutely no difference to Nature whether human beings thought the Earth was flat or not. Nature was exactly how it was.

We have created a false reality through the mind. And that false reality includes who you are, because you think that you are a Chinese, a Hungarian, a Swahili or whatever, that you were educated in such-and-such a way, that you have this or that job. You have all these ideas about what you think you *are*—and they are completely not what you are at all.

What you really are is a vast, infinite being with no boundaries. Every one of us has no boundaries and is open to the whole cosmic flux, the Cosmic Mind, the whole of Nature, both visible and invisible. We are not bound by country, nationality, religion or philosophy—things *we* created. Human society lives in an artificial creation, a creation of the human mind itself.

In reality, human intelligence is infinitely larger and vaster than that artificial creation. Can you imagine that your mind is an infinite ocean of Intelligence breathing in and out through all of Creation, rather than just your limited thinking ability? That is your real mind, the mind of the Spiritual Warrior, the mind of someone moving up the ladder of Evolution. And it is through that mind that Spiritual Warriors act.

The Spiritual Warrior Consciousness is an immense power within every one of us. It is already there, but it will not manifest by itself; we have to actually do something about it. And one of the first things we should do is learn the art of meditation, because without meditation that other Intelligence cannot manifest.

That is why meditation is supremely important. Through meditation we learn to still our minds and harmonize our emotions so that we can get a glimpse of, or awaken to, that other Consciousness. In the beginning you may only get a glimpse of it, but as your skill improves, as your internal focus and concentration improve, as your ability to stop your mind improves, you will increasingly have visions or sensations of the

---

All true meditation will drive you inside your self. Then you will begin to feel what you really are, not the ideas of what you think you are—ideas imposed *on* your mind *by* your mind. You limit yourself by your own thinking process! The ancient martial artists, who used the martial arts as the outer part of their inner training, could see immediately their limitations through the techniques of warfare, because if you make a mistake in war you are out of action. So very soon you learn where you actually are in life.

Infinite Mind until you are able to be in it all the time, until you are simply living in it. Then you can change your environment radically; then you can throw out vibrations and energies that will change the people and environment around you, and therefore the destiny of the planet.

The Warrior in Action

To become a Spiritual Warrior, therefore, you must have a basic modicum of intelligence to understand that there is such a possibility. Suppose you come from an Eastern religion: then you should have the idea that you can become a Buddha, because if you haven't even got that concept you can never become one. Suppose you come from a Christian background: you at least have to have the idea that you can become something like the Christ—wise, powerful, loving, forgiving. You must have at least developed a level of intelligence that you recognize that there is a certain possibility inside you; otherwise you will just stay on the same level of intelligence.

Personal development starts when you wake up and say, "Yes, I can become more than what I am, more than what my education gave me, more than what my parents gave me, more than what society gave me. I can become like those Great Ones because I have the power and potential to be like them." Once you acknowledge your potential, your possibility, then you can set about achieving it. Then you are a Spiritual Warrior *in action* and your actions will be towards manifesting that possibility.

One of the most important actions, one of the primary techniques, is meditation, because without that you cannot move an inch forward, that is to say, *inward*. In meditation you learn to disengage your mind in order for the Self within you to begin shining on its own accord, in its own Light, not dependent on your mental activity. And once the Self inside you shines by its own Light, then you can move to the next stage and begin to use that Light and feel how it motivates you from within and what it is doing to the people around you and to your environment. Your Warriorship begins once you understand that the energy of that

Light needs to be released in a particular situation, for example, to help alleviate suffering or bring harmony or love into the chaotic condition of the planet.

When you understand that you have another power that can be used for good, you are only a baby Warrior and you will still make mistakes. Being at the beginning stages of the Warrior Path does not mean that all your actions are perfect and you can never make a mistake. All it means is that you are learning your powers, your abilities, and learning from your mistakes. Making mistakes develops your intelligence so that there comes a day when you can completely avoid mistakes because you know beforehand the consequences of your actions.

But when you are a Spiritual Warrior and have developed some degree of Cosmic Consciousness, then you have a problem: you see precisely what people should be doing according to the Divine Plan and you also see that they are not doing it. The fact that society is out of tune with the Infinite is most obvious; there's no question about it. But then as a Spiritual Warrior you have the problem that if you try to push society, try to tell the masses or the authorities what they really should be doing, you will be persecuted.

So one of the choices of the Warrior is self-sacrifice, sacrificing yourself for a cause. For example, Mahatma Gandhi—he was a baby Warrior—knew he had to put India into a certain condition because it was in a terrible state, so he sacrificed himself. He was killed because he was stirring people in the right direction, toward manifesting the Divine Intelligence. Of course, the public did not like it, the religious authorities did not like it, and it was a religious fanatic who killed him in the end.

In the past, many Warriors went to the authorities and told them what they should be doing. They fought for their vision and got killed—and then became heroes. That is how you became a hero in those days: either the authorities declared you a hero (after they had put you out of your misery of course) or the pope canonized you. It was always the same: canonization came after they had destroyed you.

But there is another way, namely, teaching people quietly in little groups in secluded spots or ashrams like the Rosicrucians did in the Middle Ages. The Rosicrucians were part of the Warrior class, for they were knights, but they knew that if they went against the Church authorities publicly, they would be tortured and burned at the stake. Seeing the futility of such an end, they promulgated the universal doctrine of Love and Reformation in a quiet and gentle way. As a Spiritual Warrior you have these two options: either fight openly or do your work silently. This is a choice the Warrior has to make when he or she is ready to do this work.

To sum up, therefore, we all have divine powers within us, which will not manifest unless we do something about it. And one of the primary requisites is that we meditate. Unfortunately, this is a difficult thing for people to do because of the time factor. People are too busy. This is understandable because they are not monks secluded in a monastery. They have very busy lives. But there is an interesting point here: in the beginning of the Path you think that meditation and active life are two different things and therefore you resist the idea of meditating because you think you are too busy to sit down and meditate.

In the beginning it appears that your active life excludes the way of meditation. But if you manage to make time to meditate, even just five or ten minutes a day, after a while another energy current will start building up inside you, an energy current that comes from meditation itself. Soon you will find time to meditate longer. That current will keep building up and after a number of years you will notice that the time that you are meditating is no different from the time you are active, that when you are acting you are not out of tune with meditation. This is when you begin to become a Spiritual Warrior.

The Spiritual Warrior Path is a way of action. In the beginning the Warrior acts or meditates, but when you reach a certain level of internal development, action and meditation become simultaneous—you are focusing inside while you are acting outside. It is an important part of the Warrior training to know that your action *is* meditation. But the state of acting always while in a state of meditation can only come once you have gone through the preliminary stage of action-meditation, action-meditation, doing them separately.

At a later stage they fuse together and you are fully acting and at the same time in the full state of meditation. Then it changes into something else completely; it becomes meditative action. When you develop Cosmic Consciousness, your action springs from meditation. Meditation is going on inside you all the time—in the same way as the thinking process goes on in ordinary people all the time. Your state of meditation is continuous and your action process is continuous, even as you are using your mind. In a state of meditation the mind can do what it likes because your action springs not from your mind, your thought processes, but from the state of meditation.

This is when you are actually becoming a Spiritual Warrior—but still a baby because at this stage you are still functioning from your own meditative state, your own perception, or *intelligence-connections* to the Cosmic Mind. But at a much higher level, even that disappears and it is the Cosmic Mind itself that begins acting through you, and you become like a mirror or like an empty vessel or a hollow tube. The Cosmic Intelligence pours out through you, without even interfering with your own meditative process. There is no particular personality mechanism involved, nor even is your meditative state involved. You are like an open channel. That is when you become a perfected Warrior, or a perfected human, when you simply act spontaneously because the Divine acts through you.

Practice

~

MARAMA Meditation Technique

The ancient Primordial Sound Language of Humanity, which was our common language in the time of Atlantis, was made of Sound-Vibrations—pure vowels and combination of vowels and consonants that had their own meanings. They were not words that conveyed a fact or reality but sounds put together in different structures for different purposes. One of those sound-structures is MARAMA, and this combination of sounds has the power to stop your mind. This is an important Warrior technique for getting into a state of internal Ecstasy, or Bliss, which you can only do by stopping the activity of the mind.

When you begin to meditate, that is to say, turn your attention within, you will notice that the mind is active. This is not because it was inactive before; it's just that you happen to notice it because you are concentrating on your inner reality and then you suddenly realize how busy your mind is. Your physical body is continually in motion (which is why you tend to fidget when you meditate) because the physical body does not like to be still. Your mind is like that too; it does not like to be quiet and doing nothing. It is like a wound-up clock that just ticks away all the time, even at nighttime when you are sleeping (when it produces your dreams).

To be a Warrior you have to learn the technique of stopping your mind, because in the midst of battle you cannot allow your mind to go rambling on about something or other; you would be killed instantaneously. In real life situations, as a Warrior, you have to be totally in control of your mind, or else you are lost even before the battle starts.

Mind control is the key to success in life not only for Warriors but also for anybody who wants to be happy. When you are in trouble your mind keeps speeding up. Have you ever noticed that? If you are under stress, your mind works overtime, and the more stressed you are, the faster your mind goes—and that is precisely what it should *not* do. The more stressed you are, the slower the mind should become; otherwise you cannot deal with the stress.

If you want to succeed in life, you must be able to still the mind so that you make the right decisions. That is why it is so important to learn to stop your mind by saying MARAMA, a combination of three sounds that tell your mind to stop its chatter.

The meditation goes like this: You say MARAMA mentally, inside yourself, and then pause and wait in silence until the mind starts thinking again. Then say MARAMA again. Each time you say it, pause and stay in silence until the mind starts thinking, and then say it again. Later on—and this may happen during your first session or later on in your practice—you will notice that it is enough for you to only say RĀMA in order to stop your mind. And as you develop this meditation further you will notice that you no longer have to say RĀMA, just RĀM. And at an even later stage you just need to say RĀ and the mind will stand still. So there is an evolution of sounds from MA-RA-MA to RĀ-MA to RĀM to RĀ.

You might stay with MARAMA for the whole session or you might get to the next stage, RĀMA, or the third stage, RĀM, or the last stage, RĀ. But do not be in a hurry; it's not a matter of getting there quickly,

---

This is the secret of happiness and it is a secret of the ancient Warriors. That is why they could go into battle and not be afraid of death. Spiritual Warriors are not afraid of death; they can die today, tomorrow or the day after, whenever their destiny wills it. It is all the same because the Spiritual Warrior is internally established in the state of Bliss. Within the Warrior there is that shining Light blazing like a tremendous blissful reality, so the Spiritual Warrior knows whether it is time to live or die, time to act or not act, time to sow or reap; for he is in the moment, part of the flow of eternal time. To be able to do that, however, one has to be established in the state of inner joyousness, that state of internal Oneness. MARAMA is one of the Warrior techniques for achieving that state.

but a matter of *being there*. When the mind is still, other things can happen. In that stillness supernatural realities begin to manifest. That is what this meditation is about: manifesting supernatural realities. A Spiritual Warrior is a supernatural being not of this world, a supernatural being disguised in a physical body.

Notes

When you say MARAMA the syllables are of equal length, but when you say RĀMA, the first syllable is longer than the second syllable, so the frequency of the sound changes. At the next stage the sound changes again and becomes more continuous: RĀM. Each time the sound changes to a higher-frequency vibration as the Energy moves inward (up to the higher dimensions). At the fourth level the sound changes completely and becomes the Universal Sound that can be heard throughout all Creation: RĀ.

The meditation has to be done systematically so that your mind becomes finer and finer and more able to gather in Light. The meaning of MARAMA in the ancient language was "blissful light", that is to say, "pure inexhaustible joy, bliss and happiness". So as you practise this meditation, the Light begins to increase in your auric system when you say MARAMA. By the time you are ready to say RĀMA, the Light builds up in your psychic structure; at the blissful stage of RĀM, the Light is intense; and by the time you say RĀ, it is like the inexhaustible power-field of the Sun shining within you.

~

If you learn this technique you can make yourself happy instantaneously, and you can also get in touch with the source of the Light within you. This is not symbolic; it is actual. The Universe is filled with Light, the light of the visible Sun, the light of the invisible (psychic or subtle) Sun and the Light of the Spiritual Sun. You have a physical body, which is visible; a psychic nature, which is invisible; and then there is the spiritual part of you, the Immortal Soul. Similarly, the Sun is visible, psychic and spiritual and the Light is physical, subtle and spiritual. With this meditation technique you go from the physical to the subtle to the spiritual—MARAMA, RĀMA, RĀM, RĀ. When you tune into RĀ the Sun is blazing and the whole Universe is filled with glorious Light, which is Infinite Bliss and Joy.

So this technique leads you to internal bliss. It will make a huge difference to your life because you can *make yourself happy*. Can you imagine that by correctly learning this technique you can make yourself happy at any given moment in time?

Normally we look for happiness outside ourselves. We think that if we earn more money then we will be happy, or if we get the latest car then we will be happy, or if we get married to a certain person we will be happy. We always think that happiness is tied to something outside of us, and we think that if and when we get that thing we'll be happy. That is how we normally think. But here is a meditation that can make you happy without being dependent on anything on the outside. If you want to be happy, just do the meditation and you will be happy.

Just doing meditation work like this is already a blessing. I have students in different countries around the world and I keep reminding them what a tremendous blessing it is for them to be doing this work. There are seven billion people on this planet. How many of them are given this knowledge? How many of them have the opportunity to do this work? When you realize that out of all those people you have been given this chance to work on yourself, to become a Spiritual Warrior, to understand, to live an enlightened way of life, then you will really begin to appreciate it. When you realize that so many people do not have the chance to do this work or even to get near a Teacher who can teach them, you will be thankful. And then you will buckle down and really work, because the world needs you; the world needs this Teaching to be preserved and given out. ✗

~ 33 ~

From Stillness into Action, from Action into Stillness

If you can master this great Warrior Principle you will attain Enlightenment: *from Stillness into Action, from Action into Stillness.* This principle applies broadly across all the aspects of your life—the way you use your body, the way you use your mind, the way you use your emotions. If you learn to apply it, it will work for you day by day, moment by moment. It is the Universal Law of the Warrior: *from Stillness into Action, from Action into Stillness.*

Nowadays most martial arts schools do not work according to this principle. They just go into activity, using action all the time, so they are not on the Spiritual Warrior Path and do not understand what that path is about. For the true Warrior, the circle of Stillness to Action back to Stillness is everything, from the perspective of one's whole life to the individual moments and actions of life, whether those actions are thoughts, feelings or physical actions. Without this principle, Warrior training is useless.

In the true Warrior Schools of the past, when the pupils got up they went into stillness straight away: they meditated for one hour, two hours, three hours or more, depending on their level of advancement and other factors. But the idea was that everybody from the most junior member to the most senior member all went into a state of meditation, or Stillness, and then came out of meditation and started their activities—training, preparing meals, all kinds of activities. At the end of the day they went back into a state of meditation, returning to Stillness. That was the one-day cycle in the life of a Warrior.

The same cycle was repeated on a smaller scale, say, during a training session. Rather than just getting together and charging at each other, they first paused and established Stillness within themselves. Then they drew their weapons and were ready to act. After the physical training was completed, they paused and went back into Stillness. And they did this with any action, no matter how small—even sitting on a rock. First they became still, became one with the rock and the surrounding life-force, and then they did what needed to be done: they went and sat on the rock.

Everything always came out of Stillness and returned to Stillness. But what is this Stillness? Stillness (capitalized) is the connection with the Infinite Intelligence, the Divinity within you. It is a returning to your foundation, your fundamental Self-Nature—your Soul, your Higher Self, the Buddha Mind, the Fundamental Mind, your true nature, whatever

---

In the ancient Warrior Schools they started with simple physical movements before they got into training with a weapon, because the weapon first had to become alive, to take on a life of its own. Similarly, in ancient India, the musicians studied meditation first and tuned into the inner Sound within themselves and the Cosmos before they started learning how to play an instrument. They spent many years listening to the Cosmic Sound *inside* and *outside*, and when they could feel that Sound, they started learning an instrument. And when they became master musicians, the energy of the Cosmic Sound played through their instrument. That is what the ancient musicians did, what the ancient dancers did, what all the ancient people who were initiated into this secret science did. First they mastered the inner side and then expressed it outwardly. Then, whatever they did, whether it was dancing, singing, music or the martial arts, it was *magic*, because they functioned from within, *from Stillness into Action*.

you like to call it. You return to your Source, the Higher Being within you, and having established that connection, which is Stillness, you go into action.

Obviously, when you come from the depths within you and go into action, the quality and nature of that action will be infused with the quality of Stillness, the quality of Inner Harmony or Inner Realization. So much so that in a real battle situation you would know what the other person was going to do before he did it; you would be so tuned in to your self that you would be able to tune into the other person and know what he was thinking. It is similar to what master chess players do. They go into a state of silence and in their mind go over their own moves and the moves of their opponent because they have learned the art of being still and focusing within themselves. You could say that master chess players are warriors, except they just use one particular expression of the Warrior technique.

With this technique, Stillness always begins and completes an action, and as I said, it can be applied to every aspect of your life from meditation to working in the kitchen or going for a walk. And the more you practise it, the more your comprehension of this principle will grow. In the beginning you might think that Stillness is just being quiet, but later on you may get the inner connection and feel your true beingness. But first you must try to apply this idea in your life like it was applied in the ancient Warrior Schools, where they became still even for just ten seconds before they started cooking a meal or doing an action. If you do this habitually, the Stillness will automatically come even when you are not thinking of it.

Have you ever seen a video of Krishnamurti talking? First there is stillness. Then he speaks. And then there is stillness. He does this all the time, not because he is consciously thinking of it, but because he is so habituated to it. It is just the way it happens in his life. Krishnamurti was a born Warrior, of course, and his life is an example of the Warrior Principle.

When you watch two Master Warriors fighting, for example, you will notice there is always a silence or stillness before they go into action. It's a magical moment because they go through the action but the stillness is still there. And then when the action is done there is still the stillness. So the Art of the Warrior is to act in Stillness; action comes out of Stillness and returns to Stillness, and the Stillness has not been changed at all.

The ancient Warriors, in absolute Stillness, drew their sword, made a sword movement and then put the sword back and returned to Stillness again—and there was no disturbance in the atmosphere. That is because action produced in Stillness does not create disturbance. When an action is done with agitation, anger or other negative emotion, of course, it will create all kinds of disturbances in the atmosphere. But when an action is done from Stillness, it is self-completing.

Under attack from uninitiated warriors or just normal thugs charging with great noise and bluster, the initiated Warrior just stays in the state of contemplation until he feels the energy of the attackers and knows they are close enough. Then, he simply draws his sword and his sword and body will move in every direction that is necessary to neutralize the enemy—automatically. *But only if he stays in the state of Stillness.* If he

---

There is a stillness around Spiritual Warriors and every move they make is almost like slow motion, yet lightning-quick. This is because in Warrior Consciousness every millisecond of time is like a whole lifetime.

When you draw your sword as a Warrior you produce waves of energy moving through the air, as if some mighty force were cutting a line through the air. And when you fight, the energy moves and the sword becomes an energy current coming from the Third Eye or the Heart, depending on what level of Warrior you are—from the Heart if you are a Spiritual Warrior. Your weapon is an extension of your arm, an extension of your *being*, which is in tune with the flow of energy in your environment. Thus, everything follows naturally and you function from Stillness into Action and from Action into Stillness.

gets agitated or worried, if he wonders what he should do, if he is in the normal human consciousness state, he will be killed in no time.

Now, in life you normally do not use this principle. Your action is not still; it is usually motivated by anger, fear, violence, aggression, self-pity, irritation, depression or whatever. When you act while you are in one of these states, you start with the wrong energy and naturally attract the wrong energy back to you.

For example, suppose you have a difficult situation in your life, say, you have a difficult person to deal with. Normally you would be all worked up about it, tense, angry, aggressive, protective of yourself, sorry for yourself or have any number of negative emotions. So you plunge into that situation and of course you get back what you started with.

But suppose that before you enter the situation, you sit down and meditate for half an hour and withdraw into the silent space within you, completely unconcerned whether that situation exists or not, completely unworried about any results. It is just the Cosmos acting through you or creating a possibility for you to act.

So you simply withdraw into stillness and manage to retain that stillness. That is important! If you manage to retain that stillness when you go into action, the outcome will be totally different. The person will pick up the vibration coming from you, so instead of being angry with you he will be mellow and responsive and willing to drop the whole problem—all because you managed to carry that stillness into action.

Remember, there is an art to this: you don't go into stillness and then go out and act violently; that is useless. *The art is to allow that stillness to flow from the inner being into your action*, whether that action is a thought, a feeling or a physical action. If you can carry that stillness into your action, then it will change the whole course of events.

This is illustrated by the story of a disciple of Buddha who had been with Buddha for about forty years and still had not reached Enlightenment. One day they were sitting by a pond and Buddha was in a profound state of meditation, his whole consciousness filled with Stillness. When he came out of meditation he picked a lotus flower out of the pond and handed it to his disciple—but in that absolute state of Stillness. And at that moment, when the disciple took the flower, he became Enlightened. As simple as that. All because one action carried the power of Stillness to another person and that power came alive in him.

This is just an example showing that when you can act out of Stillness naturally, spontaneously, it will affect your environment in a powerful way.

When you are a Master Warrior there is no difference between action and stillness. It's only in the beginning stages that you move from stillness into action and back into stillness again, as a conscious, intelligent way of *doing* and *being*. But when you are a Master Warrior, that

---

It is important to have a correct understanding of this principle. It means that before any action, before a battle or any engagement, you just become still. You do not think about your action, what you are going to do. You are just still, as if there was nothing in your existence except stillness. And then you drop that and go into action. You know that this is the action you have to do and you just go straight into it, but without referring your mind back to stillness, or to the future, the past or anything. You just do the action.

Stillness just means stillness, nothing else. Action just means action, and nothing else. It is as simple as that. But it is difficult to do because between those two states the mind is always going on about one thing or another. If both are done correctly, however, then the action and stillness will become simultaneous and spontaneous, not because you think they are in your mind but because they actually are. That is why, in the early stages, you must not concern yourself with the other part of it. When you are still you are just still; when you act you just act.

If you can do that, you will understand what this whole thing is about, what the great Spiritual Warrior Path is about, because a shift will take place in your consciousness that enlightens you in an absolutely unbelievable way. You will understand what *Action into Stillness, Stillness into Action* means, and how you connect to the eternal through the temporal and to the temporal through the eternal.

stillness remains within you all the time, whether you are acting or not. That is why the Warrior is liberated.

The heroine in the movie *Crouching Tiger, Hidden Dragon* who jumps off a bridge and floats into Eternity was able to do that because she had attained Liberation. The idea of getting together with a boyfriend was not relevant to her. When you attain the complete Warrior Power your actions are not based on the values of society or on personal ambition or personal desire; they are not based on personal showmanship or glorifying yourself or getting people to think how great you are. Your whole inner being is enlightened with the intelligence of the Cosmic Mind, and every one of your actions is self-fulfilling, that is to say, fulfilling the harmony of the Cosmos. This happens, of course, when you become a Master Warrior. ⚔

~ 34 ~

GOING WITHIN

Going Within is one of the most important topics for anyone on the Spiritual Path, whether you follow the Way of the Warrior, Yoga, Mysticism, Sufism, Zen, Taoism, Buddhism or any other path. Going Within is the primary step toward attaining the goal of every spiritual path.

The Ocean of Life

Because people do not understand the structure of the human being and the structure of the Universe, they do not understand what it means to go inside themselves. I'll give you an analogy. Birds that can fly over the ocean see the surface ripples of the ocean, and for them, that is what the ocean is. Some birds can dive underwater and catch fish. For them, the ocean has waves and ripples on the surface and another part underneath the surface where they can catch fish. And then there are the creatures that actually live in the ocean. They can explore the surface, go to various depths of the ocean, see rocks and plants and shells, feel various currents. For them, the ocean is vast and has different regions and all kinds of things in it.

The normal human being is like the first bird that only sees the surface of the ocean. What you perceive through the physical senses is only the surface of life, because the physical senses cannot penetrate the invisible dimensions and perceive the invisible substances, energies and forces. So you have a superficial view of life. Because of that, many people build up philosophies, theologies, psychologies and systems of thought based on the superficial observation of life, because that is all they can perceive.

To understand how false that is, you need to experience the deeper regions of the Ocean through internal experience. This is why the technique of Going Within is the primary technique of any spiritual discipline: it wipes the superficial view out of your consciousness so that you begin to experience the larger and deeper regions of the Ocean.

Understanding life, therefore, starts with understanding that as a personality you are a complex being, a reflection of how the Solar System is structured. You are a microcosm, a little universe; the Solar System is a macrocosm, a larger universe. You have a physical body and the Solar System has a physical body; you have a vital body that gives life to your physical body and the Solar System has a vital body. You have an emotional body, which is technically your astral body, and the Solar System has an astral body. And you have a mental body, and so does the Solar System. What you have the Solar System has, the Earth has and all the planets have because you are a small replica of the larger.

You are a personality living in certain dimensions (layers) of the Ocean of Life. Your physical body lives on the surface of Life, your astral body slightly below the surface, your mental body deeper below the surface and your causal body (your Soul) lives in the middle range of the Ocean.

Materialists think that the mind is the brain and the emotions are chemical reactions in the brain. For them, the brain is the be-all and end-all of knowledge and reality. In truth, the brain is simply a reactive mechanism that conveys messages from one part of the body to another. The brain just follows what you are already. If you are an illumined person, your brain assumes the state of an illumined person. If you are an ignorant person, your brain assumes the state of an ignorant person. It is like a mirror: it reflects whatever you are.

Beyond that you know nothing of the depths of the ocean whatsoever. Only your Soul knows the deeper regions below the surface and only the Spirit within you knows what is right at the bottom of the Ocean.

The Ocean of Life is layered and we call these layers *planes, worlds, realms* or *dimensions*. They are layers but they are not separated; there is no door from one layer to another. You cannot say that you are now in the Physical World and you have to open a door and go to the Astral World and then you have to open another door and go to the Mental World. It is nothing like that at all. These are layers of Vibration. Within the Physical there is the Etheric; within the Etheric there is the Astral; within the Astral there is the Mental; within the Mental there is the Causal; beyond that is the great life of the Soul and beyond that is the life of the Spirit—all deeper and deeper layers of Vibration of the Ocean of Life.

So you have to start off your Journey by understanding that Life itself is a vast ocean with many regions in it, because when you begin to have mystical experiences you need to know where you are so that you do not get deluded. One of the problems of the psychics since time immemorial is that they experience certain layers of the Astral World and think they have obtained the final truth, whereas in fact they are just below the surface of the Ocean of Life and have gone no further than that.

The Nature of the Inner Worlds

If you meditate without any real understanding of the complex structure of the human being and of the Universe, it is easy to be deluded because you don't know where a particular experience is coming from. The delusion of psychics can be colossal; they can imagine themselves to be the Christ or the Buddha or even some greater entity. This is why it is important to have a Teacher who can tell you exactly where you are and what you are experiencing, whether it is physical, etheric, astral, mental or causal.

Some regions of the Astral Worlds are extremely beautiful, absolutely magical, and so are the Heaven Worlds, which are the Mental Worlds.

There you can see beautiful cities of jewels and gold and beautiful angelic beings and perfect geometric shapes and patterns. But you still have not reached the Soul; you are not even Self-Realized yet. These are still within the possibility of your personality, the self that you are now. With your astral senses, mental senses and causal senses you can sense those worlds, but still in the context of your personality; you have not touched on the World of the Soul, which includes the Buddhic dimension and the Nirvāṇic dimension, what Jesus called the Kingdom of God and Buddha called Nirvāṇa.

Those regions are where the Soul functions, not the personality, where you as a Living Soul have radically different possibilities of experience than you have as a personality. There are channellers nowadays who believe that they are channelling the Soul. The fact is that you cannot channel the Soul in the Astral World; it's impossible. You can channel someone on the Astral who tells you he is a great master and you are his special agent who will save the world, and that is fine. But in the states of the Soul there is no channelling. You do not get messages from the Soul. You have to *be* the Soul, not channel it. You are either in Soul-Consciousness or you are not.

To explore that great ocean of possibilities that we deal with on the Spiritual Path, all the possibilities within the Self, you have to go within, because with the physical senses you cannot touch on the Astral World; with the astral senses you cannot touch on the Mind World; with the mind senses you cannot touch on the Causal World, the world of the Soul; with the causal senses you cannot touch on the Buddhi, the Spiritual Soul; as the Buddhi you cannot touch on Nirvāṇa; and when you are in Nirvāṇa you cannot touch on Paranirvāṇa. In each case you have to develop senses to connect to the level above; you have to move in the *appropriate* manner to the next phase.

This involves the right internal process whereby you move from one state of consciousness or existence to another. This is the art of meditation, learning how to move from your present stage of evolution to the next. That is what meditation is about, and that is what Going Within is about.

You might ask: Why are we not aware that we have an etheric body, an astral body, a mental body and a causal body? Why are we not aware that we are Living Souls? Why are we not aware of the Divine Spirit within us? These are valid questions because the materialist says "I have never experienced these things, so they don't exist." Why do they not experience them? Because to reach the present state of human evolution, the evolutionary wave has been focusing on the material Creation for quite a few million years now. You have to understand that it has taken aeons for Humanity to reach this point of evolution. We came down from the causal dimensions to the astral dimensions and then to the etheric-physical dimensions, and after that we assumed physical bodies.

Origin of Materialism

There is an angelic hierarchy in the Astral World called the MAKARA, which means "crocodile" in Sanskrit, and they have crocodile-like features. A long time ago, when they were Pure Spirits, some of them were given a vision of the Deity, that is to say, they saw a deeper region of the Ocean and became proud; they thought that they knew everything, that they had seen the ultimate mysteries of God and Creation. They had not, but they stuck to their delusion.

They then became the "fallen angels" because they could not progress beyond that original vision. They had seen a certain aspect of Reality and they refused to move on or evolve. It was pride—not in the human sense, but in the sense that they thought they had reached their goal of evolution and had no further to go. Unfortunately, these fallen angels had a large influence on the early history of Mankind and they taught us about matter, because they were masters of matter, masters of material forces and material energies. Because they were our early instructors, and because they are still active today, we have become materialistic. We think that matter is everything there is; we can create with matter, invent all kinds of gadgets with matter; we have the keys to matter; we can conquer the materialistic world.

It was a very long journey even before we reached the Physical Plane and started to evolve in physical bodies, trying to make sense of physical life. And in time we will begin to go back through the etheric regions, the astral regions, the mental regions, the causal regions and back to Nirvāṇa, which is the beginning and end of the great cosmic cycle of Evolution.

Getting Inner Help

So we have a long way to go yet, but the good news is that you do not have to wait until the Divine Will pushes you through those vast stages of Evolution. You can motivate yourself to complete the Journey more quickly. Suppose you want to travel on the train from Berlin to Moscow. You probably need to change trains a few times, so it will take a while to get to Moscow. But if you want to make a fast trip you can go to the airport and catch a plane to Moscow. You can make the journey fast or you can make it slow—you can even walk to Moscow if you want to, but that will take a very long time.

The people who are not on the Spiritual Path, the materialistic people who are going the natural way, are walking to Moscow. If you live in materialistic consciousness you will still reach the end of the Journey, but it will take ages.

The Ancients foresaw this because the great Seers of ancient times looked into the Mind of God and saw the archetype of the human being, and they could therefore see how human beings are supposed to evolve. So they devised the Science of Meditation, the Science of Spiritual Life, in order to speed up human evolution, so that we know which plane to catch, what we will need on the trip and everything we have to do, and what we should avoid doing, in order to reach our destination more quickly.

Of course, to get there quickly you have to make an extra effort, you have to shake yourself out of materialistic consciousness and set your goal to attain Self-Realization, God-Realization, Nirvāṇa, the Kingdom of God, Spiritual Warriorship—whatever you want to call it—*in this lifetime.* You have to name your vision or goal and then start working towards it. Once you do that, help will be given to you. You may come across a book that will change your life, or meet someone and instinctively know that he or she is a Spiritual Teacher.

Everything changes once you wake up to the fact that there is a plan in life, that there is a greater purpose than what you were told by your parents. The *internal network* begins to work for you. You receive hints and tips from different sources that help you along that way of understanding. You may be walking along the street and suddenly get an inspiration to turn down a street you have not gone down before, and there is something waiting for you there. The Cosmos begins to work for you, to arrange your life to help you to attain your vision or goal of that larger horizon.

All of this is still on the personality level, the inner development of the personality, but when you have connected with your Soul, when you have had Soul Illumination, then comes another miracle: you become directed not by outer agencies but by the Divine Mind itself, internally, in waves and waves of Light, Intelligence and Understanding. You begin to understand Cosmic Destiny and you realize that the destiny of your personality is only a small part of the story.

As Saint Paul said, "When I was a child I did as children do, but now that I am an adult I do what adults do" (1 Corinthians 13: 11). Most people interpret this at face value, but what he was really saying was that when he was first on the path of discipleship, everything he did was for developing personality powers, intelligence, understanding and even psychic powers (the early Christians were into speaking in tongues, psychic healing and performing miracles). But when he became a mature adult, that is, a Soul-connected person, he realized that all those things were just childish demonstrations of personality powers.

When you are in Soul-Consciousness, you realize that there is destiny that you must fulfil as a Soul and you begin to work on your Soul destiny, which means that your Soul begins to move towards the MONAD, the One Indivisible Reality. In this internal process there is no outer guidance. The instruction is within the Soul itself, and each Soul finds its own way to approach Divinity. All the possibilities of the personality dimensions, even the miraculous powers, are still only personality experiences, whereas the Soul dimension is Pure Awareness, Pure Light, Pure Bliss, Pure Joy, Pure At-one-ment with all things. ✣

~ 35 ~

ANTAR-YĀMIN
THE INNER GUIDE

The invisible worlds surround us; they were here yesterday and a million years ago, and they will be here tomorrow and a million years from now. We are surrounded by them but we are not aware of them and, what is more important, we are not aware of our Inner Guide, or ANTAR-YĀMIN in Sanskrit.

In religions like Christianity and Islam there is the idea of a Guardian Angel, but that is not the Antar-Yāmin; the Inner Guide is something else. You can have your own Guardian Angel, although it is not usual, but everybody has an Inner Guide, which is their own Soul, that is to say, the Divine Principle within them.

It is that Inner Guide that we are disconnected from in our day-to-day living. This is because in our worldly consciousness our attention is always going outwards: towards family, towards friends, towards work, towards everything. Always going *out*. Naturally, while our attention is always going outside of us we are not in tune with our Inner Guide, and on a larger scale we are not in tune with the guiding force of the Universe, which you may call God or the Primordial Energy or the Infinite Mind, the awesome *Power* that controls the whole of Creation.

That is the tragedy of human life. Because we are out of touch with Reality we continually argue with each other, asserting that our belief system is the best, our view of life is the best. Over the last hundred thousand years, in any society, human beings have been continually arguing and fighting each other for supremacy. If we were in touch with our Inner Guide, all our ideas of supremacy over others would disappear. We would know that our Inner Guide is one with Reality, one with the Cosmic Life, and that the Inner Guide of every other human being is also one with the Infinite Ocean of Life.

We are Living Souls walking around in a physical body and using a mind—which is unfortunately the problem, because it is the mind that cuts us off from our Inner Guide. The physical body is an automaton, a machine that just does what it is told; it acts out what you feel and what you think, driven by your mind and your emotions.

On the Spiritual Path, therefore, the first thing to understand is that you have to reorient yourself and put your attention *inside* rather than outside. This means remembering that you are a divine Soul and you have a guiding force in every aspect of your life—the Antar-Yāmin.

That guiding force can come through meditation, through Warrior exercises, through many spiritual techniques, but the main thing is to *connect* to the Inner Guide within us. This involves disconnecting from our outer view of life and refocusing our attention and trying to connect to our Inner Guide. Put simply, rather than thinking *outside*, we have to try to think *inside, inwardly*.

It is therefore important to be aware and not get caught up in your life so much that you forget who you really are, beyond your *mask*. Your

---

What is inside you? What is beyond your body? What is beyond your emotional nature? What is beyond your mental activity? There must be something beyond your personality, which is what we call the *mask*. The word *personality* comes from the Latin word *persona*, which means "mask", something that hides the real. So your personality mechanism is just a mask hiding the truth of who you really are. Everyone has a personality and the question is: What does it hide?

worldly life can swamp you so that you completely miss out on what is real, the Living Soul within you. Have you ever thought about what the Soul gets out of your life? I mean, what do you as a Soul get out of your life as a personality? You say, "Well, I have this degree, I have that job, I have four wives, I've been promoted here and there, I've been decorated by the Queen." But what does your Soul get out of all that? Absolutely nothing. On the personality level, yes, you get acknowledgement; everybody thinks you are a great person and that is fine. But what about your Soul?

This is why it is important to look inward. The outer worldly life is necessary—there is nothing wrong with it—but if that is the only thing you do, you are lost. You might as well not be born because you have wasted your lifetime. Remember, you cannot take anything from this world with you to the other side: you can't take your house, your latest electronic device, your husband or wife—nothing. When you wake up on the other side you realize that all your achievements are absolutely useless; nobody cares whether you had one university degree or ten degrees, or whether you were famous or rich. Then you say, "Oh, what a waste of time that was! I should have done something about my Soul."

As Souls, we are all extremely beautiful, full of light, full of joy, full of colour vibrancy. If you could see yourself as a Living Soul in the Causal World you would be amazed. Every one of us is a bright, beautiful being, but we all put on masks and slog around in our personalities, and we only see ourselves as personalities, not as the beautiful Souls that we really are.

This is why spiritual retreats and workshops are important: they reminds us that "I have to do something about my Soul—*me* as I was before birth and as I will be after death, the real me who has never been born and has never died, who never *can* die." Whatever spiritual work you do has one purpose: to awaken you, to remind you to think about how your Soul, your Inner Guide, can work through your personality to express itself in the world, and how to make the personality become simply a vehicle, a channel for the Soul energies.

Normally the personality is not a channel or a vehicle; it just reacts like a zombie to everything going on around it. But once you are tuned in internally you can *know* that something is motivating you from the inside, something that is not your mind. This is where the Art of the Warrior comes in: to learn to distinguish your thoughts from real inner guidance, an impulse that comes from deeper within, from beyond the mind.

You may have a lot of good ideas and know what you want to do, and it is easy to mistake that as a motivation from the Inner Guide or the Soul when it is just your mind telling you to do this, that or the other thing. The motivating force of the Inner Guide is extremely subtle, a feeling that you should do something, a feeling so subtle that sometimes you don't do it because your mind tells you not to. You follow your rational mind instead of the original impulse that came from the Inner Guide. If you follow the Inner Guide you will be on the right path in life; if you do not, you are just following your own mental structure and your life will be completely different. It will be mentally directed, which is alright, but it will not be spiritually directed.

Once you touch your inner Self even slightly you will feel an inner pull and also an energy coming through you, a fine, subtle energy like a blessing. Then you will know what your purpose is in life. That is what we call the Inner Guide. Of course, you can have an external guide, a Guardian Angel, but to listen to a real Guardian Angel you have to have the same ability to tune *in*; the only difference is that you have to tune *in* to something outside of you, which is even more difficult than tuning in inwardly.

Nowadays Guardian Angels are quite fashionable and there are many books on Guardian Angels that say they will run after you like servants and do everything for you. Of course, this has nothing whatsoever to do with real Guardian Angels. Real angels are immensely powerful entities; they are not going to find you a parking space or tell you nice bedtime stories. But as I said, not many people have a real Guardian Angel, so you don't have to worry about that. You do, however, have a real Inner Guide, the Living Soul within you.

As a Living Soul you are omniscient, omnipotent and omnipresent. That may be difficult to understand on the personality level; you may say, "If I'm omniscient why do I do stupid things?" Well, you are mistaking your personality for your Soul. You are not omniscient on the personality level, only on the Soul level. So you are asking the question in a completely different world where you are not what your Soul is. But—and here is the beautiful part of it—if you follow the Spiritual Path honestly and sincerely, sooner or later you will get glimpses of your Soul, glimpses of omnipotence, omnipresence and omniscience, and you will realize, "Wow, this is Life, real Life, the Cosmic Life! This is how it is to live in the vast dimensions of the Cosmos!"

The Antar-Yāmin is the Inner Guide, but there is more to it than that. It is an inner force that can direct you—sometimes even physically. It can save you from danger, from an accident, or help you during an accident, and it can prevent some traumatic situation from happening. It is real and most people have experienced it maybe once or twice in their life. But you are not limited to experiencing the Inner Guide only once or twice in your life: you can experience it all the time.

The Inner Guide is always there, whether you are sleeping or awake, whether you are in the body or out of the body; it is you who are not in relationship to *it*. If you relate to it you will have its blessings all the time, in every situation of your life. Normally people have an amazing experience when they know they have been guided, but you can experience amazing happenings twenty-four hours a day, provided that you tune in and remain tuned in to the Inner Guide.

I would like to impress on you that the world is a crazy place, with conflicting energies sweeping through society and creating havoc in human beings, and it has basically been like that for hundreds of thousands of years—in the East, West, North and South. But we can overcome that—first individually, by learning to tune into our Inner Guide, and second communally, when many people in the community have learned to tune in. If half a million people were tuned in to their Inner Guide, imagine what a tremendous impact it would have on the world. The power, the energy-frequency of the planet would be absolutely awesome, like a high-frequency Light-Energy lighting up the whole planet, a light that can be seen for millions of miles in space.

To learn to tune in, imagine that you are not your personality but the Living Soul, and whether you do a Warrior technique or meditation, do it as a *Living Soul*, an immortal, omnipotent, omniscient, beautiful Living Soul, not as a limited personality. Try to keep that attitude no matter what you are doing; whether you are cooking, washing dishes, or whatever you need to do, you are always the Living Soul. Never forget that for a moment, because that remembrance will make a big difference in your life. Then, whatever you do turns into a magical phenomenon. You will find that somehow you have put magic into life into the human condition, and that magic will come out of you and influence people in the right direction.

So before you step on the Warrior Path, *become* the Warrior. In reality you already are the Warrior—the Soul within you is already the Master Warrior—so you just have to become that, and then everything will work itself out in amazing ways.

~ 36 ~

THE WARRIOR TRANSMITS THE ENERGY OF THE SPIRITUAL KINGDOM

Planetary Crisis

Our Spiritual Teaching is not simply the repetition of a Roman Catholic, Jewish or Muslim dogma from two thousand years ago. That is not what we are about. It is a teaching emerging in the present moment, in the here and now, right at the place and time we speak. And this new Revelation, or new Teaching, is what we call the Spiritual Warrior Path.

Those who have been students of Yoga, Mysticism, Sufism or other religions know that there are different ways and paths towards Self-Realization or God-Realization, different techniques of meditation and ways of trying to attain higher states of consciousness and find the fundamental meaning of life. But there was an ancient path, the Warrior Path, which over the last six thousand years has been forgotten. (It is not known that there even was such a path!) So we are bringing that ancient way forward now as a new energy-reality.

This revelation of the Spiritual Warrior Path is of the moment, due to certain planetary conditions that we will describe. Once you understand them, you will understand why we have to apply the Warrior Path now and why it is so important for the planet today. There is a crisis on this planet and the crisis is rooted in the lack of spiritual orientation in the mass consciousness. This crisis has always been here but at this particular time it is worse than usual. This is why we have to awaken the Spiritual Warrior Path and the Warrior techniques. Now we have to *consciously* become Warriors, otherwise the planet is going to fall apart.

In ancient times you did not worry much about what happened in other countries. You just made your living, fed your family and lived your life until you died. It was a simple lifestyle. But now the vast structure of our Solar System is being stimulated by cosmic vibrations[11], and naturally all the planets in the Solar System are also being stimulated. These high-frequency energies, of course, have sped things up and put much stress on planet Earth.

On top of the stress of cosmic vibrations, our planet has to bear the extra damage of human beings putting out as much negativity as they possibly can, century after century for thousands of years, right up until today, when the situation is particularly bad. Expressed in a different way, the planet is under huge stress due to the powerful vibrations coming from the physical dimension and the wrong vibrations from the astral and mental dimensions produced by the negative emotions and negative thought vibrations of all Humanity.

So the planet, our Mother Earth, is going to rebel more and more, which means that the twenty-first century will be much worse than the twentieth.

You might think this has nothing to do with you, but it has everything to do with you. If we want a better life on this planet, we have to start acting like responsible custodians of the planet, because we *are* the custodians of the planet. The Human Kingdom is the only kingdom that has a physical body on the physical level, an astral body in the Astral World, a mental body in the Mental World, a causal body in the Causal

---

11. For details of this stimulation and other events impacting Earth, see Imre Vallyon, "An Overview of the Coming Changes", Chap. I in *Planetary Transformation: A Personal Guide to Embracing Planetary Change* (Sounding-Light Publishing, 2010), 15–23.

World and a spiritual body in the Buddhic World. It is the only kingdom that has a continuum of vehicles of expression from the spiritual level down to the dense material level. The other kingdoms do not. The animals and the angels have only partial expressions on various levels.

> The Human Kingdom is the only one that can function on all the levels of Life, and humans are the link between the Kingdom of God (Nirvāṇa) and the Kingdom of Earth, between the highest and the lowest points of Creation. This is our function as the human race, according to the Divine Plan.

But, of course, we are not acting as custodians; we are destroying the planet, quite systematically and unintelligently. People think that because we have a scientific civilization and lots of gadgets, we are living in an ideal paradise condition. This is the delusion of materialism. Everybody is focused on material living, busy earning more money to buy more gadgets, completely forgetting our responsibility to the planet. Meanwhile, eighty percent of the disasters on this planet are caused by the warped thinking and warped emotions of humans. All the needless violence in the world is human-produced. You cannot blame the Animal Kingdom for it and you cannot blame the angels.

We as a species on this planet are failing. Mind you, we have been failing for thousands of years, but now the planet has reached a critical point. Our Mother Earth has certain bodily parts like we have. We have a heart, lungs, kidneys, liver and other organs. The planet has hierarchies which are its vital organs, such as the Angelic Kingdom and the Elemental Kingdom. The Human Kingdom—Humanity—is the *physical heart* of the planet. If the human family is maladjusted or malfunctioning, therefore, the planet will suffer from heart disease, which can be fatal. If a vital organ in your body is diseased, your body cannot function normally. And if the heart of the planet, the whole of Humanity, is sick, the planet cannot function normally. It will have to go through a crisis, and it may even die.

Every day there is so much negative energy generated on this planet that even if we stopped now it would take a thousand years to clear up the mess. How many people have negative thoughts, how many people have negative feelings, day in and day out? It all accumulates in the Astral World, which surrounds the planet in which we live, move and breathe. The amount of negativity is phenomenal and it keeps increasing because Humanity keeps generating it twenty-four hours a day, nonstop.

Group Work

We must understand that Life has an *internal* structure, so what every one of us does impacts other people and the planet. And this is where the Spiritual Warrior Path comes in. The Spiritual Warrior School has a threefold mission: first is the evolution and enlightenment of the individual; second, the energizing of the group consciousness of the Warrior School so that the group can more effectively work in the world; and third is planetary reconstruction work based on the Esoteric Teaching and spiritual exercises and techniques.

During the last six thousand years, when somebody decided to look for God or to find Self-Realization and they started meditating, whether they were Jewish, Egyptian, Chinese, Indian or whatever, they were watched from the Inner Worlds by the Spiritual Hierarchy, who gave them help individually by guiding them to a living Spiritual Teacher or by giving them inspiration from the inside. They worked case by case, when somebody was ready: "When the pupil is ready, the Master appears." But this is no longer the case. Now it is: When Humanity is ready, the Master appears. When Humanity is ready, the Kingdom comes. The Hierarchy no longer works case by case but group by group, country by country, continent by continent, and on a planetary scale.

So the idea is to work in groups, but to do that the individuals have to go beyond their personality limitations. This is a big thing. Every human being has to live in a personality, otherwise we would not be able to function on this planet. That has to be accepted; so we all have to put up with each other's personality. The primary thing, however, is: *the personality must not obstruct the group work.*

All it takes is one person to destroy a whole work. It has always been like this. Great Teachers have come, formed a group and then a selfish personality comes along and destroys the whole work—the great visions and inspired teachings of the Teacher. If you understand this principle you will watch your personality and try not to manifest those qualities that get in the way of the group work. Personality issues are actually not important whatsoever. Most people think that their personalities are very important; they are not. In the cosmic scheme of things they have no meaning whatsoever; they are just fragmentary happenings in space and time.

So do not get caught up in your own personality imperfections or somebody else's imperfections. Look beyond the personality and concentrate on the work, on what is to be achieved. In this case, it is the transformation of the individual, the group and the world through the teachings and spiritual techniques of the Spiritual Warrior Path. Understand the bigger picture of what the group is trying to do and then put your heart and soul into doing it.

The planetary situation has reached critical mass, so Humanity needs to step up and do its bit towards helping the planet, rather than

---

Pillars of the Temple of God

The ancient Egyptians had the idea that every great enlightened being or great spiritual person who realized the Divine Plan on this Earth became a *pillar of the Temple of God*. An Egyptian temple had massive pillars that held up the structure of the temple, so this saying was a symbol that every person who became enlightened was like a pillar holding up the Temple of God, which is the invisible Spiritual Kingdom. This idea is still valid, but the only difference is that now we all have to become pillars of the Temple of God. The planetary situation is so stressful now that we need pillars by the thousands, by the hundreds of thousands.

constantly destroying it. We need to start reconstructing the planet, intelligently, wilfully and purposefully by the right means—the Spiritual Warrior techniques. Of course, some people think that all you have to do to help people is give them money, but that just patches things up. The United Nations helping the victims of a disaster is good, but it does not stop the disaster from happening again. And some people think that they can help people by making up rules and regulations. Societies and religions have all kinds of rules, but do people follow them?

We need another approach, a completely different approach—*we need to change the functioning of consciousness itself*. You have to actually change the function of human consciousness itself. If a group of people can change their own individual consciousness, they will change their group consciousness, and then through meditation and other spiritual work, the group vibration can impinge on the minds and consciousness of others so that they can *think* differently, more in tune with Reality.

Giving aid is a physical help but it does not change anything. Rules are just mental ideas; they do not change anything. But by changing consciousness, within individuals and within groups, that will change the consciousness of the planet itself.

Remember that everyone's consciousness is linked to everybody else's. This is the magic of the Warrior Path: whatever the Warrior does impacts on society, and the greater the Warrior, the greater the impact. A Warrior thinks and society changes. A Warrior draws her sword and society moves. Every mental, emotional and physical action of the enlightened Warrior, who has reached the end of the Path, changes society. But even at the beginning of that Path, you are changing yourself and changing your environment by being what you are: a Warrior-in-training.

Our Spiritual Warrior School and the Spiritual Warrior Path have a grand purpose: the bringing of the Kingdom of God on Earth, which is about manifesting a divine Energy-field on the planet and annihilating the negative planetary condition.

There is an amazing possibility for our planet. We call it the *Divine Plan*, or *Cosmic Evolution*, what God has in mind for the Universe. The Infinite Mind, the Absolute Deity, which cannot be described or comprehended at all, is in charge of the vast field of Cosmic Evolution—the evolution of all the hierarchies, all the species, all the kingdoms, all the embodiments. The Universe, with its uncountable numbers of galaxies, is incredibly vast, infinite in every direction, externally *and* internally.

This great Cosmic Intelligence, what we call God, evolves the whole Cosmos according to its Plan for Cosmic Evolution, and within that Plan there is an evolutionary sub-plan for each galaxy. Our Milky Way Galaxy has its own plan of unfoldment. Within that, our Solar System has its own unfoldment plan because our Solar Logos is a Cosmic Being with a certain evolutionary standard to reach in this Creation, along with all the planets and hierarchies within the Solar System. And within that plan, our planet Earth is a Cosmic Being with her own plan of evolution.

Ideally, if all the hierarchies do the right thing, Evolution proceeds according to the Divine Plan. Unfortunately, for the last few hundred thousand years our human family has not fulfilled the requirements of our part of the Divine Plan. But we have now reached a point where we are intelligent enough to understand that life is not meaningless, not just the result of a big accident or a "big bang". Life has been *planned* right from the beginning until the very end, and it is now vital that we wake up and start working for that plan, intelligently, en masse. If we don't, the writing is on the wall.

So we have to realize that we are responsible for the planet and we must do our share of the work to save it. There is no other option. You might think that the idea of gaining Liberation for yourself is a big deal; well, liberating the planet is an even bigger deal. It is a nobler ideal, a higher ideal, because in the process you liberate yourself. The larger always includes the smaller, so if you work for Planetary Liberation you liberate yourself because you are part of the planet. So instead of working by ourselves individually, as we have been doing over the last few thousand years, we have to work together with others, for the total liberation of Humanity.

The Warrior Path is different from the Path of Yoga, the Path of Mysticism, the Path of Sufism, the Path of Zen and other paths based on the idea that you have to quit your family life and quit the world, that you stop being responsible for anything and just look for Enlightenment. In India, there are still millions of sadhus who still think that renunciation is the way. But they are way out of date, way out of tune with present-day reality. Most of their techniques were based on torturing the physical body. Those techniques have no relevance today whatsoever. They never did have relevance; they were always a wrong idea.

On the Spiritual Warrior Path you do not quit the world; you meet the world head on. And in that meeting, moment by moment, *there* is Enlightenment. The Art of the Warrior is to be enlightened every second of every day. It is not something you look forward to in the future; it is something you live *now*. The Warrior Path is always in the immediate moment, at *this* second of time, in your total relationship with the outer world and the world inside you, with the Divine Presence within you and the Divine Presence outside you. It is the conjunction between the God Within, the God Without and the Cosmos in between. This is the Way of the Spiritual Warrior, the Spiritual Path for today.

The Code of the Spiritual Warrior

No anger.

A calm mind.

A friendly Heart.

A constant readiness to serve and to help in the working out of the Divine Plan on Earth.

Respect for the Teacher.

Respect for the Teaching.

Respect for the Group one travels with on the Path.

To follow one's inborn Destiny.

To live nobly and Free.

To overcome all difficulties with dignity and strength.

To persevere upon the Path until the end, until Mastery and Perfection are gained.

This is the Code of the Spiritual Warrior.

Let this be your Guide, your Inspiration, and your Strength.

SANSKRIT PRONUNCIATION GUIDE
~

VOWELS

A AS IN FATHER
E ... THERE
I ... MACHINE
O ... GO
U ... FULL
Ṛ ... MERRILY (ROLLED)
Ṝ ... MARINE
AI ... AISLE
AU ... HAUS (GERMAN)

LONG VOWELS

Ā, Ī, Ū

THE LONG VOWELS ARE PRONOUNCED THE
SAME AS THE SHORT VOWELS, BUT ARE
OF LONGER DURATION (TWO OR THREE
MEASURES). O AND E ARE ALWAYS SOUNDED
LONG. THE LONG Ö INDICATES A PROLONGED
SOUNDING.

SEMI-VOWELS

H ... HEAR
Y ... YET, LOYAL
R ... RED
V ... IVY
   ... MORE LIKE W WHEN
   FOLLOWING A CONSONANT
L ... LULL

GUTTURAL CONSONANTS

SOUNDED IN THE THROAT.

K   ... KEEP
KH ... INKHORN
G   ... GET, DOG
GH ... LOGHUT
Ṅ   ... SING (NASAL)

PALATAL CONSONANTS

SOUNDED AT THE ROOF OF THE MOUTH.

C   ... CHURCH
CH ... CHAIN
J   ... JUMP
JH ... HEDGEHOG
Ñ   ... SEÑORITA

CEREBRAL CONSONANTS

SOUNDED WITH THE TONGUE TURNED UP TO
THE ROOF OF THE MOUTH.

Ṭ   ... TRUE
ṬH ... ANTHILL
Ḍ   ... DRUM
ḌH ... REDHAIRED
Ṇ   ... NONE

SANSKRIT PRONUNCIATION GUIDE
~

DENTAL CONSONANTS

SOUNDED WITH THE TIP OF THE TONGUE AT
THE FRONT TEETH.

T	... WATER
TH	... NUTHOOK
D	... DICE
DH	... ADHERE
N	... NOT

LABIAL CONSONANTS

SOUNDED AT THE LIPS.

P	... PUT, SIP
PH	... UPHILL
B	... BEAR
BH	... ABHOR
M	... MAP, JAM

SIBILANTS

THE SIBILANTS ARE HISSING SOUNDS.

S	... SAINT
Ś	... SURE
Ṣ	... SHOULD, BUSH

NASAL SOUNDS

THE NASAL SOUNDS ARE SOUNDED AS A
HUMMING IN THE ROOT OF NOSE. THE
FOLLOWING REPRESENT INCREASING DEGREES
OF NASALIZATION:

M, Ṁ, Ṅ (NG), Ṅ

ASPIRATED SOUNDS

H	ASPIRATED OUT-BREATHING
Ḥ	DEEPER OUT-BREATHING

VARIATIONS

THE VOWELS Ṛ AND Ṝ ARE SOMETIMES
WRITTEN AS ṚI, RI OR RĪ WHEN FALLING AT
THE END OF A WORD.
FOR EXAMPLE: SĀVITRĪ

SOME COMMON EXAMPLES OF ANGLICIZED SPELLINGS

CAKRA	... 'CHAKRA'
ṚṢI	... 'RISHI'
SVĀMĪ	... 'SWAMI'
ŚAKTI	... 'SHAKTI'
ĀKĀŚA	... 'AKASHA'
KṚṢṆA	... 'KRISHNA'
ĀŚRAMA	... 'ASHRAM'
AVATĀRA	... 'AVATAR'

ANGLICIZED SPELLINGS APPEAR IN
THIS WORK ONLY IN THE CONTEXT
OF POPULAR USAGE.

ABOUT THE AUTHOR

~

Born in 1940 in Budapest, Hungary, Imre emigrated to New Zealand at the age of sixteen. Since 1980 he has dedicated his life to teaching the Wisdom Science through his extensive writings and through workshops and retreats conducted around the world.

Imre's extraordinary knowledge of human spirituality is derived not from scholarly research, but issues forth from his own Interior Realization. He spans the full spectrum of human experience: reaching through time, illuminating the great Spiritual Teachings and Sacred Languages of our planetary history while pointing the way to the future. Imre's work is one of synthesis. His writing is universal, not biased towards any particular religion or tradition.

Presenting a complete cross section of Planetary Spirituality, Imre's vast Teaching has been recorded on over four thousand CDs and DVDs. He was awarded first place in the prestigious Ashton Wylie Charitable Trust Awards, and won a gold medal in the Living Now Awards, for the four-volume spiritual treatise *Heavens and Hells of the Mind.*

SELECTED TITLES
~

The Journey Within
ISBN 978-0-909038-70-0

The New Heaven and The New Earth
ISBN 978-0-909038-68-7

The New Planetary Reality
ISBN 978-0-909038-65-6

Planetary Transformation
ISBN 978-0-909038-61-8

Heavens & Hells of the Mind
ISBN 978-0-909038-30-4

The Magical Mind
ISBN 978-0-909038-11-3

The Warrior Code
ISBN 978-0-909038-64-9

The Sedona Talks
ISBN 978-0-909038-54-0

The Divine Plan
ISBN 978-0-909038-53-3

Heart to Heart Talks
ISBN 978-0-9038-55-7

The Art of Meditation
ISBN 978-0-9038-56-4

Please refer to our catalogue for a full list of products.

FOR MORE INFORMATION
~

Online
www.soundinglight.com
www.thefhl.org
info@soundinglight.com

Americas
PO Box 14094
San Francisco
CA 94114
United States of America

Asia-Pacific
PO Box 771
Hamilton 3240
New Zealand

Europe
PO Box 134
2000 AC Haarlem
The Netherlands

www.soundinglight.com